BACKROADS & BYWAYS OF

GEORGIA

BACKROADS & BYWAYS OF
GEORGIA

Drives, Day Trips &
Weekend Excursions

SECOND EDITION

DAVID B. JENKINS

Countryman Press

An Imprint of W. W. Norton & Company
Celebrating a Century of Independent Publishing

For Louise, who perseveres . . .
I will love you forever.

For information about permission to reproduce selections from this book, write to
Permissions, Countryman Press, 500 Fifth Avenue, New York, NY 10110

For information about special discounts for bulk purchases, please contact
W. W. Norton Special Sales at specialsales@wwnorton.com or 800-233-4830

Manufacturing by Versa Press
Series book design by Chris Welch
Maps by Michael Borop (sitesatlas.com)
Production manager: Devon Zahn

Countryman Press
www.countrymanpress.com

An imprint of W. W. Norton & Company, Inc.
500 Fifth Avenue, New York, NY 10110
www.wwnorton.com

978-1-68268-684-3 (pbk)

10 9 8 7 6 5 4 3 2 1

Earth is crammed with heaven
And every bush aflame with God.
But only those who see
Take off their shoes.
    —Elizabeth Barrett Browning

Soli Deo Gloria

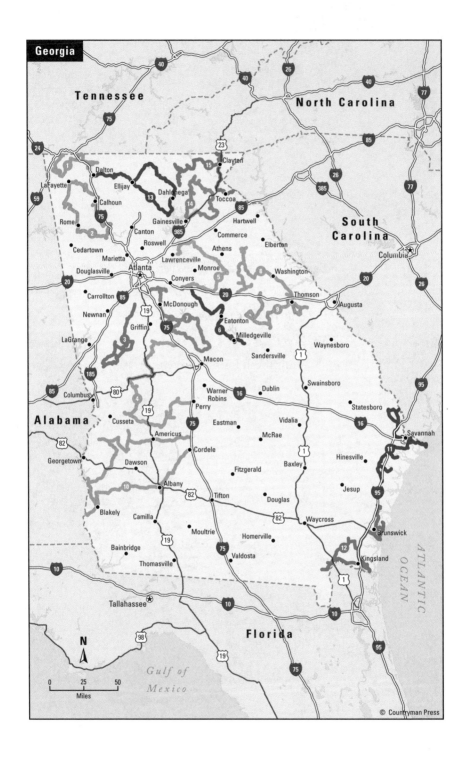

Contents

Introduction

Georgia is a big state—the largest in land area, in fact, east of the Mississippi River—and it's densely packed with interesting things to see and do. Travelers buzzing through on Interstates 16, 20, 75, 85, and 95 can get off at just about any exit and find something worth seeing within a few miles—often even closer.

Since I don't know any of you, my readers, personally, and have no way of knowing what you like, I decided to write this book for myself, visiting places that interest me and seeing the kinds of things I like to see.

So, what do I like to see?

I am a visual historian of mid-20th-century America and a recorder of the interface between man and nature, a keeper of vanishing ways of life.

I'm drawn to the old, the historic, the quirky and offbeat, the strange and unusual, and the beautiful. Old houses, old churches, old courthouses, old mills, covered bridges, and historic sites.

The backroads and little towns are where you find many of these things, so I've tried to stay away from towns of any size. We go through the larger towns when necessary, of course, and sometimes around them, but they are not "off the beaten path," and so the many worthwhile things to see in Georgia's cities are left to be explored in a different book.

The purpose of this book is not to build traffic for tourist attractions; however, some such sites are included when they offer interesting things to see and experience that are relevant to the overall theme.

Likewise, I've given preference to local restaurants and lodgings, especially bed and breakfast inns rather than hotel and restaurant chains. If you're not interested in something different, why leave home? One Holiday Inn is pretty much the same as another, while bed and breakfast inns are infinite and delightful in their variety. And good luck finding a Cracker Barrel or a Ruby Tuesday in many of the places on our itinerary. You might

PRATER'S MILL ON COAHULLA CREEK IN WHITFIELD COUNTY IS ONE OF GEORGIA'S MANY BEAUTIFUL OLD MILLS

find some of the local eateries surprisingly good. Or maybe not. That's life. Suck it up.

The listings for restaurants and lodgings are as correct as I can make them, but things do change. Phone numbers are provided for most facilities, and it's always a good idea to call ahead.

I hope enough of you will like the same places and things I like to make this book a success. I need the money. But seriously—I really do love to get off the beaten path. Sometimes, way off. So if that's what you like too, hang with me, 'cause we're going to see some country!

MAPS, GOOGLE MAPS, AND GPS

All in all, I prefer paper maps. However, while they are usually accurate, they can be hard to read and often don't give sufficient detail, especially when you're searching for obscure byways.

Google maps can be helpful in that regard, but they aren't always totally accurate. Although Google was very helpful in *planning* these tours, I found *actually driving* them was full of surprises. I hope I've got all the surprises worked out, so that you won't have any unpleasant ones of your own as you drive the tours.

I find GPS most useful in urban areas. When traveling the backroads, you can use it, but don't rely on it. You will sometimes find yourself out of range of a cell tower.

ODOMETERS AND APPROXIMATIONS

You might notice that I use the words "about" and "approximately" a lot when talking about distances. That's because no two odometers seem to read the same. We once owned two Dodge Grand Caravans, one of which registered the distance to a certain crossroads on the way to Chattanooga as 17.1 miles, the other as 17.8 miles. As they say online, YMMV—"Your Mileage May Vary."

GEOGRAPHY AND TOPOGRAPHY

Georgia has three main geographic divisions. In the north, you have mountains, dwindling down to the rolling Piedmont Plateau, which forms a belt across the middle of the state. South and east of that is the coastal plain, which is mostly flat to slightly rolling. Even though it's large, Georgia is an easy state to get around in because it has very good roads, at least at the level of state and federal highways. County roads vary widely.

THE UPSON COUNTY COURTHOUSE IN THOMASTON

DIRT ROADS ARE STILL COMMON IN MANY COUNTIES IN GEORGIA

THE GLORY OF GEORGIA
(AND A PROBLEM NO ONE TALKS ABOUT)

The glory of Georgia is its courthouses. One hundred and fifty-nine of them, to be exact. Only Texas has more, and it's a much larger state. The people of Georgia have obviously taken great pride in erecting the finest courthouse possible in each county, even though the county seat may be too tiny and poor to sustain a restaurant where the lawyers can eat lunch on court days.

So what's the problem? The problem is that the citizens of each county are paying the costs of workspace, equipment, and salaries of county officials and workers from top to bottom. For many of the smaller and poorer counties, this is a crushing load. And that's why we have so many unpaved county roads in Georgia.

Can something be done about it? Like, maybe, consolidating several of those smaller counties into one larger one? Well, what do you think? Does the sheriff of Jones County want to work as a deputy under the sheriff of Jasper County? Do the County Commissioners of Catoosa County want to look for jobs in the administration of the Walker County Commissioner?

So you'll be traveling a few gravel and clay roads as you follow some of these tours. Just deal with it.

FOR PHOTOGRAPHERS

Most of the photographs in this book were made with either a Canon 6D or a micro 4/3s Olympus OMD-EM5 camera, both digital. On the 6D, I used an old Nikon Nikkor 35mm PC (perspective control) lens mated to the Canon with an adapter for a great many of the building shots to ensure that vertical lines remained vertical and parallel. In extreme situations (e.g., the Barker's Creek Mill photo), I pulled out a Canon 17–35mm ultra wide-angle zoom. A Panasonic 14–140mm Version II zoom lens (equivalent to a 28–280mm lens on the 6D) stayed pretty much glued on the Olympus, although I occasionally used a Panasonic 12–32mm lens (equivalent to a 24–64mm zoom on the 6D) in situations that called for a wider angle.

I like both camera kits for different reasons: the Canon for its reliability, ease of use, and beautiful files; the Olympus for its exceptional color and light weight, even with a very wide-ranging zoom lens attached. In fact, two

BAXTER MILL IN HANCOCK COUNTY WAS BUILT IN THE EARLY 1800S

Olympus bodies and all four of the lenses I own for the system weigh about the same as the Canon with one mid-range zoom!

In 2017, I made my first major equipment change in more than 20 years—from Canon to the Fujifilm system, which combines the file quality of the Canon with the light weight and small size of the Olympus. Any new photographs in this second edition were made with my Fuji cameras and lenses.

All photographs were made in RAW mode and processed in Capture One to render jpeg files of exceptional clarity. Only a few needed further work in Photoshop to express my vision, which is basically WYSIWYG—What You See Is What You Get.

PREFACE TO THE SECOND EDITION

I traveled nearly 11,000 miles to map out the 15 tours in the first edition of this book. For the second edition, I didn't go so far—only about 8,000 miles—to retrace every tour, make sure all directions were correct (I'm embarrassed to say a few weren't), and to confirm that each point of interest was still there. Almost all were still present, and I was even able to add a few new ones.

It was a great pleasure to once again drive Georgia's backroads and revisit familiar scenes. I hope using this book will give you as much enjoyment as creating it has given me.

A Word About the COVID-19 Pandemic

I have contacted all the restaurants, accommodations, attractions, and events listed in the first edition and have found substitutes for those that are no longer available. Phone numbers are listed for each facility, so remember: **Always Call First!**

Acknowledgments

I must first of all acknowledge my gratitude to my wife, Louise Devlin Jenkins, who has endured my mental and physical absences with a great deal of grace. She even accompanied me on three trips, which calls for special grace, given that when I'm traveling and working on a project I tend to focus on the work to the exclusion of all else.

It did become a bit too much for her, however, when she elected to spend the day by the pool at our hotel in Brunswick while I went off to the Okefenokee Swamp. Distracted by my quest for "just one more" photo, I failed to leave in time and got locked in, with a weak to non-existent cell phone signal. As we say in the South, "When Mama ain't happy, ain't nobody happy!"

Quite a few books and a great number of websites were researched as I planned trips and wrote the various tours. Deserving of very special recognition is Brian Brown, statewide traveler and creator of the website www.vanishinggeorgia.com, for the vast amount of information about what is where and how to find it in rural Georgia. Brian appears to be about as ubiquitous as one human being can be.

Also deserving special recognition are Sonny Seals and George S. Hart, founders of Historic Rural Churches of Georgia and custodians of the website www.hrcga.org, which is a massive and still growing compilation of information about Georgia's old rural churches. I would also like to put in a plug for their beautiful book *Historic Rural Churches of Georgia*, published by the University of Georgia Press.

Another organization to which I owe gratitude is SPOOM—The Society for the Preservation of Old Mills. They have voluminous and detailed listings of old mills, not only in Georgia, but also nationwide. If old mills are a special interest of yours, you can join for free and receive their lists. Their website is www.spoom.org/index.php.

1

MILLS, MANSIONS, AND MOUNTAINS

Northwest Georgia

The total length of this tour is about 90 miles and includes Whitfield, Catoosa, Walker, and Dade counties.

Begin at Interstate 75 Exit 341, the Tunnel Hill exit, and go west on GA 201/North Varnell Street. GA 201 will curve left (south) and will eventually become South Varnell Street. Turn right on Dogwood Street, then left on Jordan Street. Cross the railroad tracks and turn left on Clisby Austin Drive to the **Western and Atlantic Railroad Tunnel**, the **Heritage Center Museum**, and the **Clisby Austin House**.

Built to connect the Port of Augusta with the Tennessee River Valley, the Western and Atlantic tunnel is the oldest in the Southeast. Begun in 1848, the 1,477-foot tunnel through Chetoogeta Mountain was completed in just 22 months without the aid of any kind of power equipment—a remarkable feat of engineering.

Today, visitors can step back into history with guided tours of the tunnel and visit the nearby museum and Clisby Austin House. Guided tours are $12 per person (call 706-876-1571 for reservations) and self-guided tours are $10. The charge for children 4–10 is $10 for all tours. The Heritage Center Museum and Tunnel are open 10 a.m.–4 p.m. Monday through Saturday. Austin, who moved from East Tennessee in 1845 because he believed the proposed tunnel would bring great economic opportunity, built the house in 1848. It served as a hospital during the Civil War Battle of Chickamauga and, in 1864, served as General William T. Sherman's headquarters for the Battle of Dalton. Many believe that it was here that he planned the Atlanta Campaign.

Although tours of the Austin House are available through the museum,

LEFT: THE GORDON LEE MANSION IN CHICKAMAUGA WAS BUILT IN THE 1840S

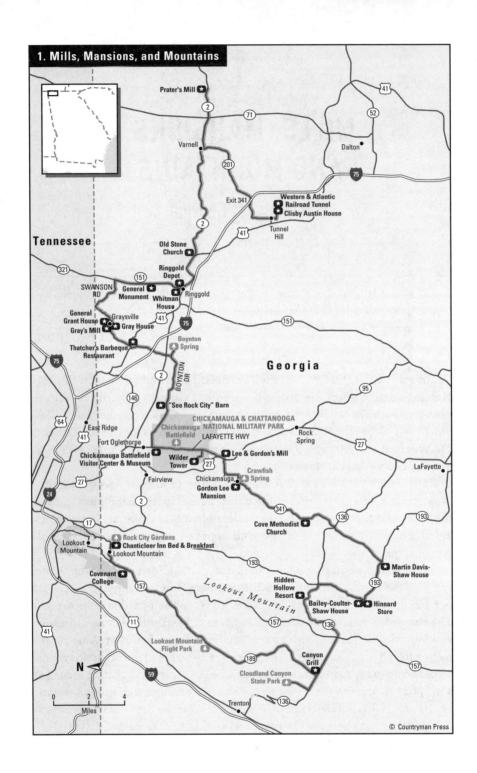

1. Mills, Mansions, and Mountains

Prater's Mill
Varnell
Dalton
Tennessee
Western & Atlantic Railroad Tunnel
Clisby Austin House
Tunnel Hill
Exit 341
Old Stone Church
Ringgold Depot
SWANSON RD
General Monument
Whitman House
Ringgold
General Grant House
Graysville
Gray House
Gray's Mill
Thatcher's Barbeque Restaurant
Boynton Spring
Georgia
BOYNTON DR
"See Rock City" Barn
CHICKAMAUGA & CHATTANOOGA NATIONAL MILITARY PARK
East Ridge
Chickamauga Battlefield
LAFAYETTE HWY
Rock Spring
Fort Oglethorpe
Chickamauga Battlefield Visitor Center & Museum
Wilder Tower
Lee & Gordon's Mill
LaFayette
Fairview
Chickamauga
Crawfish Spring
Gordon Lee Mansion
Cove Methodist Church
Rock City Gardens
Chanticleer Inn Bed & Breakfast
Lookout Mountain
Lookout Mountain
Martin Davis-Shaw House
Covenant College
Lookout Mountain
Hidden Hollow Resort
Bailey-Coulter-Shaw House
Hinnard Store
Lookout Mountain Flight Park
Canyon Grill
Cloudland Canyon State Park
N
Trenton
Miles
0 2 4
© Countryman Press

THE CLISBY AUSTIN HOUSE WAS BUILT IN 1848

if you just want to see the house, continue on Clisby Austin Road for about a half-mile and turn right on Hunt Road to the entrance to the property.

From the tunnel, go back to I-75 and continue on GA 201 for 4.7 miles. Turn right on GA 2 and go 3.3 miles to **Prater's Mill**, at 5845 GA 2, Dalton. Built in 1855 on Coahulla Creek by Benjamin Franklin Prater, the mill was operated by the Prater family for a hundred years.

In 1971, an all-volunteer foundation took over the mill and has done extensive restoration and preservation of the site, financed by the Prater's Mill Country Fair, a highly-rated arts and crafts festival held on Columbus Day weekend each October. Prater's Mill Heritage Park also includes old barns, the Prater residence, and the General Store. The site is open to the public every day, dawn to dusk, at no charge, and tours can be arranged by appointment. Country Fair hours are 9 a.m.–6 p.m. on Saturday and 9 a.m.–5 p.m. on Sunday. Admission is $7, and free for children under 12.

Leaving Prater's Mill, turn right and stay on GA 2 for approximately 10 miles to the intersection with US 41. The **Old Stone Church** will be on your right at 41 Catoosa Parkway, Ringgold.

Originally the Chickamauga Presbyterian Church, construction began in 1850 and was completed two years later, using locally quarried stone. The pews came from an earlier building; during the Civil War, they were used as horse-feeding troughs. The church became a headquarters and as a hospital at various times during the war, and bloodstains from surgeries are still visible on the ancient heart pine floorboards.

THE PRATER'S MILL COUNTRY FAIR IS HELD ON COLUMBUS DAY WEEKEND EACH YEAR

Used by several different denominations over the years, the gospel hymn *Leaning on the Everlasting Arms* had its first public performance at the Old Stone Church in 1887. The building was acquired by the Catoosa County Historical Society in 1995 and is now a museum of local and Civil War history. Admission is free and the hours are Thursday through Sunday, 1 p.m.–5 p.m.

Turn right on US 41/GA 2 and continue 2.4 miles to Ringgold. You will be passing through Ringgold Gap, with the highway following the route of Tiger Creek with Taylor's Ridge on the left and White Oak Mountain on the right. Until the construction of Interstate 75 in the 1960s, much of the traffic from the upper Midwest to Florida passed through Ringgold Gap on that narrow, two-lane ribbon of blacktop.

FACE-PAINTING IS VERY POPULAR WITH THE YOUNGER SET AT PRATER'S MILL COUNTRY FAIR

Immediately after the railroad underpass in Ringgold, turn right on Depot Street. The **Ringgold Depot** was built in 1849 and has been in continuous use since 1850. It now also serves as a community center and event venue. Just north of the depot on Nashville Street is Ringgold's old commercial district, with buildings from the 1850s to the early 1900s still in use.

From the depot, continue on Depot Street three blocks and turn left on High Street to the intersection with GA 151. The **Whitman House** will be directly in front of you.

Built of handmade bricks by William Whitman in 1858, it was used by Union General Ulysses S. Grant as his headquarters after the Battle of Ringgold. When he and his staff left, they offered Mrs. Whitman $50 in US greenbacks. She insisted on being paid in Confederate money instead, causing General Grant to remark, "She certainly is not whipped yet!"

Turn right on GA 151 and continue approximately 1.5 miles to the **"General" Monument** on the left side of the highway.

In April 1862, as Union forces closed in on Chattanooga, Tennessee, a spy named James J. Andrews undertook to cut off supplies from Atlanta to the Confederates defending Chattanooga by sabotaging the Western and Atlantic rail line. In disguise, he and a group of about 20 Union soldiers made their way to Big Shanty, Georgia, now Kennesaw, stole a locomotive named "The General," and steamed northward, intending to tear up tracks, burn bridges, and cut telegraph lines.

However, pursuit began immediately, and they were unable to do much damage. In fact, they were followed so closely that they did not have time to take on enough water and wood to keep going, and so they ran out of steam just north of Ringgold, where all the raiders were captured. Eight men, including Andrews, were hanged and are now buried in the National Cemetery at Chattanooga. The others escaped or were exchanged.

GENERAL ULYSSES S. GRANT WAS PHOTOGRAPHED ON THE UPPER PORCH OF THIS HOUSE IN GRAYSVILLE DURING THE CIVIL WAR

The monument marks the spot where Andrew's Raiders abandoned the General. There is a place to pull off the highway, but it is very small and the highway is usually pretty busy. The monument sits in a narrow strip of land between the highway and the railroad tracks.

Andrew's raid was the inspiration for the 1956 movie, *The Great Locomotive Chase*, starring Fess Parker and Slim Pickens.

Continue 2 miles north on GA 151, then turn left on Swanson Road for 3.5 miles to the village of Graysville. Turn right on Vaughn Street for one block and the two-story **"General Grant House"** will be directly in front of you. The Catoosa County Historical Society has a photograph of General Ulysses S. Grant on the second-floor porch of this house, taken during the Civil War. The owners of the house appear to be doing some much-needed restoration at this writing.

Turn left on Sparks Street for a block, then

THIS ROCK CITY BARN ON OLD GA 2 IS ONE OF ABOUT 85 STILL BEING PAINTED BY ROCK CITY GARDENS

left again on Blackford Street. The turrets of the Queen Anne–style **Gray House** will be on your right.

In 1883, Dr. William T. Blackford, a Chattanooga physician, built a Queen Anne–style house and moved his practice to Graysville. In 1916 a member of the Gray family bought the house from Dr. Blackford's daughters. It has had numerous owners in the intervening years and was at one time a restaurant, The Graysville House.

CANNON AT CHICKAMAUGA BATTLEFIELD NATIONAL MILITARY PARK

John D. Gray, the English-born major contractor who built the Western and Atlantic Railroad, including digging the tunnel at Tunnel Hill, liked the Northwest Georgia area so much that he bought 4,000 acres on Chickamauga Creek and laid out the town of Graysville in the late 1840s.

Turn right on Front Road and continue to the stop sign, then turn left on Graysville Road and cross the railroad tracks to the bridge over Chickamauga Creek. John Gray built a mill dam, which still stands, and a large grist mill, which was burned during the Civil War.

It was rebuilt in 1869 and operated into the 1950s, but was burned again by vandals in the late 1970s and a three-story home was later built on the mill foundation.

From the mill site, continue on Graysville Road for approximately 2 miles to the intersection with US 41. Turn left on 41. The highly rated **Thatcher's Barbecue Restaurant** will be on the left at 2929 US 41, Ringgold.

Continue for about a quarter-mile and turn right on Three Notch Road. Go about 2 miles south, cross four-lane Battlefield Parkway, which is new GA 2, and go about 0.2 mile to Boynton Drive, old GA 2. (For a quick side trip, go left on Boynton Drive for about a half-mile to **Boynton Spring**, a large spring where people come from miles around to fill their jugs with pure, natural drinking water.)

Returning to the Three Notch Road intersection, continue about 3 miles to a large barn on the right with a SEE ROCK CITY **sign**. Rock City Gardens on Lookout Mountain ran one of the most successful outdoor advertising campaigns in history by painting "See Rock City" on more than 800 barns in 19 states, covering most of the Southeast and much of the Midwest.

Go a short distance farther and enter **Chickamauga National Battlefield Park**. Boynton Drive becomes Reeds Bridge Road at that point. In about 2 miles, you will come to the intersection of US 27. Turn left (south) on US 27 and the park's **Visitor Center and Museum** will be on your right.

THE SNODGRASS CABIN ON SNODGRASS HILL WAS THE SCENE OF INTENSE FIGHTING DURING THE BATTLE OF CHICKAMAUGA

WILDER TOWER ON CHICKAMAUGA BATTLEFIELD WAS BUILT IN HONOR OF COL. JOHN T. WILDER AND HIS "LIGHTNING BRIGADE"

A part of the Chickamauga and Chattanooga National Military Park, which was authorized by Congress in 1890, the first such park in the US, Chickamauga Battlefield was the scene of a horrendous engagement between Union and Confederate forces in September 1863. The bloodiest battle in American history, with more than 36,000 casualties, it had no clear-cut winner, and yet it was in fact the beginning of the end for the Confederacy.

At the visitor center, you can see exhibits and a large collection of military weapons and view a film about the battles in the Chattanooga area. You can also pick up a map for the 7-mile, self-guided driving tour and explore to your heart's content. If you're not into maps, just dial 585-672-2619 on your cell phone and follow the tour instructions.

Chickamauga Battlefield has something like 1,400 monuments and historical markers, so depending on your level of interest in Civil War history, you could easily spend hours or days in the park. In fact, some people have spent large portions of their lives there.

Be sure to watch out for the deer, which are numerous, and for the bikers and hikers, which are perhaps even more so. Also, be sure to see **Wilder Tower**, about 1.5 miles off US 27, near the south end of the park on Glenn-Viniard Road.

Leaving the park by the south exit on US 27, turn left at the intersection with US 27 Bypass, go about 0.2 mile, then left again on Lee and Gordon Mill Circle for about 0.3 mile to **Lee and Gordon's Mill**, on the left.

Built by James Gordon on Chickamauga Creek in 1836, the mill was in operation until 1967. After the mill had been dormant for years, Frank Pierce, long-time mayor of Chickamauga, bought the property in 1995 and began a six-year process of restoring the building and the dam. Now fully operational, the mill and general store are a fascinating museum covering an ear-

COVE METHODIST CHURCH HOSTS ANNUAL FALL REVIVALS AND CHRISTMAS SERVICES

lier century. The mill and general store are open Tuesday through Saturday, 9 a.m.–5 p.m., and 1–5 p.m. on Sunday. By all means, call first! The mill is also a popular venue for weddings and other events. Call 706-375-6801 for more information or to arrange a tour.

From the mill, turn right and go to the top of the hill, then make a sharp left and continue to the traffic light at US 27. If you're hungry by this time, you have several good choices: If you would like good Southern country cooking, turn left and go about a quarter-mile to **Greg's Restaurant** on the left. If you have a taste for barbecue, turn right and go about a quarter-mile to **Choo Choo BBQ & Grill** on the right. If you're thinking about great Mexican food, then continue through the traffic light into the lovely village of Chickamauga. As you cross 27, the street will become Lee and Gordon's Mill Road. Go a half-mile to the next traffic light and turn left on Crittenden Street for about a mile. At the traffic light in downtown Chickamauga, turn right to **Los Potros Mexican Restaurant**, about half a block on the left, or turn left (south) at the light on Cove Road/GA 341. The **Gordon Lee Mansion** is about 200 yards along on your right, just past the Methodist Church. It was built between 1840 and 1847 by James Gordon, who had earlier built the grist mill. During the Battle of Chickamauga it was used as a hospital.

After the death of James Gordon, the property was purchased by James Lee, who was one of the principal organizers of the nearby Elizabeth Lee Memorial United Methodist Church, named after his wife. After her death, the property was acquired by her son Gordon Lee, who served in the US House of Representatives for 20 years. Across the street from the Gordon Lee Mansion is **Crawfish Spring**, a large spring in a natural amphitheatre. It is a lovely and peaceful place.

Continue south on Cove Road/GA 341 for 4.5 miles to **Cove Methodist Church** on the right at the intersection with Kensington Lane. Erected in 1894 to replace an earlier structure from 1872, the architecture is New England Colonial. Although it has not had a congregation for many years, the church is kept alive largely through the efforts of Mrs. Mary Agnes Fine and her son Lamar. The annual Fall Revival and Christmas Service are standing-room-only occasions. It is also a popular wedding venue.

From the church, continue on 341 for 5.2 miles (crossing GA 136 as you go) to the intersection with GA 193 at Davis crossroads.

Cross GA 193 and go about a hundred yards to the **Martin Davis-Shaw House** on the right. A one-and-a-half-story, dogtrot-style frame house, it was built in the early 1850s by Martin Davis, who had moved to Georgia with his family from Lumpkin County in 1850. The stone wing in the rear was added by his son John in 1884. The last resident was Frank Clement "Bug" Shaw, who built a number of outbuildings adjacent to the house to depict a rural, 19th-century village. Before his death, Mr. Shaw transferred the property to

LAUNCHING A HANG GLIDER INTO THE WIND AT MCCARTY'S BLUFF, LOOKOUT MOUNTAIN

the Martin Davis House Foundation. Reservations for tours can be arranged by calling 706-539-2244.

From the Martin Davis House, go back to the crossroads and turn left (west) on GA 193 for about 2.5 miles to the intersection with West Cove Road and turn left. On your immediate right, behind its white picket fence, will be the **Bailey-Coulter-Shaw House**, built by Wiley Bailey around 1850. Typical of Northwest Georgia mountain architecture, the style is Plantation Plain with additions; however, the double front porches are an unusual feature. The property was purchased by William Michael Coulter in 1874 and the current residents are the fifth generation of his family to live in the house.

Next door is the old **Hinnard Store**. The date when it was built is not known, but it was listed on a Confederate Civil War map in the early 1860s.

Go back to GA 193 and turn left. On your immediate left, set back from the road about a hundred yards, is the distinctive board-and-batten exterior of the former **Methodist Parsonage**, built in 1887. The church is long gone, but the parsonage remains as a private residence.

Continue on GA 193 for 2.7 miles to the intersection with GA 136. Turn left and go 7.8 miles to the top of Lookout Mountain and **Cloudland Canyon State Park**.

Hidden Hollow Resort will be on the right just as you start up the mountain. Located on the western rim of Lookout Mountain, the 3,488-acre Cloudland Canyon State Park is one of the largest and most popular in the state. Its most prominent feature, of course, is the canyon itself—more than a thousand feet deep. Park facilities include 16 cottages, 72 campsites, 30 walk-in campsites, picnic shelters, 30 miles of hiking and mountain biking trails, 16 miles of horseback riding trails, caving, and a 600-step staircase to the two waterfalls at the bottom of the canyon.

The park is open 7 a.m.–10 p.m. every day. There is no admission charge, but a $5 parking pass is required.

Leaving Cloudland Canyon State Park, turn left on GA 136 and go just under a mile to the intersection of GA 189.

As soon as you turn left onto GA 189, you will see the **Canyon Grill** on the right. The Canyon Grill has a touch of rusticity, but the food is upscale—in fact it has been voted the best restaurant in the Chattanooga area more than once. Call 706-398-9510 or check their website (www.canyongrill.com) for current days and hours. Reservations are not required but are recommended.

Continue north on GA 189. Known as "Scenic Highway," the road runs along the western brow of Lookout Mountain, with many spectacular views. In 7.3 miles, you will arrive at Lookout Mountain Flight Park on McCarty's Bluff, one of the premier hang gliding sites in the United States.

Located on the western brow of the mountain, prevailing winds from the west make it possible for hang gliders to take off most days of the year. The bluff has been the site of numerous world-class hang gliding competitions. On a good day, you can spend an interesting half-hour watching the gliders launch. Or if you're feeling adventurous, you can try it yourself, flying in tandem with an instructor, or you can even sign up for a day of hang gliding lessons.

From the flight park, continue on GA 189 for 6.6 miles to **Covenant College**, on your left. Covenant is a four-year liberal arts college of the Presbyterian Church in America. The school moved to the North Georgia area from St. Louis in 1964 and purchased an old resort hotel known as the Castle in the Clouds. The castle has been renovated, and numerous other buildings have been added.

From Covenant College, go 0.9 mile and turn right on GA 157/McFarland Road. Stay on GA 157 for about a mile through the town of Lookout Mountain, which used to be named Fairyland and still has street names like Peter Pan Road and Red Riding Hood Trail. Turn right at the Rock City sign onto Mockingbird Lane, and go about 0.2 mile to the entrance to one of the South's premier tourist attractions, **Rock City Gardens**.

"A ten-acre tract of massive stone formations on the eastern cliffs of Lookout Mountain overlooking Chattanooga, Tennessee and the North Georgia countryside, Rock City is," as I wrote in my book *Rock City Barns: A Passing Era* (Silver Maple Press, 1996), "an oddly pleasing blend of magnificent natural beauty and a charming naiveté.

"The naiveté comes in the form of trailside elfin figurines, walking 'storybook' characters (Mother Goose, Humpty-Dumpty, Rocky, the Rock City elf), and Fairyland Caverns, a man-made 'cave' featuring black-lighted dioramas of nursery rhyme scenes. This is what family entertainment was like before Disney World and video games, and the place still holds a special fascination for kids of all ages."

Although the rocks have been there for a long time, Rock City as a tourist attraction is the brainchild of Garnet Carter, whose wife had made the place her own nature garden. He widened the trails, made more plantings, and opened the place to the public in 1932. However, it was not until the barn painting program began around 1937 that Rock City really took off.

Is it really true that you can "See Seven States" from Rock City? Come find out. You owe it to yourself to "See Rock City."

By the way, as you make the turn onto Mockingbird Lane toward Rock City, you will pass the **Chanticleer Inn Bed and Breakfast** on the right. If you arrive late in the day or finish your tour of Rock City late in the day, you would most definitely enjoy spending the night at the Chanticleer.

This is the end of our northwest corner of Georgia tour. From here, you can take GA 157 down the mountain to Chattanooga, where you can connect with I-24 East to its junction with I-75 South into Georgia.

THE SWING-ALONG BRIDGE AT ROCK CITY IS SAFE, BUT IT CAN FEEL A BIT SCARY

IN THE AREA

Accommodations

CHANTICLEER INN BED AND BREAKFAST, 1300 Mockingbird Lane, Lookout Mountain. 706-820-2002. stayatchanticleer.com.

THE GARDEN WALK BED AND BREAKFAST INN, 1206 Lula Lake Road, Lookout Mountain. 706-820-4127. www.gardenwalkinn.com.

HAMPTON INN, 6875 Battlefield Parkway, Ringgold. 706-935-4800.

HIDDEN HOLLOW RESORT, 463 Hidden Hollow Drive, Chickamauga. 706-539-2372.

Dining

CANYON GRILL, 28 Scenic Highway 189, Rising Fawn. 706-398-9510. www.canyongrill.com.

CHOO CHOO BBQ & GRILL, 12960 North Highway 27, Chickamauga. 706-375-7675. www.choochoobbqgrill.com.

GREG'S RESTAURANT, 12560 North Highway 27, Chickamauga. 706-375-4788.

LOS POTROS MEXICAN RESTAURANT, 201 Lee Avenue, Chickamauga. 706-375-4111.

THATCHER'S BARBECUE, US 41 at Three Notch Road, Ringgold. 706-935-6465.

Attractions and Recreation

CHICKAMAUGA BATTLEFIELD NATIONAL MILITARY PARK, 3370 Lafayette Road, Fort Oglethorpe. 706-866-9241.

CLOUDLAND CANYON STATE PARK, 122 Cloudland Canyon Park Road, Rising Fawn. 706-657-4050.

LOOKOUT MOUNTAIN FLIGHT PARK, 7201 Scenic Highway 189, Rising Fawn. 706-383-1292. www.flylookout.com

ROCK CITY GARDENS, 1400 Patten Road, Lookout Mountain. 706-820-2531. www.seerockcity.com.

TUNNEL HILL HERITAGE CENTER, 215 Clisby Austin Road, Tunnel Hill. 706-876-1571.

For more information on any Georgia State Park or Historic Site, visit the state parks website: www.georgiastateparks.org.

Events

Catoosa County

1890s Days Jamboree, Ringgold, Memorial Day weekend.

Dixie Highway 90-Mile Yard Sale, Old US 41, June.

Dade County

New Salem Mountain Festival, New Salem, October. www.newsalem mountainfestival.com/index.html.

Walker County

Down Home Days, Chickamauga, first Saturday in May.

Honey Bee Festival, LaFayette, June.

Candlelight Tours of the Gordon Lee Mansion, Chickamauga, first and second weekends in December.

Enchanted Garden of Lights, Rock City Gardens, late November through December 31.

Whitfield County

Battle of Tunnel Hill Civil War Reenactment, Tunnel Hill, September.

Dixie Highway 90-Mile Yard Sale, Old US 41, June.

Prater's Mill Country Fair, Varnell, Columbus Day weekend.

2

POSSUM TROT TO PARADISE
Northwest Georgia

The total length of this tour is about 175 miles and includes Gordon, Bartow, Floyd, Chattooga, and Walker counties.

Beginning at the intersection of I-75 and GA 225, go north 1 mile on GA 225 to **New Echota**.

In 1819, the Cherokee Council began holding their annual meetings at New Town, a village near the headwaters of the Oostanaula River. In 1825, the Council adopted a resolution renaming the village New Echota and making it the capital of the Cherokee nation.

More civilized than many of their white neighbors, the Cherokees developed their own alphabet and published their own newspaper, *The Cherokee Phoenix*. They even sued the State of Georgia in the United States Supreme Court and won. However, President Andrew Jackson refused to enforce the verdict, and in the winter of 1838–39 the Cherokees were assembled at New Echota and other points and driven west in the infamous "Trail of Tears," one of the most shameful chapters in American history. One fourth of the 15,000 people died along the way.

The New Echota site has twelve original and reconstructed buildings. The **James Vann Tavern**, built in 1805, is original to the era, although it was moved here from a site in Forsyth County. The only other original building is the **Samuel Worcester House,** built by Worcester, a Presbyterian missionary, in 1828 as a mission station and family home. Working with Elias Boudinot, the first editor of *The Cherokee Phoenix*, he translated parts of the Bible and many hymns into the Cherokee language and, as a faithful minis-

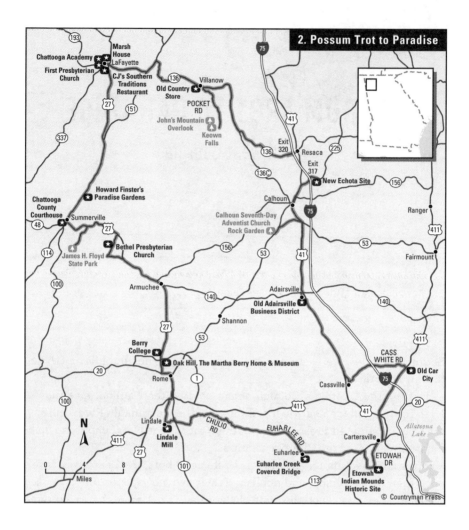

ter, went with the Indians when they were moved west. New Echota is open Tuesday–Saturday 9 a.m.–5 p.m. and on Sundays 1 p.m.–5 p.m. Admission is $5.50 for ages 6–17, $7 for ages 18–61, and $6.50 for seniors 62 and older. The site is closed on Sundays December through March.

Leaving New Echota, go left (south) on GA 225 for 2 miles to the intersection with US 41. Slant left (south) and follow US 41 through **downtown Calhoun** for 4 miles to the intersection of GA 53. Go right (west) on GA 53 for 3 miles to the Seventh Day Adventist Church on the right. **The Rock Garden** is behind the church.

A unique acre or so of folk art, the garden is made up of miniature castles and cathedrals, forts, and fantastical fairytale villages, all lovingly constructed from pebbles, shells, bits of ceramic tile, pieces of glass, and cement by volunteers whose only goal was to serve their faith by creating a place of relaxation and meditation for whomever might choose to spend a few minutes enjoying the peace and beauty of the site. The garden is open daily 8 a.m.–7 p.m. No admission charge, although there is a box for donations.

THE CHEROKEE ALPHABET INVENTED BY SEQUOYAH MADE IT POSSIBLE FOR THEM TO HAVE THEIR OWN NEWSPAPER, PRINTED AT NEW ECHOTA

From the Rock Garden, go back to the intersection of GA 53 and US 41 and turn right (south) on 41 for 7 miles to the intersection of GA 140. Go right for 0.1 mile and then left on Hill Street, which is the original route of US 41. In about 0.6 mile, slant right at the United Methodist Church onto Public Square and **the old Adairsville business district**. Like many small towns in the South, the storefronts in old downtown Adairsville are lined up in a row, facing the railroad tracks.

At the south end of the business section, turn left on Gilmer Street and go back to US 41. Turn right for about a mile until it intersects with the present-day route of US 41 and continue south 7 miles to Cassville Road, which slants left immediately after crossing the bridge over Two Run Creek.

THE JAMES VANN TAVERN ONCE SERVED TRAVELERS ON THE OLD FEDERAL ROAD NEAR GAINESVILLE

THE ROCK GARDEN NEAR CALHOUN CONTAINS MORE THAN 50 TINY BUILDINGS

Go 0.8 mile to the old Cass Grocery Store at Cass White Road and turn left. Follow Cass White Road for about 6 miles to the traffic circle, then continue straight for another 0.2 mile to the junction with US 411 and turn left for 0.3 mile. **Old Car City** will be on the right at 3098 US 411 in White, GA.

Begun in 1931 as an auto dealership and still owned and operated by the same family, Old Car City is now the world's largest-known classic auto junkyard, covering 34 acres with 6 miles of walking trails and more than 4,000 cars. Also on display are Elvis Presley's last automobile and a large styrofoam-cup folk art collection.

Old Car City is open Wednesday through Saturday, 9 a.m.–4 p.m. Admission for ages 7–12 is $10. For adults, admission is $25 if you plan to take photographs; $15 if you don't. Go figure. Interesting place, though.

Leaving Old Car City, go left (south) on US 411 for about 6 miles and curve left onto North Tennessee Street (US 41 South) in Cartersville for about 2 miles, then right onto Main Street. In 0.4 mile, turn left onto Etowah Drive. From there it's about 2.5 miles to **the Etowah Indian Mounds Historic Site**.

With three principal mounds and three smaller ones on a 54-acre plot on the northern banks of the Etowah River, this is the best-preserved site of the Mississippian Culture in the Southeast. It was inhabited from about 1000 A.D. to 1550 A.D. by people who were probably the ancestors of the Muscogee (Creek) Indians.

The highest mound, called the Temple Mound, is 63 feet high. That's as tall as a six-story building. It was probably the home of the priest/chief. Only about nine percent of the mounds have been excavated, but it appears that nobles, dressed in elaborate costumes, were buried in another mound.

Etowah Mounds Historic Site is open Tuesday through Saturday, 9 a.m.–4:30 p.m. Admission is $6 for adults, $5 for seniors, $4 for ages 6–17, and $2 for children under six.

From the Etowah Indian Mounds, turn left onto Indian Mounds Road for 0.8 mile to the T intersection with Douthit Ferry Road. Turn right for about 2 miles, left on Rockmart Highway for about a half-mile, then right on Euharlee Road and then continue for 6 miles to Covered Bridge Road. The old Presbyterian Church and cemetery are on the left just before the turn. Turn left, and in 0.4 mile the **Euharlee Creek Covered Bridge** will be on your left.

A Town truss lattice design, the bridge was designed by famed freed slave and bridge builder Horace King and built in 1886 by his son Washington King. The 138-foot bridge carried traffic across Euharlee Creek for 90 years before being bypassed in 1976. "Euharlee," by the way, is a Creek Indian word meaning "she who laughs."

Leaving the bridge area, go back to Euharlee Road and go west 7.2 miles, at which point Euharlee Road becomes Chulio Road. Continue on Chulio for 5.6 miles, then turn left onto Boyd Valley Road. In 0.7 mile, turn right onto Pleasant Valley Road. Go 1.6 miles and turn right onto GA 101. In 0.2 mile,

THIS JALOPY IS ONE OF MORE THAN 4,000 CARS AT OLD CAR CITY

THE TEMPLE MOUND, AS SEEN FROM THE SECOND-HIGHEST MOUND

turn left onto Jack Street/GA 101 Spur for 0.7 mile, then turn right on Old Rockmart Road. After 0.5 mile, turn left on Maple Road. Go about 0.1 mile, cross the bridge over Silver Creek, and turn into the parking lot on the left. The **Lindale Mill** will be on the left across the creek.

An overshot wheel design, the mill was erected in 1832 by slave labor, using bricks made from clay near the site. Larkin Barnett was the original owner. After being damaged by Union soldiers during the Civil War, it was restored by Captain Jacob Hoss, and for many years it was known as Hoss' Mill. In 1840, a bag of flour processed at the mill won First Prize at the Paris World's Fair.

Leaving the mill area, turn right on Park Avenue, which will become Maple Rd. In about 2.5 miles, turn right onto the US 27/ 411 north ramp. Continue on US 27, which will become East Second Avenue as you go north. After about 3 miles, East Second Avenue will become Martha Berry Blvd. Go about 1.5 miles, then turn right on Veterans Memorial Highway (GA 1). The entrance to **Oak Hill, the Martha Berry Home and Museum** will be just over 100 yards on the right.

Oak Hill was originally built in 1847, but after being damaged by fire in 1884, was rebuilt in Greek Revival style. Tours guided by Berry College students begin at the museum, where visitors can trace the evolution of Martha Berry's schools into Berry College, and include Oak Hill,

THE EUHARLEE CREEK COVERED BRIDGE WAS BUILT ON PIERS HIGH ABOVE THE CREEK BECAUSE A FLOOD HAD CARRIED AWAY A PREVIOUS BRIDGE

the outbuildings, and the extensive gardens. The facilities and grounds are open from 10 a.m. until 5 p.m. Monday through Saturday, except for holiday weekends. Call 706-368-6789 or visit the website (www.berry.edu/oakhill) for information about tours and the museum. Reservations are necessary for the tour.

THE EUHARLEE CREEK COVERED BRIDGE TRUSSES ARE FASTENED TOGETHER WITH WOODEN PEGS

Martha Berry, born in 1865, was brought by her parents to live at the mansion they called Oak Hill in 1871. She lived there the rest of her life, never marrying but dedicating her life to the education of the children of the North Georgia Mountains. In the late 1890s, she began holding Sunday School sessions for poor children in a small cabin that still stands on the Oak Hill grounds. She also started Sunday schools in a small building that she built across the highway on 83 acres given to her by her father and in an abandoned church at Possum Trot.

In 1902, she opened a small boarding school for boys, and in 1909 she opened the Martha Berry School for Girls. Over the years, these small schools grew into Berry College, one of

THE OLD GRIST MILL AT LINDALE, JUST SOUTH OF ROME, WAS MADE OF BRICKS HAND-MADE BY SLAVES

the most highly rated schools in the South and, with more than 27,000 acres, the world's largest college campus.

From the Oak Hill exit, turn right on US 27 and continue for about a mile to the second entrance to **Berry College**, on the left. The best way to find your way around the campus is to pick up a map from the attendant at the entrance. The castle-like **Ford Buildings**, donated by automaker Henry Ford, will be on the right as you enter. Mr. and Mrs. Ford began to take a

THE 42-FOOT WATER WHEEL AT THE BERRY COLLEGE MILL WAS BUILT BY STUDENTS

great interest in Martha Berry's school in 1921, ultimately providing most of the financing for the gothic complex, which was begun in 1928 and completed in 1931.

From the Ford Buildings, follow the map to the Mountain Campus and the **Old Grist Mill** and **Possum Trot Church**.

Built in 1930, the Old Grist Mill ground flour and meal for the Berry College kitchens. It was operated by students under the supervision of a miller as part of their practical training. The overshot water wheel, 42 feet in diameter, is one of the largest in the nation.

Possum Trot Church was built around 1850 and was originally home to the Pleasant Valley congregation but had been abandoned by the late 1800s. In 1900, Martha Berry began a Sunday School there and soon became known as "The Sunday Lady of Possum Trot." In the 1930s, classrooms were added, and Possum Trot became a grammar school. No longer in use except for special occasions, the old church is maintained by Berry students and alumni volunteers.

Leaving Berry College, go left (north) on US 27 for 11.6 miles and turn left on Silver Hill Road. Go 1.7 miles, then turn right on Unity Church Road for 1.3 miles. Turn left on a dirt road for a short distance to **Bethel Presbyterian Church**, built in 1849, and Bethel Yard, its large and very old cemetery, which predates the church.

In one of the graves lies the Reverend T.C. Crawford, who founded Bethel Church and pastored it until his death in 1885. He also established at Bethel a school called Armuchee Academy, the first high school in Chattooga County.

In this obscure place, in a community called Dirt Town, once existed several thriving churches and an academy that drew students from as far away as Alabama and Tennessee. Now only the cemetery and empty buildings remain. Bethel, at least, is being well cared for. I encountered no one when

POSSUM TROT CHURCH WAS ABANDONED UNTIL MARTHA BERRY STARTED A SUNDAY SCHOOL THERE AROUND 1900

BETHEL YARD, THE CEMETERY AT BETHEL PRESBYTERIAN CHURCH, IS OLDER THAN THE CHURCH ITSELF

I visited the church, but when I looked inside I saw scaffolding, which indicated that someone was repairing the ceiling.

From Bethel Church, continue on Unity Church Road for another 1.3 miles and turn left on US 27. In about 3.5 miles, the entrance to **James H. (Sloppy) Floyd State Park** will be on the left.

The 561-acre park offers outstanding fishing in two stocked lakes, boat ramps, four cottages, 25 campsites, picnic shelters, and 3 miles of hiking trails. It's only a 1.6-mile hike to the trailhead of the scenic, 60-mile Pinhoti Trail. The park is open 7 a.m.–10 p.m. every day. There is no admission charge, but there is a $5 parking fee.

Go back to US 27 and turn left for about 3 miles to downtown Summerville and the Neoclassical Revival **Chattooga County Courthouse**, built in 1909, on the left.

From the courthouse, continue on US 27 about 2.9 miles to Rena Street on the right. Watch for the **Howard Finster's Paradise Gardens** sign on the side of a concrete block building. (If you come to the Wal-Mart, you've gone about a half-mile too far.) Follow Rena Street for three blocks. Paradise Gardens will be on the right.

One of America's most famous folk artists, Howard Finster was a Baptist minister who believed God had called him to spread the gospel through art. In 1961, he bought four acres near Summerville and began filling it with his art. He first attracted outside attention in 1975, when an Atlanta TV station did a story about him. *Esquire* magazine also did a story about him and his art museum, which they named "Paradise Garden." The name stuck.

Finster gained national fame through the album covers he designed for the bands R.E.M. and Talking Heads in the 1980s. The cover he did for the Talking Heads album *Little Creatures* was selected as Album Cover of the Year in 1985 by *Rolling Stone*.

Through all the fame, he remained focused on religious outreach through his paintings and found-object sculptures. Paradise Garden contains more than 46,000 pieces of his art, which simply must be seen to be appreciated. As he said, "I took the pieces you threw away and put them together by night and day."

Finster died in 2001 at the age of 84. In 2011, Chattooga County purchased Paradise Garden and now maintains and operates it through the Paradise Garden Foundation. The Garden is open to the public Thursday through Sunday, noon to 5 p.m. Admission is $15 for adults, $10 for seniors, and $5 for students. No charge for children under 12.

From Paradise Garden, go back to US 27 and turn right (north). In 12.8 miles, turn left onto South Main Street, LaFayette, and go 0.2 mile to **CJ's Southern Traditions Restaurant**, on the left at 640 South Main Street. Located in the Patton-Moore House, built in 1860, CJ's features Southern cooking (some folks say cuisine, but around here we call it cookin') and some of the best fried catfish you will ever taste. Like many businesses, their hours have changed because of the pandemic, so check their website (c-js-southern .edan.io) for current information.

From CJ's, turn left and continue north on South Main through the town square to **First Presbyterian Church**, on the left. Erected in 1848 and still very much in use, it served as a hospital for both Confederate and Union wounded after the Battle of LaFayette in June of 1864.

Turn right on Withers Street, across from the Presbyterian Church, then left at the next corner (Duke Street), and go north a few blocks until you see the parking for **Chattooga Academy** and the **Marsh House** on the left.

Chattooga Academy, built in 1836 of bricks made at Rock Spring, a few miles north of LaFayette, is believed to be the oldest brick schoolhouse in Georgia. It cost $815 to build and has one large room on each floor with a chimney at each end. The Presbyterians used it as their meeting house until their church was built in 1848.

Just north of the Academy is the Marsh House, also known as the Marsh-Warthen House. Built in 1836 by Spencer Stewart Marsh, a prominent businessman who founded a major cotton mill in Trion, the house was owned by his descendants for 150 years.

During the Civil War, Union cavalrymen stabled their horses in the house. Bullet holes from the Battle of LaFayette are still visible in the walls. Check the Marsh House website for their tour schedule, because it varies consider-

THE HUBCAP TOWER AT HOWARD FINSTER'S PARADISE GARDEN

ably depending on the time of the year (marshhouseoflafayette.org) or call 423-994-8485.

Leaving the Chattooga Academy/Marsh House parking lot, go right on Duke Street back to the traffic light at East Villanow. Turn left and continue across the bypass, at which point the road will become GA 136. Follow 136 for

CHATTOOGA ACADEMY IN LAFAYETTE IS THE OLDEST BRICK SCHOOL BUILDING IN GEORGIA

about 10.8 miles over Taylor's Ridge to Concord Road on the right. Follow the road for about a mile to Concord Methodist Church on the left. Organized in 1844, the present structure was built in 1882. The church property was the site of camp meetings for many years, with as many as 1,500 in attendance. Monthly services were held at the church until recently, but they may have been discontinued. The church's signs have been removed. The cemetery, about a quarter-mile from the church on Ben Smith Road, has graves of many early Walker County settlers and Civil War veterans. Leaving Concord Methodist Church, go back on Concord Road to GA 136. Turn right and go 1.2 miles to **the Old Country Store** at Villanow, believed to have been built by Joseph Warren Cavender around 1840. There is some dispute about this, but if it is true, it was the longest operating stand-alone country store in the state.

In its heyday, the Cavender store was the center of the remote Villanow community, selling everything from buggies to caskets. Cavender also had a blacksmith shop and cotton mill on the property. Sadly, the old store is now a chiropractor's office. But at least it's being preserved.

If you'd like a short side trip and maybe even feel up to a little hiking, continue on 136 to the top of the hill past the Old Country Store and turn right on Pocket Road for about 2.5 miles to the **Keown Falls Recreation Area** in the Chattahoochee National Forest. The parking area is about a mile from the highway on a well-maintained gravel Forest Service road, and from there it's a hike of a little over a mile to the falls.

Leaving the falls area, turn left, and watch for the road to **John's Mountain Overlook** on your left. John's Mountain is about 1,880 feet high, and the overlook has a great view of the surrounding area. Going back to GA 136, turn right and follow it through Snake Creek Gap to the Exit 320 intersection with Interstate 75 on the north side of Calhoun. Go south for 2 miles to Exit 318 and you will have completed the loop.

IN THE AREA

Accommodations

ADAIR MANOR BED AND BREAKFAST INN, 110 Church Street, Adairsville.

THE CLAREMONT HOUSE BED AND BREAKFAST INN, 906 East Second Avenue, Rome.

FAIRFIELD INN AND SUITES, 1002 GA 53, Calhoun. 706-629-8002.

Dining

THE CITY CELLAR, 72 Railroad Street, Cartersville. 770-334-3170. thecitycellar.com.

CJ'S SOUTHERN TRADITIONS RESTAURANT, 640 South Main Street, LaFayette. 706-639-9443.

DUB'S HIGH ON THE HOG, 349 South Wall Street, Calhoun. 706-602-5150.

SAM'S BURGER DELI, 3170 US 27, Rome. 706-295-0733. Great burgers!

Attractions and Recreation

ETOWAH INDIAN MOUNDS HISTORIC SITE, 813 Indian Mounds Road, Cartersville. 770-387-3747.

HOWARD FINSTER'S PARADISE GARDEN, 201 North Lewlis Street, Summerville. 706-808-0800. paradisegardenfoundation.org.

JAMES H. (SLOPPY) FLOYD STATE PARK, 2800 Sloppy Floyd Lake Road, Summerville. 706-857-0826.

THE MARSH HOUSE, 308 North Main Street, LaFayette. 423-994-8485. www.marshhouseoflafayette.com.

NEW ECHOTA HISTORIC SITE, 1211 Chatsworth Highway, Calhoun. 706-624-1321.

OAK HILL & THE MARTHA BERRY MUSEUM, 24 Veterans Memorial Highway, Rome. 706-368-6789. www.berry.edu/oakhill.

OLD CAR CITY, 3098 US 411, White. 770-382-6141. oldcarcityusa.com.

For more information on any Georgia State Park or Historic Site, visit the state parks website: www.georgiastateparks.org.

Events

Bartow County

Arts Festival at Rose Lawn, Cartersville, September.
Dixie Highway 90-Mile Yard Sale, Old US 41, June.

Chattooga County

Steam into Summerville Railroad Days, Summerville, every Saturday in October and November.

Gordon County

Dixie Highway 90-Mile Yard Sale, Old US 41, June.

New Echota Heritage Day, New Echota Historic Site, November.

Harvest Fest, Calhoun, October.

Walker County

Down Home Days, Chickamauga, first Saturday in May.

Honey Bee Festival, LaFayette, June.

Tours of the Gordon Lee Mansion, Chickamauga, www.friendsofthegordon leemansion.org.

Enchanted Garden of Lights, Rock City Gardens, late November through December 31.

3

A PRESIDENTIAL PICNIC

West Central Georgia

The total length of this tour is about 135 miles and includes Fayette, Coweta, Meriwether, Harris, and Pike counties.

Begin at the **Old Fayette County Courthouse** in downtown Fayetteville (GA 54 at GA 85).

Designed and built by Finley G. Stewart in 1825, this vernacular structure is the fourth-oldest courthouse in Georgia. The Second Empire clock tower was added in 1888.

Many courthouses have benches in front of them, but the Fayette County courthouse has undoubtedly the longest—a 58-foot, hand-hewn heart pine beam that was taken from the courthouse interior when it was reconstructed in 1965.

From the courthouse square, go south on North Glynn Street/GA 85/92. Stay on GA 85 south for 8.8 miles to **Starr's Mill** on Whitewater Creek. It's on the right side of the highway.

The first mill at this site was built by Hananiah Gilcoat sometime before 1825, but it was Hilliard Starr, who owned the property from 1866 to 1879, whose name stuck. The first two mills, both of which burned, were of logs. The current mill, built by William T. Glower in 1907, was in service until 1959 and at one time included a cotton gin and a dynamo that generated electricity for nearby Senoia. There are some beautiful old mills in Georgia, but I rate this as one of the top two.

From Starr's Mill, continue south on GA 85 for 2.4 miles, and turn on Seavy Street, the first right after the Senoia city limits sign. In 0.8 mile, the **Senoia United Methodist Church**, built in 1898, will be on the left on Bridge Street.

LEFT: STARR'S MILL ONCE POWERED A DYNAMO THAT PROVIDED ELECTRICITY FOR THE TOWN OF SENOIA

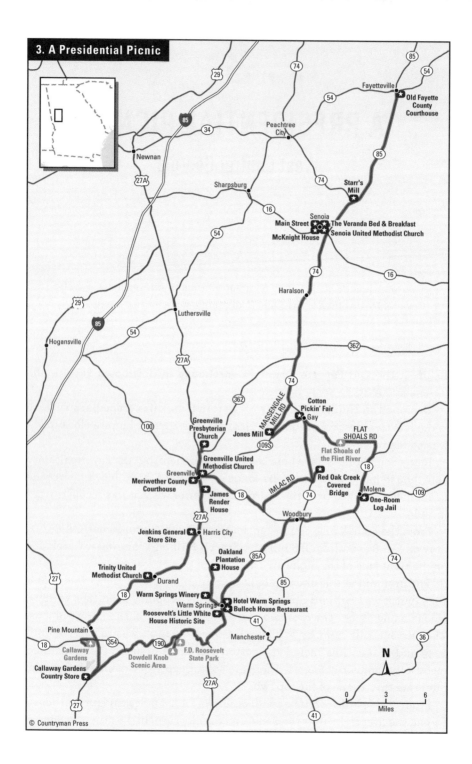

3. A Presidential Picnic

29

85

74

54

Fayetteville

54

Old Fayette
County
Courthouse

85

34

Peachtree
City

85

Newnan

27A

54

Sharpsburg

74

Starr's
Mill

16

Senoia

Main Street

The Veranda Bed & Breakfast

54

McKnight House

Senoia United Methodist Church

74

16

Haralson

29

Luthersville

85

54

362

27A

Hogansville

74

362

MASSENGALE MILL RD

Cotton
Pickin' Fair

FLAT
SHOALS RD

100

Greenville
Presbyterian
Church

Jones Mill

Gay

Flat Shoals of
the Flint River

109S

18

Greenville United
Methodist Church

IMLAC RD

Red Oak Creek
Covered
Bridge

Greenville

Meriwether County
Courthouse

James
Render
House

18

74

Molena

One-Room
Log Jail

109

27A

Woodbury

Jenkins General
Store Site

Harris City

85A

74

Oakland
Plantation
House

27

Trinity United
Methodist Church

Durand

85

18

Warm Springs Winery

74

Warm Springs

Hotel Warm Springs

Roosevelt's Little White
House Historic Site

Bulloch House Restaurant

41

Pine Mountain

Manchester

36

18

Callaway
Gardens

354

190

F.D. Roosevelt
State Park

N

Callaway Gardens
Country Store

Dowdell Knob
Scenic Area

27

27A

0   3   6

Miles

41

© Countryman Press

THE HEART-PINE BEAM IN FRONT OF THE FAYETTE COUNTY COURTHOUSE IS PROBABLY THE LONGEST ONE-PIECE COURTHOUSE BENCH IN THE COUNTRY!

Some consider Senoia Methodist, still very much in active service, to be the best example of Queen Anne architecture in Georgia.

Continue on Seavy for 0.2 mile to **The Veranda Bed & Breakfast**, on the right at number 252, at the intersection with Barnes Street. An 8,000-square-foot 1906 Greek Revival mansion with nine guest rooms, it was originally the Holberg Hotel and is also an event venue. The granddaughter of a long-time

DOWNTOWN SENOIA IS A POPULAR LOCATION FOR MOVIE-MAKERS

friend was married there a few years ago, and the breakfast they served was absolutely the best I've ever eaten.

The Veranda is also just one block from **Senoia's historic Main Street**, with many interesting shops, including **Holberg Furniture Store**, in business since 1894.

Crossing Main Street, go 0.2 mile and turn left on Pylant Street. Pylant slants right after crossing the railroad tracks. From there, it's 0.1 mile to the Neoclassical **McKnight House** at number 258, built by Captain W. D. Linch in 1905 as a wedding gift to his daughter, Mary McKnight. Legend says that the reason the front door is offset to the left is because Mary wanted to make room for her grand piano in the chamber on the right. The McKnight House is just one of the many interesting things to see in Senoia. Pick up a historical tour brochure at the Senois Welcome Center, 68 Main Street. They're open Wednesday through Saturday, 11 a.m.–3 p.m. Their number is 770-727-9173.

Go back on Pylant to Gin Street (not marked, but just before the railroad tracks) and go right for 0.1 mile. Turn right again on Broad Street, go 0.1 mile, and go left on Wells Street/GA 16 for 0.6 mile back to GA 74/85. Turn right and continue south on GA 85 about 13.3 miles to Massengale Mill Road.

Turn right and follow Massengale Mill Road for 2.3 miles to **Jones Mill and millpond**. As you cross the old bridge over the millpond, the mill will be on your left. This is about all that's left of a once-thriving farming community. Long abandoned, Jones Mill is currently being reconstructed. I have no idea what it will look like by the time this book is published.

BASKETMAKING IS JUST ONE OF THE TRADITIONAL CRAFTS ON DISPLAY AT THE GAY COTTON PICKIN' FAIR

From Jones Mill, continue 0.4 mile on Massengale Mill Road to GA 109 Spur. Go left, and in about 2.5 miles you'll rejoin GA 85 at the only traffic light in the metropolis of Gay, GA. There probably won't be much happening in Gay, unless it's the first full weekend in May or October, in which case you may find yourself in the middle of a traffic jam as thousands flock to the **Gay Cotton Pickin' Fair**, an arts, crafts, and antiques festival on the old Gay family farm.

An institution that dates back to 1972, the Cotton Pickin' Fair is one of the Southeast Tourism Society's Top Twenty Events. The Fair has also been the backdrop for three movies: *The War* in 1993, *Lawless* in 2011, and *In Dubious Battle* in 2014.

From Gay, go south on GA 85 for 4.9 miles to the well-marked intersection with Covered Bridge Road on your left. **Red Oak Creek Covered Bridge** is about a mile back on Covered Bridge Road.

RED OAK CREEK COVERED BRIDGE IN MERIWETHER COUNTY IS THE ONLY BRIDGE BUILT BY HORACE KING STILL IN USE

Dating to the 1840s, this is Georgia's oldest covered bridge, and at 391 feet, the longest, if one includes the approaches. The covered portion is about 140 feet long, using Town lattice construction with criss-crossed planks held together by approximately 2,500 wooden pegs. It was built by the legendary Horace King, a freed slave and master bridge builder. At one time, much of the traffic in the Deep South crossed its streams on bridges built by King, but time moves on, and the Red Oak Creek bridge is the last of King's bridges still in use.

Returning from the bridge to GA 85, go right (north) for less than 50 yards and turn left onto Imlac Road for 4.9 miles to GA 18/109. Go right and continue 5.8 miles to Greenville. In the center of the town square is the Queen Anne–design **Meriwether County Courthouse**, built in 1903.

On the right hand corner as you enter the square is the **Greenville United Methodist Church**, erected in 1895 by a congregation organized in the early 1830s.

Turn right at the Methodist Church and go north on GA 41/US 27 ALT for 1.9 miles to GA 362. Turn right, go 0.2 mile, then turn left on Rocky Mount Road for 0.6 mile to the **Greenville Presbyterian Church**, on a small knoll on the left. The congregation was organized in 1829 and this building was erected in 1836, at a time when the West Georgia area was very much raw frontier. The church has weekly services and the building is obviously lovingly maintained, with a modern parish house in the rear. The cemetery is

THE QUEEN ANNE–STYLE MERIWETHER COUNTY COURTHOUSE IN GREENVILLE WAS BUILT IN 1903

very old—I didn't spend much time looking, but I easily found a gravestone with a death date of 1818.

Returning to the courthouse square, stop at the visitor information center on the north side of the square and pick up a driving tour brochure. You can even download a driving tour app for your phone.

Greenville has a number of very interesting old structures. One such is the Three Gables House. From the west side of the square, take LaGrange Street west for 0.2 mile. The Three Gables House, built in 1870 by Confederate veteran and prominent local citizen Samuel Monroe Davidson is at No. 418.

Go back to the courthouse square and take US 27 ALT/GA 41 south 0.8 mile to the **James Render House** on the left.

Render, who came to Meriwether County about 1832, established a large cotton plantation and built a Plantation Plain-style home. By 1850 his holdings had expanded to 1900 acres, growing a variety of crops in addition to cotton. He had eleven children, and among his descendants have been a governor of Georgia and a Chief Justice of the Alabama Supreme Court. Render's grandson James L. Render expanded the house to its present Neoclassical style in the early 1900s.

GREENVILLE PRESBYTERIAN CHURCH CLOSED IN 1963 BUT REOPENED IN 1972

THE JAMES RENDER HOUSE WAS THE CENTER OF A 1,900-ACRE PLANTATION

Continue south on US 27 ALT/GA 18/41 for about 3.2 miles to the traffic circle at Harris City. Take the first exit (GA 18) and look on your immediate right for a small stone arch, a couple of steel girders, and behind them, some broken-down walls. This is all that remains of **Jenkins General Store**, established by George W. Jenkins at Harris City in the early 1900s. It was here that his son, George, Jr., learned the rudiments of the grocery business. He graduated from Greenville High School, and in 1925 moved to Florida, where he worked for Piggly Wiggly for five years. In 1930 he opened the first Publix store in Winter Haven, and the rest, as they say, is history.

So believe it or not, these ruins on a remote West Georgia highway could be considered the progenitor of Publix, the well-known grocery chain (and my favorite store because they bake five-grain Italian bread that is to die for!).

Continue south on GA 18 for 5.5 miles to the ghost town of Durand. **Trinity United Methodist Church** will be on your right. Built in 1910, the classically beautiful sanctuary replaced the original 1854 structure that was destroyed by a tornado in 1908.

Go 6.5 miles farther on GA 18 to the intersection with US 27 and turn left (south) on 27 for 2.6 miles through the town of **Pine Mountain**. US 27 intersects with GA 354 at the south edge of Pine Mountain. Turn right and take GA 354 West for 1.2 miles, then left on GA 18 for 1.6 miles to the main entrance to **Callaway Gardens**.

With 13,000 acres, Callaway Gardens is so many things that it's almost impossible to summarize it in a few paragraphs. It's a resort with lakes, beaches, boating and fishing, water sports, championship golf courses, tennis courts, eight walking trails, and bicycle trails. There are nine restaurants, nine shops, an inn, cottages, and villas. It is also an event venue and a conference center.

Callaway Gardens has one of the country's largest butterfly conservatories and North America's largest azalea garden, with more than 20,000 native and exotic species lining the winding trails and reflecting their beauty in the Mirror Pond and Valley Stream. It is a spring spectacle that must be seen to be believed. I once spent an entire day walking the trails and photographing the azaleas.

From mid-November to New Year's, visitors can drive a 5-mile trail of illuminated scenery, or ride a trolley if you prefer, in Callaway Gardens' **Festival of Lights**, made up of eight million lights on 725 miles of light string.

Leaving Callaway Gardens, take GA 18 back to GA 354 and turn right. Turn right again on US 27 South and go 3 miles to the intersection with GA 190. The **Callaway Gardens Country Store** will be on the right. Make a sharp left on 190 and follow the signs for 3 miles to the entrance of **F. D. Roosevelt**

THE REMAINS OF JENKINS' STORE IN HARRIS CITY, WHERE THE FOUNDER OF THE PUBLIX CHAIN WORKED AS A TEENAGER

MORE THAN 20,000 VARIETIES OF AZALEAS GROW IN CALLAWAY GARDENS

State Park. With 9,049 acres and 42 miles of trails, the park is a hiker's and backpacker's paradise. It has 2 lakes, 21 cottages, 115 RV campsites, and 16 backcountry campsites. It also offers picnicking, swimming, birding, and fishing. The park is open at 7 a.m. daily, There is no entrance fee, but a $5 parking pass is required.

Continue on GA 190 for about 5.5 miles along the spine of Pine Mountain and turn right at the sign for **Dowdell Knob Scenic Area**. It's 1.3 miles back to the overlook, which was one of President Franklin Delano Roosevelt's favorite places for contemplation and picnics. Always the aristocrat, he had a grill built so he could picnic in his preferred manner, sitting in a chair at a linen-draped table, eating hot food with silverware. His statue at Dowdell Knob depicts him sitting on one side of a bench, as if inviting someone to come sit beside him. The statue is remarkable in that it is the only public depiction of Roosevelt with the leg braces necessitated by his polio worn on the *outside* of his trousers, rather than under them.

Leaving Dowdell Knob, go back to GA 190 and turn right. From that point, it's about 3 miles to the intersection of GA 190 and US 27 Alt/GA 85. Go left for about 3 miles to the entrance to **Roosevelt's Little White House Historic Site**. From the entrance, it's about a half-mile back to the Little White House grounds.

Roosevelt first came to Warm Springs in 1924, hoping that the 88-degree spring waters would cure the polio that had struck him in 1921. The waters helped, but were not a cure. Nevertheless, he kept coming back, making 41 trips between 1924 and his death.

In 1932, while governor of New York, he had a six-room house built at Warm Springs, the only home he ever owned. He died of a stroke at the Little White House in 1945, with World War II victory in sight.

Today, visitors can tour his home, which has been carefully preserved very much as he left it. The site is open from 9 a.m. to 4:45 p.m. every day except Thanksgiving, Christmas, and New Year's Day. The admission charge is $12 for adults, $10 for seniors, $7 for ages 6–17, and $2 for ages five and under.

Exiting the Little White House area, turn left on US 27 Alt/GA 85, go 0.4 mile to the intersection of GA 41, and turn right. On your left as you enter Warm Springs' block-long commercial district is the **Warm Springs Hotel**.

Built in 1907, the hotel has been owned, operated, and extensively (and

THE FRANKLIN D. ROOSEVELT STATUE AT DOWDELL KNOB ON PINE MOUNTAIN

PRESIDENT ROOSEVELT HAD A GRILL BUILT FOR HIS PICNICS AT DOWDELL KNOB, ONE OF HIS FAVORITE PLACES

authentically) restored by vibrantly active septuagenarian Gerrie Thompson since 1988. During Roosevelt's visits to Warm Springs, it was home to staff people, the press, and international dignitaries. As a photographer, I had the interesting privilege of spending two nights in a room whose bathroom was used by press photographers to process their film at the time of Roosevelt's passing.

Hotel Warm Springs features rooms furnished with unique antiques and also furniture made in Eleanor Roosevelt's family furniture factory, combining the ambience of the past with every up-to-date amenity. A "Southern Breakfast Feast" and evening refreshments are part of the package, and an ice cream parlor and fudge shop are on the premises.

At the other end of the block and on the other side of the street is the **Bulloch House Restaurant**.

The original Bulloch House was built in 1893 by Benjamin F. Bullock, cofounder of the town of Warm Springs. It was converted into a restaurant in 1990, and was purchased by Peter and Sandy Lampert in 2011, who continue the Bulloch House's tradition of fine Southern cuisine.

Unfortunately, the house burned to the ground in 2015, but the Lamperts moved the business to a storefront at 70 Broad Street and carried right on, with an all-you-can-eat buffet lunch on Tuesdays through Sundays as well as dinner on Fridays and Saturdays.

From Warm Springs, take GA 85 ALT north for 8.6 miles and turn right on

THE HOTEL WARM SPRINGS IS NOW A UNIQUE BED AND BREAKFAST INN

THE LOG JAIL IN MOLENA WAS BUILT AROUND 1900. APPARENTLY ONE CELL WAS ENOUGH IN THOSE DAYS

GA 18/109 through Woodbury's old downtown. Go 6.4 miles to Molena and turn right on GA 18/109 at the flashing traffic signal. The **One-Room Log Jail**, dating from about 1900, will be on the immediate left. It does not look like a very comfortable place to be incarcerated.

From Molena, stay on GA 18 for 3 miles and turn left on Hamilton Road (well-maintained gravel) for 1 mile. Stay left at the Y intersection. Turn left on Flat Shoals Road for a little over 2 miles to the bridge over **the Flat Shoals of the Flint River**, so called because the Flint, a fairly small river above that point, flows over an area of large, flat rock outcroppings perhaps 300 yards wide before returning to its normal width downstream. The shoals form a natural footbridge that was part of the Oakfuskee Trail, a major Creek Indian trade route.

From the Flat Shoals bridge, continue for 3.5 miles to Gay and the end of this tour.

IN THE AREA

Accommodations

HOTEL WARM SPRINGS, 47 Broad Street, Warm Springs. 706-655-2114. www.hotelwarmspringsbb.org.

MOUNTAIN CREEK INN, 17800 US 27, Pine Mountain. 800-852-3810. www.callawaygardens.com.

THE VERANDAH BED AND BREAKFAST, 252 Seavy Street, Senoia. 866-598-3905, 770-599-3905. verandabandbinn.com.

Dining

BULLOCH HOUSE RESTAURANT, 70 Broad Street, Warm Springs. 706-655-9068. www.bullochhouse.com.

THE COUNTRY KITCHEN, 16275 US 27, Pine Mountain Valley. 844-227-5245.

NIC & NORMAN'S, 20 Main Street, Senoia. 770-727-9432. www.facebook .com/nicandnormansofficialpage.

THE OYSTER HOUSE, 113–463 West Harris Street, Pine Mountain. 706-489-3233.

Attractions and Recreation

CALLAWAY GARDENS, 17800 US 27, Pine Mountain. 800-852-5292. www .callawaygardens.com.

F. D. ROOSEVELT STATE PARK, 2970 GA 190, Pine Mountain. 706-663-4858.

ROOSEVELT'S LITTLE WHITE HOUSE HISTORIC SITE, 401 Little White House Road, Warm Springs. 706-655-2311.

For more information on any Georgia State Park or Historic Site, visit the state parks website: www.georgiastateparks.org.

Events

Coweta County

Cruisin' to the Oldies Car Show, Senoia, September.

Harris County

Annual Plant Fair and Sale, Callaway Gardens, Pine Mountain, March.

Sky High Hot Air Balloon Festival, Callaway Gardens, Pine Mountain, Labor Day weekend.

Fantasy in Lights, Callaway Gardens, Pine Mountain, November–December.

Meriwether County

Roosevelt Days, Warm Springs, April.

Harvest Hoe-Down, Warm Springs, October.

Gay Cotton Pickin' Fair, Gay, first full weekend in May and October.

Spring Fling Festival, Warm Springs, April.

4

PATSILIGA, PASAQUAN, AND PEACHES

West Central Georgia

The total length of this tour is about 190 miles and it includes Monroe, Lamar, Upson, Taylor, Talbot, Marion, Schley, Sumter, Macon, and Peach counties.

From Interstate Exit 185 at Forsyth, take GA 18 west. After about 13 miles, US 41/GA 18 turns left as you approach the outskirts of Barnesville. Stay to the right and continue straight on Forsyth Street for about a mile to downtown. One block before the intersection of Forsyth and Main Streets, the **Barnesville City Hall**, surely the funkiest city hall in the entire United States, will be on the left.

At the intersection of Forsyth and Main Streets, **Jackson C. Smith Barnesville Buggies** will be on the corner on your right. Currently, they're selling cell phones instead of buggies. Times change.

Turn left on Main and go 0.8 mile. In a few blocks, Main will become Thomaston Street, lined with really fine old homes.

One of the last houses in the historic district, at 901 Thomaston Street, is the **Barnes-Keifer House**, built in 1870 by William and Sarah Barnes Keifer, the daughter and son-in-law of Gideon Barnes, tavern-keeper and founder of Barnesville.

Turn right on Rose Street, at the corner by the Barnes-Keifer House, and go about 0.6 mile. Cross the bypass and continue on Burnette Street/GA 18 for 2.6 miles to the **Benjamin Gachet House**, at 951 GA 18.

This nearly pristine Plantation Plain-style home was built by Benjamin Gachet, a French nobleman who came to the US from Santo Domingo. He began buying up land in what is now Lamar County in 1825, built his home in 1828, and unfortunately died in 1829, leaving his widow, Caroline Stubbs

LEFT: THE BARNESVILLE TOWN HALL. SURELY AMERICA'S FUNKIEST

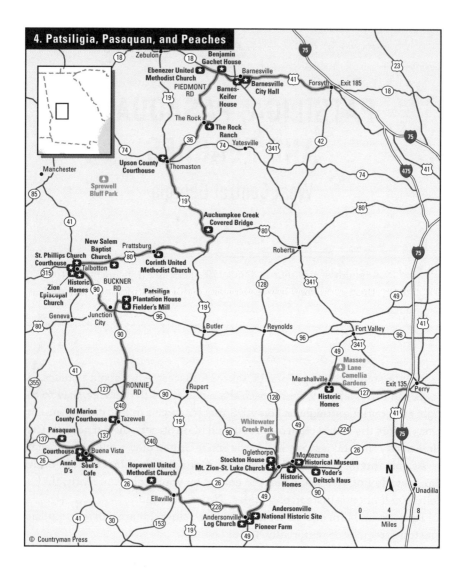

Gachet, with young children. It appears that she supported her family by operating the house as an inn and stagecoach stop.

From the Gachet House, continue on GA 18 for another 2 miles to **Ebenezer United Methodist Church** at the intersection of GA 18 and Meansville Road/GA 109. According to congregational records, the church was built around 1840 and still holds regular services.

From Ebenezer Church, go back on GA 18 about 2.1 miles and turn right on Piedmont Road for 4.1 miles. Turn left onto The Rock Road for another 4 miles. Somewhere along the way it becomes Piedmont Road again. At the intersection with GA 36 turn left, go 0.6 mile, and **The Rock Ranch** will be on the right at 5020 GA 36.

The Rock Ranch was founded by S. Truett Cathey, the businessman who founded Chick-Fil-A, and is dedicated to "growing healthy families." At its base, it's a 1500-acre working cattle ranch, but it's also much more. It's a farm, growing and selling fresh produce and grass-fed natural beef. It's an amusement park with train rides, zip lines, a carousel, fishing, pedal boats and pedal carts, pony rides, and more.

The ranch hosts numerous events and festivals throughout the year. They also have lodging and camping facilities, facilities for corporate meetings and company and group picnics, and field trips. Everything at The Rock Ranch has one ultimate purpose: to build family values and enrich the lives of others through service and love.

Visit their website (www.therockranch .com) for information and tickets, or call 706-647-6374.

BRONC RIDER SCULPTURE AT THE ROCK RANCH

The little town named "The Rock," just south of The Rock Ranch, got its name from the fact that it had no train station. Passing trains would leave or pick up mail at a large rock near the tracks. Mail to a resident of the community would often be addressed to "Ed Jones at the rock," and so the town became "The Rock."

Leaving the Rock Ranch, turn left and continue on GA 36 for 2.1 miles and turn right on Delray Road for 4.8 miles to US 19. Go left on 19 for 0.6 mile, then right on Jeff Davis for 1.2 miles, then left on Hannah's Mill Road for 0.1 mile to the old Hannah's Mill on Tenmile Creek. The mill is on the right—still standing, but pretty dilapidated.

From the mill, continue on Hannah's Mill Road for 2.8 miles, then left on West Main Street for 0.6 mile to downtown Thomaston. Go right on GA 36 for one block, left on West Gordon for a block, then right on US 19. But before you leave Thomaston, be sure to see the Neoclassical Revival **Upson County Courthouse**, built in 1908, which dominates the town square.

A worthwhile side trip from Thomaston is **Sprewell Bluff Park**, on the Flint River. It's about 12 miles west, via GA 74 and Old Alabama Road. The 1,372-acre park is spread along 3 miles of the Flint River.

From Thomaston, take US 19 south for 12 miles, turn left on Allen Road and go 0.8 mile to **Auchumpkee Creek Covered Bridge**. Built in 1892 by the firm of Herring and Alford, the bridge is 96 feet long and uses the Town lattice truss design.

After being destroyed by a flood in 1994, the bridge was rebuilt on

EBENEZER UNITED METHODIST CHURCH WAS BUILT AROUND 1840 AND STILL HOLDS REGULAR SERVICES

the creek bank in 1997 by Arnold Graton of New Hampshire, who used a team of horses to pull the restored bridge into its place over the creek. It is no longer open to traffic, but parking and a picnic area are available at the bridge.

From the covered bridge, go back to US 19, turn left, and go about 4 miles to the junction with US 80. Go right on US 19/US 80 for about 1.5 miles, then right on US 80 for about 5.5 miles to **Corinth Methodist Church** on the left side of the highway in Prattsburg. The town was founded in 1828, the same year the church was organized. The town sign, by the way, says "Unincorporated, But Not Dead."

A beautiful Greek Revival structure, the Corinth church is very similar to Mt. Zion Presbyterian Church in Hancock County, but in better condition. Erected in 1869, it has not been in regular use since 1965, but someone is doing a good job of maintaining it, even to the point of keeping electric candles alight in the windows.

From Corinth Methodist Church, continue for 5.8 miles to **New Salem Baptist Church**, also on the left. I don't have any history on this church, but it's probably not quite as old as Corinth Methodist. The congregation has fairly recently moved to new facilities. From New Salem Church, it's about 5.5 miles to downtown Talbotton.

Just after New Salem church comes PoBiddy Crossroads. There's nothing much there, but the name has always intrigued me.

In Talbotton, go to the Chamber of Commerce at the corner of South Washington and East Madison and pick up a tour guide. There's also a website (talbotcountychamber.org/online-tour.php) that you can access on your cell phone or iPad to guide you on your tour.

You can't, of course, miss the Queen Anne–style **Talbot County Courthouse**, built in 1892 (truly a banner year for Georgia courthouses). Some other sites I found especially interesting are the following:

The **Warner-Simpson-Jordon House**, at 126 Monroe Street, on the southwest corner of Monroe and Clay. A Plantation Plain house built in 1832 by Judge Hiram Warner, a Justice of the Georgia Supreme Court, as his home and law office. During the Civil War the house was raided by Yankee soldiers. Warner, a prominent Rebel leader, resisted and was sentenced to hang. The Yankees hanged him from a tree in his own yard and left him for dead, but he was cut down by a family slave, revived, and lived 16 more years.

Cata-cornered across the intersection, on the northeast corner of Monroe and Clay at 106 Monroe, is the **Thelma Hill House**. You would not suspect

AUCHUMPKEE CREEK COVERED BRIDGE WAS DESTROYED BY A FLOOD IN 1994 BUT REBUILT IN 1997

THE CORINTH METHODIST CHURCH IN PRATTSBURG IS BUILT IN THE GREEK REVIVAL STYLE SO POPULAR IN THE EARLY 19TH CENTURY

that this modest cottage was once the famous two-story Mansion House Hotel, headquarters of the Federal officers in the district following the Civil War. The building was cut into two sections and the bottom floor was moved to this location, while the top floor occupied the lot next door. That lot is now empty because the erstwhile top floor was destroyed by a storm in the 1920s.

St. Phillips African Methodist Episcopal Church, at the southwest corner of Tyler and Elizabeth Wright Streets, is an historic black congregation founded in 1870. The building dates from 1875, replacing an earlier structure that was destroyed by a storm. For many years, the only school for black children in Talbot County was in the basement of St. Phillips. The great educator Elizabeth Wright was born just up the hill, one of a family of 27 children, and received her early schooling at St. Phillips before going on to graduate from Tuskegee Institute, where she was mentored by Booker T. Washington himself.

Zion Episcopal Church, on Jackson Street between Clark and Polk Streets, is a Tudor-Gothic structure which would look right at home in an English village. Master craftsmen put it together with handmade iron nails and wooden pegs, making the altars, communion rails, and pulpit of native walnut, and hanging doors that open with a five-inch brass key. The rare

THE QUEEN ANNE–STYLE TALBOT COUNTY COURTHOUSE IN TALBOTTON WAS BUILT IN 1892

THE STRAUSS-LEVERT MEMORIAL HALL IN TALBOTTON IS ALL THAT REMAINS OF LEVERT COLLEGE

Pilcher pipe organ, installed in 1850, is the oldest one still in working use in the United States.

A $257,000 project to restore the exterior of the church was completed in November 2020. Worship services are held quarterly.

The **Talbotton United Methodist Church**, at 225 College Avenue, was organized in 1830, and a wooden building was erected on this site. It was replaced in 1857 by the present Greek Revival brick structure. Talbotton was an important center for Methodism in the pre–Civil War years, with two Methodist colleges in the town.

One of those colleges was LeVert College, founded in 1856 as one of the first schools for young women in Georgia. Its most prominent building was the **Straus-LeVert Memorial Hall**, on the northwest corner of Clark Street and College Avenue, also built in 1856. The school closed in 1907, but the building was renovated through the generosity of the Straus family.

Lazerus Straus, a German Jew, immigrated in 1853 and came to Talbotton in 1854, peddling goods from a wagon. He settled in the town, brought his family from Germany, and established a successful dry-goods business on the town square. He moved his family to New York in 1865, and by 1896 the Straus family were the sole owners of Macy's Department Store.

The **Pew-Hill-Dean House**, built in 1852, is a fine example of Greek Revival architecture. It is set back from the road, on the right, at Number

864 on US 80/GA 22/41 south of town. Unfortunately, you won't be able to see its most unusual feature: two-story columns at the rear of the house to match those in front!

The **Towns-Persons-Page House**, several blocks out on West Monroe, is a bit hard to see because it is on a hill set well back from the right side of the road with no place to park. A classic Greek Revival design, it was built in 1830 by George Washington Towns, a cousin of the Creek Indian Chief William McIntosh, who built the McIntosh House at Indian Springs in Butts County in 1823.

Many of the original outbuildings were made of brick and are still standing, including a seven-seat brick outhouse!

The **Pew-Thornton-Olive-Calhoun House** is on the southwest corner of Adams and North Jefferson. Another Greek Revival design, it is an imposing mansion built in 1836. It was the home of Captain Seaborn W. Thornton, who served under General Robert E. Lee in the Army of Virginia during the Civil War.

There are quite a few other interesting and significant sites, so enjoy the tour. When you're finished, take GA 90 (Clark Street) south for about 6 miles and merge left onto GA 96. After 2 miles, turn left on Buckner Road for about 1.5 miles, then right on Fielder Mills (dirt) for 0.8 mile to **Fielder's Mill,** at 780 Fielder Mills, Junction City.

The mill is a water-powered turbine type, built in 1930 on the site of the circa-1840 John Downs Mill, which had burned. The mill is very rustic-looking but is still functioning. In fact, it is one of the oldest continuously operating businesses in Talbot County.

THE MILLSTONES AT FIELDER'S MILL NEAR JUNCTION CITY ARE STILL GRINDING OUT CORNMEAL, FLOUR, AND GRITS

The real surprise for me was finding an 1840 manor house on the property— **Patsiliga Plantation House**. The entire property is a museum, dedicated to preserving the industrial equipment used from 1830 to 1930—powered by water, hand, horse, steam, gasoline, and electricity. Patsiliga, by the way, is pronounced "patchy-leggy," according to Mike Buckner, who runs the place and should know. It's a Creek Indian word meaning "pigeon roost."

To provide an opportunity to experience the sights, sounds, and smells of this bygone era, Patsiliga Plantation hosts a festival the first full weekend of each November— **Harvest Days in Old Talbot**. The mill will be

REPLACED WHEN THE COUNTY SEAT MOVED TO BUENA VISTA IN 1850, THE OLD MARION COUNTY COURTHOUSE IN TAZEWELL IS STILL HOME TO A MASONIC LODGE

grinding meal, flour, and grits. The sugar cane mill will be squeezing cane to be cooked into syrup, and JACK the locomotive will be giving rides. Plus, there are many demonstrations, exhibits, vendors, and activities. Admission is $10 for adults, and those 18 and under are free.

From the mill, go back to Buckner Road, turn left, and go back to GA 96. Cross it, and continue on GA 90 for 6.9 miles, then turn right on GA 127. You will be driving through sand country, with large sand pits on both sides of the road. Go 3 miles and turn left on GA 240 Connector to GA 240. Merge left to Tazewell and the vernacular, wood-framed **Old Marion County Courthouse**. Erected in 1848 to replace one that had burned in 1845, only one court session was held there before the voters decided to move the county seat to Buena Vista.

From Tazewell, go right on GA 137 for 6.2 miles toward Buena Vista. As you enter the town, GA 137 will turn sharp right and follow 3rd Avenue. Continue about 0.3 mile, then turn left on Broad Street to the town square and the Neoclassical **Marion County Courthouse**, built in 1850. If you're hungry, there are, at the time of this writing, three restaurants around the square—a pizzeria, a Mexican restaurant, and the very up-to-date **Coffee Club**, which serves breakfast and sandwiches. There's also **Annie D's**, off the square at 123 North Broad Street, claiming it serves the "best fried chicken in town."

From the square, go back on Broad Street to 3rd Street/GA 137 and turn left. Stay on GA 137 for about a mile, and when GA 137 and GA 41 divide, keep left to stay on 137. Go about 4 miles, then turn right on Eddie Martin Road and go 0.7 mile to **Pasaquan**, on the right at 238 Eddie Martin Road, certainly the most unusual place you will visit on this tour.

Born poor in Marion County in 1908, Eddie Owens Martin escaped to New York while still a teenager. While sick with a high fever, he had a series of visions in which he was visited by three "people of the future" from a place called Pasaquan, who informed him that he had been chosen to create art that would portray a peaceful future for the human race. He began calling himself St. EOM, from his initials.

Instructed by his spirit guides to return to Georgia and "do something," Martin did so in the early 1950s, having inherited an old farmhouse and a few acres of land near Buena Vista from his mother. In 1957, he began work on Pasaquan, expressing his eccentric and highly individualized vision in concrete and paint until his creations filled seven acres. His work simply has to be seen to be believed.

Pasaquan fell into neglect after St. EOM's death in 1986 but has been restored by the Kohler Foundation in cooperation with the Pasaquan Preservation Society and Columbus State University. The foundation provided a grant and the university acts as steward for the property.

EDDIE O. MARTIN FILLED SEVEN ACRES WITH HIS OTHER-WORLDLY VISION AT PASAQUAN IN MARION COUNTY

Pasaquan is open Thursday, Friday, and Saturday, 10 a.m. to 5 p.m. It's closed on Federal and bank holidays and during the months of July and December. Admission is $10 for adults, $5 for seniors, and $3 for students. Call 706-507-8306 for more information or visit their website (pasaquan .columbusstate.edu).

From Pasaquan, go back to the square in Buena Vista and take GA 26 east about 10.8 miles to Hopewell Church Road. Turn left and go 0.3 mile to **Hopewell United Methodist Church**. The sanctuary was built circa 1870, while a section with Sunday School rooms was added later. The church is very much alive and in business.

Leaving Hopewell Church, go back to GA 26, turn left, and go 3.1 miles to Ellaville. The Romanesque Revival **Schley County Courthouse** on your right was erected in 1899.

From Ellaville, continue on GA 26 for about 0.7 mile. Turn right on US 19, go 1.4 miles, turn left on GA 228 for 10.3 miles, then left on GA 49 to the entrance to **Andersonville National Historic Site**.

The most horrific of Confederate prisoner of war camps, Andersonville Prison was essentially a small valley rimmed by a stockade of logs planted vertically in the ground to form walls 12 feet high, enclosing an area of sixteen acres. A small stream ran through the valley to bring in fresh water at one end and to carry away sewage at the other. It succeeded at neither.

A REPLICA OF THE STOCKADE AT THE ANDERSONVILLE CIVIL WAR POW CAMP, WHERE 13,000 PRISONERS DIED

Built to hold 10,000 prisoners, Andersonville actually housed 33,000 at one point. All told, approximately 45,000 Union prisoners were in the camp at various times. They had little or no clothing, and the only shelters were worn-out tents and brush wickiups. It can be no surprise that exposure, starvation, and disease, especially dysentery, took the lives of 13,000 of them. They are buried nearby in the Andersonville National Cemetery, which was established largely through the efforts of Clara Barton, founder of the American Red Cross.

The **National Prisoner of War Museum**, established in 1998 to commemorate all American prisoners of war, is also the visitor center for the Andersonville Historic Site. It is open 9 a.m.–4:30 p.m. daily except for Thanksgiving, Christmas, and New Year's Day. Visit the website (www.nps.gov/ande/index.htm) or call 229-924-0343 for more information. The park grounds are open 8 a.m.–5 p.m. daily.

Directly across GA 49 from the Historic Site exit is the town of **Andersonville** itself. Although the tiny downtown is tourism-focused, there are some worthwhile things to see. Continue on West Church Street past the monument to Captain Henry Wirz, the POW Camp Commander who was hanged in 1865 as a war criminal, to the **Village Hall**, built in 1843, and the **St. James Pennington Log Church**, built in 1927.

The Village Hall began life as a Baptist church about 5 miles from Andersonville. It was moved to its present site in 1890 and continued to be a church until 2010, when its last surviving member gave it to the Andersonville Guild.

The Pennington Log Church was designed by noted architect Ralph Adams Cram, who also designed the Cathedral of St. John the Divine in New York City. It was built for Dr. James Bolan Lawrence and his Episcopal congregation in Pennington, a few miles to the east. After his death it was given by his family to the Andersonville Guild and moved to its present site in 1963.

On a seven-acre site behind the storefronts of East Church Street is a recreated **Pioneer Farm**, complete with restored buildings and an operating grist mill built circa 1850. There is no admission charge and the Pioneer Farm is open daily, 9 a.m. to dusk.

History comes alive each year on the first full weekend in October, when the town hosts the **Andersonville Historic Fair**, with Confederate and Union encampments; mock Civil War battles; old-time craftsmen at work; dealers in arts, crafts, antiques, and collectibles; live entertainment, and activities for children. The fair is open 10 a.m.–5 p.m. both Saturday and Sunday, and admission is $4 for adults and $1.50 for children 12 and under. Call 229-924-2558 for more information or visit their website (www.andersonvillegeorgia.info).

From the town of Andersonville, go left on GA 49 for about 8 miles to

Oglethorpe. The Romanesque Revival **Macon County Courthouse**, built in 1894, will be on the right at the traffic light.

Although Oglethorpe currently has a population of about 1,300 inhabitants, in the mid-1850s it was one of the largest cities in the state, with a population of 16,000, and missed becoming the state capital by just one electoral vote. Things are much quieter these days.

Other than the courthouse, most of the interesting buildings in Oglethorpe are on Randolph Street. So from the courthouse, go back on GA 49/Chatham Street for two blocks and turn right on Randolph.

First up is the **Stockton House**, on the left at Number 201. A coastal-style cottage built in 1850, the house has an unusual upstairs-downstairs design, with twin front staircases leading to the upper level. During the summer, the family lived upstairs to avoid the harmful "vapors" at ground level that were believed to cause fever.

Continuing on Randolph Street, the **Mt. Zion-St. Luke Lutheran Church** is on the left at Number 401. This structure was erected in 1911, but was preceded by at least three others at different locations following the organization of the congregation in 1827. The land for a church in Oglethorpe was donated by Martin Luther "Luke" Shealy, in whose honor the church was renamed Mt. Zion-St. Luke. The church has historic ties to St. Mark's Lutheran Church in Sumter County (recently moved to Webster County).

THE STOCKTON HOUSE, OGLETHORPE. THE FAMILY LIVED UPSTAIRS IN SUMMER AND DOWNSTAIRS IN WINTER

Across the street from Mt. Zion-St. Luke is the **Oglethorpe United Methodist Church**, built in 1892 by a congregation founded in the 1850s. The bell from the original 1850s building is in the belfry. It was requisitioned by the Confederate government to be melted down into bullets, but fortunately was returned unharmed when the war ended.

At Number 405, just beyond Mt. Zion-St. Luke, is the **Keen House**, a Greek Revival plantation mansion built in 1853 with vernacular details such as tall, boxed columns and unusually large windows.

Just 5 miles from downtown Oglethorpe is **Whitewater Creek Park**, a 482-acre camping, fishing, picnicking, and hiking facility. It's open year-round, 7 a.m. to 10 p.m. There's a boat ramp, and five cabins are available for overnight rental. Call 478-472-8178 for more information.

To get to the park, take Sumter Street north from downtown. In a half-mile, it will merge into GA 90. Continue for about 2 miles, turn right on Pond Church Road, go 0.4 mile, turn left on GA 128, go 1.7 miles, and turn left on Whitewater Road. From there, it's 0.3 mile to the park.

Leaving Oglethorpe, continue on GA 49 for about a half-mile and turn left on Buck Creek Bypass for one block to the Oglethorpe Seventh-Day Adventist Church, on the right. This unusually beautiful structure was built in 1895 by the Oglethorpe Baptist congregation. In the 1950s, the Baptists built a new church and sold this building to the Adventists, who moved it to its present location in 1956.

Go back to GA 49 and continue for about 1.5 miles to downtown Montezuma and the **Carnegie Library** at 101 North Dooly Street. Built in 1907 with a grant from the Andrew Carnegie Foundation, it's the oldest standing Carnegie Library in Georgia. It now houses the **Macon County Welcome Center** and Chamber of Commerce.

Across from the library is the old **Central of Georgia Railroad Depot**. Built in 1890, it was used as a warehouse after the railroad discontinued passenger trains in the 1970s, but it has been renovated and is now the home of the **Macon County Historical Museum**.

From the library and railroad depot, pass between the storefronts of downtown Montezuma to 510 South Dooly—the **House on Literary Hill**, a neoclassical home built in 1885 by prosperous businessman and landowner Captain J.E. DeVaughn for his new second wife, schoolteacher Mary Elizabeth Porter.

If you're hungry for some really good food, continue on South Dooly to Walnut Street, which is Georgia 26, and turn left to **Yoder's Deitsch Haus Restaurant and Bakery** at 5252 GA 26 E in Macon County's large Beachy Mennonite community. The Mennonites are famous for good cooking, and they serve lunch Tuesday through Saturday 11:30 a.m.–2 p.m. and dinner Tuesday, Thursday, Friday, and Saturday 5:30–8 p.m. Call 478-472-2024.

Going back past the library and depot on GA 49/North Dooly street, there

THE GEORGE H. SLAPPEY HOUSE IN MARSHALLVILLE BEGAN AS A FOUR-ROOM FRAME HOUSE

is a handsome brick **Colonial Revival home**, built in 1885, on the left at 301 North Dooly.

Just up the street, on the right at 322 North Dooly, is the **Watson-Mathews Funeral Home**, with an unusual conical porch and oval entrance hall. It was originally a private residence but has been a funeral home since 1969.

Continuing north on GA 49 for about 12 miles to the outskirts of Marshallville, the distinguished, circa 1850s **Slappey-Camp-Liipfert House** is on the right at 500 West Main Street. Originally a much smaller four-room frame house built by E. S. Crocker, it was bought by George H. Slappey around 1860 and expanded to the two-story Greek Revival Mansion that it is today.

A little farther along, on the left at 401 West Main, is the Greek Revival **Frederick-Wade House**. Daniel Frederick built the house on his plantation around 1843, and in 1928 his nephew, Dr. John Donald Wade, pulled it to its present location with teams of mules.

And on the right at 204 West Main, is the **Marcus Sperry House**, built around 1870 and the very essence of quaintness. The story is that Sperry's wife was an artist and designed the house according to her artistic notions. It would be hard to find a better representative of the architectural style known as "eclectic."

Across the street is the **Samuel Henry Rumph (Rumph-Meyers) House** at 209 West Main Street, a 17-room brick mansion built in 1904. It is not architecturally significant except for its lavishness. The important story behind the house is where the money to build it came from, because it was on the Rumph plantation that the Georgia peach industry was born.

In 1857, Lewis Rumph received a gift of an assortment of peachtree plantings of various varieties. He planted them in the family orchard, where they eventually blossomed and bore fruit. Mrs. Rumph saved some of the seeds from the peaches and dropped them in a work basket, forgot about them, and left them there for a dozen years.

When her grandson, Samuel Henry Rumph, began plant experiments at his plantation, Willow Lake, she remembered the mummified seeds and gave them to him. That was in 1870. He planted them, and five years later, they bore fruit—and what a fruit! Because of the magic of cross-pollination, which must have occurred when the original trees were all planted in proximity to each other back in 1857, this delicious, golden, new peach could be broken in half easily and the stone could be removed by hand. Moreover, it was firm enough for shipment to East Coast markets.

Samuel Rumph named the peach "Elberta," for his wife. And that is how the great Georgia peach industry began.

For flower lovers, or anyone who loves beauty, **Massee Lane Camellia Gardens** is a great, easy side trip from Marshallville. Take GA 49 north from downtown for 2.4 miles, then turn right on Massee Lane for 0.4 mile to the gardens.

Headquarters of the American Camellia Society and an International Camellia Society "Garden of Excellence," Massee Lane is nine acres of one of the world's finest collections of camellias. Begun as a private garden by David C. Strother in the 1930s, it was donated to the ACS in 1966.

February is a special time for camellias, but new varieties are blooming every day from September through April. The gardens are open Tuesday through Saturday: 10 a.m.–4:30 p.m. Sunday: 1 p.m.–4:30 p.m. Admission is free for members of the American Camellia Society and children under 12, $5 for adult non-members, and $4 for seniors.

From the Massee Lane Gardens, go back to Marshallville and turn left on GA 127. Immediately after crossing the railroad tracks in downtown Marshallville, notice the **Frigidaire Sign** on the side of a building on the left.

FRIGIDAIRE NO LONGER DOMINATES THE REFRIGERATOR MARKET, BUT ITS SIGN IN MARSHALLVILLE STILL LOOKS GOOD

You don't see many of those nowadays! Frigidaire is still in business but no longer dominant in the industry. I can remember when "Frigidaire" was often used as a generic term for any refrigerator.

From Marshallville, take GA 127 for 11.2 miles east to Interstate 75, Exit 135 at Perry and the end of this tour.

IN THE AREA

One thing to keep in mind as you tour the West Central Georgia back country is that food is where you find it. It will probably be country cooking, and it will most probably be good. But it probably won't be haute cuisine. *Likewise, there are many places to stay along I-75, but nothing at all in Talbotton or Buena Vista. So keep these things in mind as you plan.*

Dining

ANNIE D'S, 123 North Broad Street, Buena Vista. 229-277-0058.

THE BIG CHICK, 148 Washington Avenue, Talbotton. 706-665-8318.

THE COFFEE CLUB, 108 East 4th Avenue, Buena Vista. 229-583-4622.

NORRIS'S FINE FOODS, 695 Short E Street, Thomaston. 706-647-8216.

RIVERBEND RESTAURANT, 202 Riverbend Road (GA 36 West), Thomaston. 706-647-9738.

YODER'S DEITSCH HAUS RESTAURANT AND BAKERY 5252 GA 26 East, Montezuma. 478-472-2024.

Attractions and Recreation

ANDERSONVILLE NATIONAL HISTORIC SITE, GA 49, Andersonville. 229-924-0343. www.nps.gov/ande/index.htm.

MASSEE LANE GARDENS, 100 Massee Lane, Fort Valley. 478-967-2358. americancamellias.com/massee-lane-gardens.

PASAQUAN, 238 Eddie Martin Road, Oglethorpe. 706-507-8306. pasaquan .columbusstate.edu.

THE ROCK RANCH, 5020 Barnesville Highway (GA 36), The Rock. 706-647-6374. www.therockranch.com

SPREWELL BLUFF PARK, 740 Spewell Bluff Road, Thomaston. 706-646-6026.

WHITEWATER CREEK PARK, 165 Whitewater Road, Oglethorpe. 478-472-8171.

Events

Lamar County

Buggy Days, Barnesville, third week in September (a Southeast Top 20 event). Barnesville BBQ & Blues Festival, April.

Macon County

Beaver Creek Festival, Montezuma. montezuma-ga.org/downtown/beaver creekfestival.html.

Sumter County

Andersonville Historic Fair, Andersonville, first full weekend in October. 229-924-2558. www.andersonvillegeorgia.info.

Talbot County

Harvest Days in Old Talbot, Fielder's Mill, Junction City, first full weekend each November. For information call 706-269-3630.

Upson County

Flint River Poker Float, June. 706-647-9686.

5

ON THE ANTEBELLUM TRAIL

Central Georgia

This tour is about 115 miles in length and includes Gwinnett, Barrow, Jackson, Oconee, Morgan, Walton, and Newton counties.

Begin at the intersection of GA 316/US 29/University Parkway and Sugarloaf Parkway between mileposts 11 and 12 on the east side of Lawrenceville.

Exit GA 316/US 29/University Parkway and go south on Sugarloaf Parkway for 0.6 mile. Take the Campbell Road exit. From the ramp, turn left for 0.2 mile and left again on Alcovy Road SE. Go 0.6 mile and Freeman's Mill Park entrance will be on the right at 1401 Alcovy Road, Lawrenceville.

Freeman's Mill, also known as Swann's Mill and Alcovy Mill, was built between 1868 and 1879 on the Alcovy River by John and Levi Loveless. It was in operation until 1996. Gwinnett County purchased the property in 2001, restored the mill, and made it the centerpiece of a 12-acre park with a half-mile paved trail, playground, and restrooms. As part of the restoration project, the mill was raised 5 feet above the Alcovy River's floodplain to avoid future damage. The mill dam is about 100 yards upstream from the mill and is an especially beautiful spot.

From Freeman's Mill Park, turn left (east) on Alcovy Road SE for 2 miles to Harbins Road. Turn left and go 1.2 miles, crossing Winder Highway/US 29 Business. Harbins Road will become Dacula Road at that point. Go about 3 miles to the **Elisha Winn House** on the right at 908 Dacula Road, Dacula. Built circa 1812, it is the oldest surviving structure in Gwinnett County and very likely the oldest building in metro Atlanta. The first Gwinnett County elections were held at this house, and for a time in the early days it served as the county courthouse. An 1820s log jail is also on the property. The Elisha

LEFT: THE ELISHA WINN HOUSE IN DACULA MAY BE THE OLDEST STRUCTURE IN METRO ATLANTA

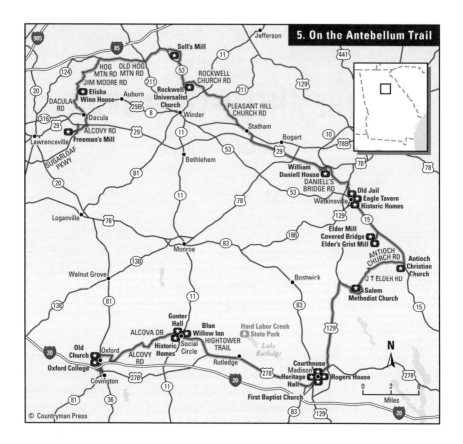

Winn House is managed by the Gwinnett County Historical Society and is open for tours from March to September on the third Saturday of the month from noon to 4:00 p.m. The Elisha Winn Fair is held on the first weekend of October, with the house and all the outbuildings open.

From the Elisha Winn House, go right (north) on Dacula Road for 0.5 mile and turn left on GA 324. Go 0.3 mile, then turn right on Jim Moore Road for 1.7 miles. Turn right on Hog Mountain Road, go 2.6 miles, then turn right on GA 124.

In 2 miles, stay right on Old Hog Mountain Road for 4.9 miles. As you go, the name of the road will change to Covered Bridge Road, then to Peachtree Road. When you reach the intersection with GA 53, turn right on 53 for 0.7 mile to Jackson Trail Road and turn left. Go 0.9 mile to Sell's Mill Park, which will be on the right at 8783 Jackson Trail Road, Hoschton.

Sell's Mill, like Freeman's Mill, has been made the centerpiece of a county park.

Early settler Jonathan Sell purchased 500 acres around Indian Creek in 1815. Sometime around 1890, his youngest son, Frank Sell, dammed the creek and built a three-story mill with an overshot wheel where he not only

FREEMAN'S MILL DAM ON THE ALCOVY RIVER NEAR LAWRENCEVILLE

ground corn but also generated electricity. His mill is still in working condition. The property was purchased by Jackson County in 2000, with ren-
ovations completed in 2007. The park also features a covered pavilion with
picnic tables, a playground, restrooms, and walking trails.

Leaving Sell's Mill, turn right (east) for 0.5 mile on Jackson Trail Road to
Bill Watkins Road. Turn right onto Bill Watkins Road, go 1.2 miles, then turn
left onto GA 53 and go 2.4 miles to the intersection with Rockwell Church
Road. **Rockwell Universalist Church** will be on the left at the corner of GA 53
and Rockwell Church Road.

Organized in 1839, the Rockwell church is the second-oldest Universalist
church in Georgia. This sanctuary was built in 1881, using volunteer labor
and materials donated by the community.

Universalism has never had a large following in Georgia, but the Rockwell church appears to still be in use, at least on an occasional basis, and has
been well-maintained by its congregation.

Exiting the churchyard, go right on Rockwell Church Road for 2.7 miles.
When you cross GA 11, Rockwell Church Road will become GA 211. Continue
8.6 miles to Statham and turn left on Broad Street for a block, then right on
Jefferson. Cross the railroad tracks and turn right on Atlanta Highway for a
block, then left on Bethlehem Road for about a mile and turn left on US 29/
GA 316 for about 8 miles. Turn right on the Oconee Connector, go 0.2 mile
and turn left on Daniell's Bridge Road.

FREEMAN'S MILL AND ITS WHEEL HAVE BEEN RAISED FIVE FEET ABOVE THE FLOODPLAIN, BUT THE FLUME IS STILL AT THE ORIGINAL LEVEL

In 0.5 mile, turn right on Founder's Blvd. The **William Daniell House** is 0.2 mile down on the right at 1170 Founders Blvd.

After the death of his first wife, with whom he had eleven children, Revolutionary War veteran William Daniell married 17-year-old Polly Melton, and in 1790, he built a new, Plantation Plain-style house for her. Fortunately, the house was quite large, because the couple had thirteen children together. Daniell lived to be 97, and the home he built for Polly is now thought to be the oldest house in Oconee County. In fact, it may well be the oldest house in North Georgia, although that depends upon where one draws the line between North and Central Georgia. The Thomas Ansley Rock House near Thompson was built in 1785, and the Jacob Burkhalter House in Warrenton is even older, dating from around 1778.

On the National Register of Historic Places, the house is owned by the county and is used for weddings, receptions, family reunions, and other meetings and events.

Go back to Daniell's Bridge Road, turn right, and follow it for 2.4 miles, then turn left on Hog Mountain Road. Go 0.7 mile to the intersection with US 441. Turn right, go 0.5 mile, and turn left on US 129/441 Business/GA 15. In about a mile GA 15 will become Main Street in Watkinsville.

On your left, across from the courthouse, is the **Eagle Tavern**, at 26 North Main Street. Built around 1801, it was an important inn, tavern, and stagecoach stop on the route between Milledgeville and Athens. The tavern also has a rich history of ghostly tales and is considered by some to be the most haunted building in North Georgia.

Today, the Eagle Tavern is a history museum depicting frontier life in Georgia 200 years ago. It is open for tours Monday through Friday, 10 a.m.–4 p.m. There is no admission charge, but a donation of $2 or more is requested.

The visitor information center is across from the Eagle Tavern at 21 North Main Street. They will be happy to provide guidance about tours and points of interest in Watkinsville.

Also across from the Eagle Tavern, behind the courthouse, is the **Old Jail**, which in 1905 was the scene of one of the worst incidents of racial violence in Georgia's history, when a mob took nine men, eight black and one white, out of the jail, dragged them outside the town, and lynched them, supposedly for raping a white woman.

Going south, the **Haygood House**, circa 1827, at 25 South Main Street, was the birthplace of two prominent Methodists: Bishop Atticus G. Haygood, born in 1839, was president of Emory College from 1875 to 1884, and his sister Laura Haygood, born in 1845, was one of the first Christian missionaries to China.

SELL'S MILL IS THE CENTERPIECE OF A JACKSON COUNTY PARK

THE WILLIAM DANIELL HOUSE NEAR WATKINSVILLE MAY BE THE OLDEST BUILDING IN NORTH GEORGIA

From the Haygood House, turn left and go back to GA 15. Turn right and go about 4 miles to Elder Mill Road. Turn right again and go 0.8 mile to **Elder Mill Covered Bridge**.

Originally built by Nathaniel Richardson over Calls Creek on the Watkinsville-Athens Road in 1897, the bridge was moved by wagon (don't ask me how they did that) to its present location over Rose Creek in 1924. It uses the sturdy Town lattice construction, with heavy planks fastened together with wooden pegs. The 99-foot-long bridge is in daily use and is one of very few covered bridges in Georgia to carry traffic without underlying steel support beams.

Elder's Grist Mill, built around 1900, is about 100 yards downstream from the bridge. The entrance is on the left just before the bridge; however, it is a private drive and may be closed. The mill can also be viewed from a path at the other end of the bridge that leads downstream along Rose Creek, but foliage blocks much of the view, except in winter. The mill ceased operation in 1941, and the overshot wheel is long gone; however, the building itself appears to be in fairly good shape, with a new metal roof.

From the covered bridge, go back to GA 15 and turn right (south) for 4.6 miles to Antioch Road. Turn right again for 0.3 mile to **Antioch Christian Church**, on the right, at 1100 Antioch Church Road. First organized in

1807, Antioch Christian has great historical significance. It may be difficult to imagine, but this small church on a country road in an obscure part of Georgia is the Mother Church of the Christian Church (Disciples of Christ) denomination's 69 congregations, with nearly 70,000 members in Georgia. An area that today appears to be a backwater was in earlier times a very important and influential part of the state.

The present building was erected in 1886 on the site of the original 1807 building and is in active service to this day. In fact, I happened to come by the church during a Sunday morning service that was extremely well attended, judging from the number of cars present.

Leaving the church, continue west on Antioch Church Road for about 3.5 miles to Colham Ferry Road. Go left for 0.1 mile and then right on J T Elder Road (a well-maintained gravel road with a one-lane bridge) for 1.8 miles to Salem Road. Go left 0.6 mile. **Salem Methodist Church** will be on the right, set well back in a field, at 3280 Salem Road.

The Methodist Church in Salem was organized in 1820, not long after the town was incorporated in 1818, settled mostly by Scots-Irish migrants from

THE EAGLE TAVERN IN WATKINSVILLE IS REPUTED TO HAVE AN ASSORTMENT OF RESIDENT GHOSTS

THE ELDER MILL COVERED BRIDGE IS STILL IN REGULAR USE

Virginia and North Carolina. It was a good-sized village in its day, but now the Methodist Church is all that's left of Salem. The present structure, built in 1896 on the site of the original building, is well cared for and used for special occasions, but no regular services have been held in the church for many years.

ELDER MILL COVERED BRIDGE AS SEEN FROM DOWNSTREAM ROSE CREEK

Leaving Salem Church, turn right for 0.1 mile and turn right again on Old Salem Road. In 1.7 miles, turn left on Tappan Spur Road and go left for 1.4 miles to US 129/441.

Turn left (south) for about 9 miles to the intersection with US 278 (James Madison Parkway) in Madison. Turn right and follow the parkway for about 1.5 miles to Main Street in **Madison**.

Madison was spared destruction by General Sherman's 1864 "March to the Sea" that broke the back of the Confederacy because it was the home of pro-Union Georgia Senator Joshua Hill. Because of that act of mercy, Madison contains one of the largest collections of antebellum structures in the South.

Madison has been called "one of the ten most beautiful towns in the Southern states" by *The Culture Trip,* and even "one of the sixteen most beautiful towns in the world" by *Budget Travel Magazine.*

Travel Holiday Magazine named it the "#1 small town in America." And those praises are nothing new. Madison was described more than 170 years ago in the *1845 Guide to Georgia* as the "most cultured and aristocratic town on the stagecoach route from Charlestown to New Orleans."

So with those accolades to whet your appetite, go to the **Historic Madison Welcome Center** on the square at 115 East Jefferson Street and pick up a self-guided tour brochure and other information about the town's attractions. There are also guided tours available—the welcome center will have information about them.

A good place to begin your tour is **Heritage Hall**, at 277 South Main Street, headquarters of the Morgan County Historical Society. A sophisticated example of Greek Revival architecture built in 1811 by Dr. Elijah Jones, it is authentically decorated and open for tours.

Here are some other buildings I liked. You will certainly have your own favorites:

ANTIOCH CHRISTIAN CHURCH IN OCONEE COUNTY IS THE "MOTHER CHURCH" OF THE DISCIPLES OF CHRIST DENOMINATION IN GEORGIA

The **Morgan County Courthouse** was built in 1905 in the Beaux Arts style and sits in an unusual location just off one corner of the town square.

Just down the street from the courthouse is the Plantation Plain-style **Rogers House**, at 179 East Jefferson, built around 1810, which makes it one of the oldest houses in Madison. It is open daily for tours. Next door is **Rose Cottage**, the home of former slave Adeline Rose.

The **First Baptist Church**, at 328 South Main, was erected in 1858, using bricks made by slaves on the plantation of John Byrne Walker. It looks surprisingly modern, even today.

Just down the block, at 382 South Main, is the **Presbyterian Church**, built in 1842. The design is Old English, with Tiffany stained glass windows. In 1866, Ellen Axson, the pastor's daughter, married Woodrow Wilson, who would later become the 28th president of the United States.

The Gothic Revival **Church of the Advent** at 338 Academy Street was built circa 1842 by a Methodist congregation but was sold to the Episcopalians in 1960. The original slave gallery has been converted to an organ loft.

The **Stagecoach House**, at 549 Old Post Road, was built circa 1810, at about the same time as the Rogers House. It was an inn and stagecoach stop when Old Post Road was part of the route between Charleston and New Orleans.

From downtown Madison, continue east on Main Street/US 278 for 8.5 miles and turn right on Newborn Road to the town of **Rutledge**.

Completely leveled by Sherman's forces, the town now offers interesting shopping and excellent dining. And just 2 miles north of Rutledge is Georgia's largest state park, 5,804-acre **Hard Labor Creek**. Best known for its golf course, the park also offers camping, cabin rentals, fishing, 22 miles of hiking trails, horseback riding, swimming, and a beach.

Going back to US 278, turn right, go about 4 miles, and then slant right on East Hightower Trail for 3.7 miles, then turn right to stay on Hightower Trail to the town of **Social Circle**, incorporated in 1832 and named, so the local legend says, on a Saturday night when a newcomer commented to a group of local people, "This surely is a social circle!"

As you come into town, you will see on your right, at 222 East Hightower Trail, the **Josiah Clark Townhouse**. Built in 1838, it was the home of Josiah Clark, who operated the Social Circle Dinner Club, a restaurant that fed passengers and crew when trains stopped at the local station.

Continue on East Hightower to the welcome center, on the left about half

THE ROGERS HOUSE IS ONE OF THE OLDEST HOUSES IN MADISONVILLE AND WAS BUILT ON ONE OF THE ORIGINAL TOWN LOTS

THE EPISCOPAL CHURCH OF THE ADVENT IN MADISONVILLE WAS ORIGINALLY BUILT IN 1842 BY A METHODIST CONGREGATION

a block before the traffic light, and pick up a walking tour brochure if you would like to spend some quality time in this fascinating village.

With brochure in hand, go on to the traffic light and turn right on North Cherokee to reach the **Blue Willow Inn**, at number 294. It's actually not an inn but a restaurant, considered by many to be one of the finest in the entire Southeast. It is located in the historic **John and Bertha Upshaw House**, built in 1917. Like many businesses, the Blue Willow Inn was affected by the recent pandemic and is closed as of this writing. The owners say the closing is temporary, so the inn may well be open again by the time this book is published. A meal at the Blue Willow is an experience you won't want to miss, so call them at 770-464-2131 to check on their current status.

From the Blue Willow, go back to the traffic light at Hightower and turn right on West Hightower Trail to the **Gibbs-Burton-Herndon House**, on the left at 309 West Hightower. Originally a three-room log structure, it was renovated in the 1830s. The second story and columns were probably added in the 1840s. Legend says that Alonzo Herndon, founder of the Atlanta Life Insurance Company, was born a slave in this house.

THE STAGECOACH HOUSE WAS AN INN AND STAGECOACH STOP ON THE OLD POST ROAD FROM CHARLESTON TO NEW ORLEANS

THE GIBBS-BURTON-HENDON HOUSE IN SOCIAL CIRCLE WAS ORIGINALLY A THREE-ROOM LOG CABIN

Continue on West Hightower to **Gunter Hall**, on the left at number 403, behind the public library. Also known as the Nebhut-Akridge-Gunter House, it is presently the headquarters of the Historic Preservation Society of Social Circle. Built 1840–55, it originally stood on North Cherokee Road, but was moved in 1911 and then again in 1992 to its present location.

Leaving Gunter Hall, turn right on West Hightower and go back to the traffic light at the intersection of Hightower and Cherokee. Turn right on South Cherokee and follow it to its merger with GA 11. Continue south on 11 to Interstate 20 and the end of this tour.

IN THE AREA

Accommodations

THE BRADY INN BED AND BREAKFAST, 250 North Second Street, Madison.

THE JAMES MADISON INN BED AND BREAKFAST, 260 West Washington Street, Madison. 706-752-7170. jamesmadisoninn.com.

A wide variety of hotels can be found along Interstate 20 near Madisonville and Social Circle.

Dining

BLUE WILLOW INN, 294 North Cherokee Road, Social Circle. 770-464-2131. www.bluewillowinn.com.

CHOPS AND HOPS, 2 South Main Street, Watkinsville. 706-310-1101. www.chopsandhops.com.

RICARDO'S KOUZINNA, 271 West Washington Street, Madison. 706-342-0729.

THE TOWN 220 RESTAURANT, 220 West Washington Street, Madison. 706-752-1445. www.town220.com.

Attractions

EAGLE TAVERN MUSEUM, 29 North Main Street, Watkinsville. 706-769-5197.

HARD LABOR CREEK STATE PARK, 5 Hard Labor Creek Road, Rutledge. 706-557-3001.

For more information on any Georgia State Park or Historic Site, visit the state parks website: www.georgiastateparks.org.

Events

Gwinnett County

Elisha Winn Fair, Dacula, first weekend in October. in-georgia.com/who-was-elisha-winn.

Morgan County

Madisonfest Arts and Crafts Festival, last Saturday in April.

Madison in May Spring Tour of Homes, Madison.

Christmas Tour of Homes, Madison, December.

Rutledge Country Fair, Rutledge, May.

Oconee County

Oconee Farmers' Market, May–October Fall Festival, October.

Blues & BBQ, Watkinsville, mid-September.

6

STONE BIRDS AND TALKING RABBITS

Central Georgia

This tour is about 90 miles in length and includes Newton, Jasper, Putnam, and Baldwin Counties.

Beginning from Exit 98 on Interstate 20, follow GA 11 south for 4.3 miles, then turn left on GA 142 for 3.5 miles to **Newborn**. The **Childs General Store**, built in 1870, is on the right at the flashing traffic signal. It is currently home to the town hall and library.

Just a block or so farther along, on the left, is the **John Gay House**, dating from the 1840s and listed on the National Register of Historic Places.

From Newborn, continue on GA 142 for about 11 miles to **Shady Dale**.

A Creek Indian village was here long before the first settlers arrived, and for many years it was a local trading post. Located near the road from Augusta to New Orleans, and later, on the railroad, Shady Dale became an important and prosperous little town. Even today, it is the only incorporated city in Jasper County other than Monticello.

At the intersection of GA 142 and GA 83, turn left and go 0.2 mile to **Calvary United Methodist Church**, on the left. Built in 1859, the church appears to have stopped holding regular services.

Go back toward the intersection of GA 83 and 142. On the left as you go is the former **Bank of Shady Dale**, built in the early 1900s and the only survivor of a row of commercial storefronts. Since its banking days, it has served as the post office, town hall, and library.

At the intersection, slant left on Providence Street, which becomes Machen Street and leads to the gleaming steeple of **Providence Baptist Church**, organized in 1810. The current building dates from 1906.

LEFT: THE FIRST UNITED METHODIST CHURCH IN EATONTON WAS BUILT IN 1857

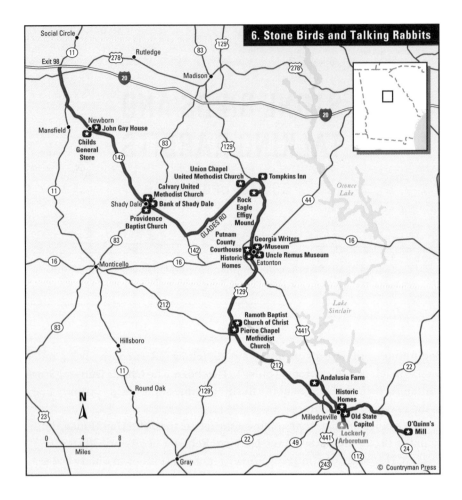

Leaving the church, go back to GA 142, turn right, and continue southeast for about 5.4 miles to Glades Road. Turn right and go about 3 miles, then right at the T intersection for 0.2 mile, then turn left and continue on Glades Road/ County Road 300 for 5.2 miles to **Union Chapel United Methodist Church**, built circa 1855. The building is quite large for a church of that era and still stands on its original foundation of stacked fieldstones. Also on the church grounds is a one-room school building which was in use from 1913 until 1946. The church now uses it as Sunday School space.

From the church, continue on County Road 300 for 1.2 miles. Go right on US 441/GA 24 for about 0.2 mile to the **Tompkins Inn**, at 1388 Madison Road/ US 441/GA 24. It's on the left and set well back from the highway.

Dating from around 1810, the Inn was a stagecoach stop on the route from Milledgeville to Athens. It was probably built by George Bird, but Giles Tompkins bought the property in 1812 and it remained in his family for several generations, so the Tompkins name has stuck. It has been owned by

CHILDS GENERAL STORE IN NEWBORN IS LISTED ON THE NATIONAL REGISTER OF HISTORIC PLACES

the Eatonton-Putnam County Historical Society since 1983 and has recently been renovated. The old inn is looking pretty good, but I have to confess a bit of nostalgia for the rustic, old, weathered boards.

From the Tompkins Inn, continue south on US 441/GA 24 for 1.4 miles and turn right on Rock Eagle Road. **The Rock Eagle**, a prehistoric First American site, is located on the grounds of the 1500-acre Rock Eagle 4-H Center, a natural retreat center with extensive facilities for conferences and group meetings. It also hosts Georgia 4-H Club Summer Camps and offers adult and family programs year round.

To get to the Rock Eagle effigy, go about 0.6 mile on Rock Eagle Road, slant right at the Rock Eagle Effigy sign, go 0.1 mile, turn left, and go 0.1 mile to the parking lot. The best way to view the mysterious bird is from the tower at the opposite end from the parking lot.

A mound of thousands of small to medium-sized milky quartz rocks in the shape of a bird, the Rock Eagle is 120 feet from head to tail, 102 feet from wingtip to wingtip, and eight feet high at the breast. There is also another bird effigy in Putnam County—the Rock Hawk at Lake Oconee near Wallace Dam—but it is in much poorer condition. The two bird effigies are on two of the highest points in the county, and are the only ones known east of the Mississippi.

Although archeologists think they were most likely created by the Woodland Indian culture between 1000 BC and 1000 AD, no one really knows for sure. The Muscogee Creeks who were living in the area told the first white settlers that even their ancestors did not know who created the effigies nor

UNION CHAPEL UNITED METHODIST CHURCH STILL
STANDS ON ITS ORIGINAL FOUNDATION OF STACKED
FIELDSTONES

when. It's not likely the mystery of the Rock Eagle and Rock Hawk will ever be solved.

From the Rock Eagle parking lot, go back to US 441/129, turn right, go 5.2 miles, and turn left onto N Jefferson Avenue/Business US 129/US 441/GA 24 for 1.5 miles to downtown Eatonton.

The impressive Neoclassical Revival **Putnam County Courthouse**, built in 1824, is the third-oldest courthouse in Georgia and the oldest still in use as a courthouse. It occupies what is said to be one of the largest public squares in Georgia.

In front of the courthouse, turn right on West Madison, go one block, then turn right on North Madison for 0.2 mile to the Plaza Arts Center on the left, where the Tourist Information Office is located, and pick up a brochure for the self-guided tour of Eatonton's more than one hundred historic buildings. I especially liked the **Bronson House** at 114 North Madison, which began life in 1816 as the **Eagle Tavern**. In 1852, the columns were added and other changes made to convert the house into a Greek Revival mansion. It is now the headquarters of the Eatonton-Putnam County Historical Society.

I also liked the circa 1836 **Thomas-Nisbet-Taliaferro House** adjacent to the **First United Methodist Church**, for which it serves as the parsonage. Both are directly across from the Plaza Arts Center. The church itself was built in 1857 but was partially destroyed by fire in 1979. It was restored and reopened in 1981.

As the birthplace of Joel Chandler Harris, author of the Uncle Remus–Brer Rabbit stories, and Alice Walker, whose best-known novel is *The Color Purple*, Eatonton is a natural home for the **Georgia Writers Museum**. Located at 109 South Jefferson Street, the museum hosts frequent lectures and workshops by well-known writers. It is open Thursday and Friday 10 a.m.–5 p.m., Saturday 10 p.m.–3 p.m., and Sunday through Wednesday by appointment (www.georgiawritersmuseum.org).

From the Writers Museum, go south on South Jefferson for about three blocks to the intersection of Jefferson and Madison Avenues and turn right into the parking lot of the **Uncle Remus Museum**.

A log cabin made from two old slave cabins from Putnam County, the museum is similar to the cabin lived in by Uncle Remus, the character made famous by author Joel Chandler Harris. Scenes and mementos depict antebellum plantation life. Turner Park, where the museum is located, was part of the original home place of Joseph Sidney Turner, the "Little Boy" in the Uncle Remus stories.

THE ROCK EAGLE IS ONE OF ONLY TWO PREHISTORIC BIRD EFFIGIES EAST OF THE MISSISSIPPI

NOW KNOWN AS THE BRONSON HOUSE, THE EAGLE TAVERN WAS BUILT IN 1816. IT IS CURRENTLY THE HOME OF THE EATONTON-PUTNAM COUNTY HISTORICAL SOCIETY

The Uncle Remus Museum is open daily 10 a.m. to 5 p.m. Sunday hours are 2 p.m. to 5 p.m. It is closed on Tuesdays from November through March. Check their website (www.uncleremusmuseum.org) for current information.

Leaving the Uncle Remus Museum, and assuming you're ready to leave Eatonton, turn right (south) on South Jefferson/US 129/441/GA 24 for about 2 miles. Cross the bypass and continue straight on US 129/GA 44 for about 6.5 miles, cross the bridge over Murder Creek, go 0.2 mile to the top of the hill and slant left onto an unmarked gravel road. It looks deserted, but in 0.2 mile you will come to a T intersection with another gravel road. Go left about 50 yards to **Ramoth Baptist Church of Christ**, built in 1836 or '37. Although no regular services have been held since the 1940s, the church has been lovingly restored by Lynn and Carling Brackey "in honor of the original church members and in memory of their descendants, many of whom are buried in the adjoining cemetery."

Leaving the church, go straight at the T intersection. In 0.2 mile you will come to **Pierce Chapel Methodist Church** on your left, another lovely old building, although not nearly as old as the Ramoth Church, having been founded in 1899.

From Pierce Chapel, continue about one hundred yards to US 129 and go left for about 0.3 mile, then turn left on GA 212. From there, it's 13 miles to the intersection with GA 22. Go left on 22 for about 2.5 miles and turn right on North Wilkinson to downtown Milledgeville.

Only two cities in the United States were laid out specifically to be capitals. One, of course, is Washington, D.C. The other is **Milledgeville, Georgia**, capital of the state from 1804 to 1868. As the once-upon-a-time state capital, it is, in a word, stately, with wide, tree-lined streets and parkways adorned with distinguished old structures, which fortunately survived Sherman and his march to the sea. Most of Milledgeville was spared, because, it is said, Sherman had relatives in the city.

There's so much to see in Milledgeville that one hardly knows where to begin. But a good place to start is the Convention and Visitors' Bureau at 200 West Hancock Street at its intersection with North Wilkinson, where you can pick up information about self-guided driving or walking tours. Guided tours are also available, and the Historic Trolley Tour is especially recommended if you're looking for a relaxed way to see Milledgeville. The trolley leaves from the Convention and Visitors' Bureau at 10 a.m., Monday through Friday, and 11 a.m. on Saturday. Admission is $12 for adults, $10 for seniors, and $5 for ages 6–13.

Also, don't miss browsing through downtown Milledgeville, with its many shops and restaurants and gracious, old-south lifestyle. Milledgeville has a surprisingly cosmopolitan air for a smallish, off-the-beaten-track town. Perhaps it's due to the two colleges located here: Georgia Military Academy and

THE UNCLE REMUS MUSEUM IS BUILT OF LOGS FROM TWO OLD SLAVE CABINS

Georgia State College and University. I wanted to stay and relax with the crowds at the sidewalk tables in front of many of the restaurants. But duty calls. I had a job to do and a deadline to meet.

Here are some don't-miss places to see (and there are lots more!):

The **Old Georgia State Capitol**, built in 1807, was the first public building in the United States to be designed in the Gothic Revival Style. Today, it is part of the campus of Georgia Military College and houses a regional history museum. It was damaged by Sherman's Union troops, but left standing.

The Old Governor's Mansion, at 120 South Clarke Street, was built in 1839 and was home to Georgia's governors for nearly 30 years until the state capital was moved to Atlanta during reconstruction days. It was designed by Charles Clusky, who built the first lighthouse on St. Simon's Island, and is considered to be one of the finest examples of High Greek Revival architecture in the US. It is now the most treasured building on the campus of Georgia College and State University and serves as an historic house museum.

St. Stephen's Episcopal Church, at 220 South Wayne Street, is just down the slope from the Old State Capitol. Dating from 1843, it is Milledgeville's oldest standing church building. In 1864, Sherman's troops burned the pews

THE OLD STATE CAPITOL WAS DAMAGED, BUT NOT DESTROYED, BY SHERMAN'S ARMY IN 1864

THE OLD GOVERNOR'S MANSION IN MILLEDGEVILLE WAS THE RESIDENCE OF GEORGIA'S GOVERNORS FROM 1839 TO 1868

and poured syrup down the organ pipes. A new organ was donated by George Perkins of New York in 1909.

The **Joseph Stovall House**, at 141 South Wilkinson Street, was originally built in the Federal style circa 1825, but Greek Revival elements were added later. The thirteen columns are thought to represent the original thirteen colonies. It now houses a firm of attorneys.

The **Paine-Jones House**, at 201 South Liberty Street, is a private residence. Built circa 1820 by Connecticut native Dr. Joshua Paine, the house originally had four rooms—two down and two up.

The **Orme-Sallee House**, at 251 South Liberty Street, is another private residence. The circa 1822 house is considered one of the most beautiful in the city, with its fanlighted doorways and trellised balcony.

The **Major Edward White House**, a private residence at 247 South Clarke Street, is one of the oldest houses in town. Built in 1806 on West Greene Street, it was moved to its present location in the late 19th century.

And the magnificent **Sanford-Powell-Binion-Mara-Hogg-Mims-Thornton-Simms House** (with a name like that it would have to be pretty great), at 330 West Greene Street, was built circa 1824 by General John W. A. Sanford with just four columns in front. Over the years the portico was gradually extended around the sides of the house until there were fourteen columns.

ST. STEPHEN'S EPISCOPAL CHURCH IS THE OLDEST CHURCH BUILDING IN MILLEDGEVILLE

The family home of the great Georgia writer Flannery O'Connor is just down the street at 311 West Greene Street, a two-story, Federal-style clapboard house built in 1820. The Ionic columns are original, hand-carved from solid timbers.

Although she lived to be only 39, O'Connor is considered by many to have been one of the most influential writers of the 20th century. Her most pro-

TOP: THE JOSEPH STOVALL HOUSE HAS 13 COLUMNS WHICH SOME BELIEVE REPRESENT THE ORIGINAL 13 STATES
BOTTOM: THE ORME-SALLEE HOUSE HAS FAN-LIGHTED DOORWAYS AND A TRELLISED BALCONY

ductive years, from 1951 until her death from lupus in 1964, were spent at **Andalusia Farm** near Milledgeville.

Now managed by the Flannery O'Connor–Andalusia Foundation, Andalusia is open for self-guided tours 10 a.m. to sunset on Thursday and 10 a.m. to 5 p.m. Friday, Saturday, and Sunday, April through September. From downtown Milledgeville, take GA 22 west to the intersection with North Columbia Street/US 441 north for about 0.5 miles to #2628. The entrance to Andalusia is on the left, across from Badcock Home Furnishings.

About 1.5 miles south of downtown Milledgeville on South Wayne Street/Business US 441 is **Lockerly Arboretum**, a 50-acre outdoor horticultural laboratory presided over by the circa 1852 Greek Revival **Lockerly Hall**. It's open Monday–Friday 8:30 a.m.–4:30 p.m. and Saturday 10 a.m.–4 p.m., March 1 through November 15 (www.lockerly.org).

Running along the east side of Milledgeville is the **Oconee River Greenway**, with hiking and biking trails, places to fish, and canoeing and kayaking in the shoals and rapids of the Oconee River.

If you're a dedicated mill buff, you might enjoy a side trip to **O'Quinn's Mill** on Town Creek, one of the oldest mills in Georgia. Built in 1807, O'Quinn's

THE SANFORD-POWELL-BINION-MARA-HOGG-MIMS-THORNTON-SIMMS HOUSE IS ONE OF MILLEDGEVILLE'S MOST IMPRESSIVE HOMES

ANDALUSIA FARM WAS THE HOME OF WRITER FLANNERY O'CONNER DURING HER MOST PRODUCTIVE YEARS

was in operation until just a few years ago. When I was working on the first edition of this book, the owners told me they hoped to interest the state or county in taking over the mill, restoring it, perhaps making it into a park, as has been done with other old mills in Georgia. They say it could be made operable again with very little difficulty.

Apparently they had some success, because a parking lot, a flagpole, and a large deck now overlook the dam and millpond. The mill itself has not yet been renovated and leans slightly to the left.

From downtown Milledgeville, take GA 22 E/GA 24 S for about 4 miles. When GA 22 splits off to the left, continue straight on 24 for about 3 miles and turn left onto Deepstep Road (unmarked, as far as I can tell). From there it is 1.4 miles to the mill, which will be on the left at 243 Deepstep Road.

Return to Milledgeville and the end of this tour.

IN THE AREA

Accommodations

HAMPTON INN, 2461 North Columbia Street, Milledgeville. 478-451-0050.

HOLIDAY INN EXPRESS, 2600 North Columbia Street, Milledgeville. 478-295-1114.

THE INN ON NORTH JEFFERSON, 210 North North Jefferson, Milledgeville. 912-604-4843. www.theinnonnorthjefferson.com.

THE LODGE ON LAKE OCONEE, 930 Greensboro Road, Eatonton. 706-485-7785. thelodgeonlakeoconee.com.

Dining

AUBRI LANE'S, 3700 Sinclair Dam Road NE, Milledgeville. 478-454-4181. www.aubrilanes.com.

BIBA'S ITALIAN RESTAURANT, 2803 North Columbia Street, Milledgeville. 478-414-1773. italianrestauranthixson.com.

THE SILVER MOON, 1977 Greensboro Road, Eatonton. 706-485-5698.

Attractions and Recreation

ANDALUSIA FARM, 2628 N Columbia Street, Milledgeville. 478-454-4029.

GEORGIA WRITERS MUSEUM, 109 South Jefferson, Eatonton. 706-991-5119. www.georgiawritersmuseum.com.

LOCKERLY ABORETUM, 1534 Irwinton Road, Milledgeville. 478-452-2112. lockerly.org.

MILLEDGEVILLE HISTORIC TROLLEY TOUR, 200 West Hancock Street. 478-452-4687.

UNCLE REMUS MUSEUM, 214 South Oak Street, Eatonton. 706-485-6856. uncleremus.com/museum.

Events

Eatonton-Putnam County

Putnam County Dairy Festival, June.

Makers and Music, June, July, August.

A Taste of Eatonton, October.

Scarecrow Contest, October 31.

Christmas Parade, December 10 and 11.

Milledgeville-Baldwin County

Old Governor's Mansion Tours, third Tuesday–Sunday, weekly.

Deep Roots Festival, October.

Joe's Farmers' Market, Elbert Street, Saturdays.

7

BARBECUE AND
FRIED GREEN TOMATOES
Central Georgia

The total length of this tour is about 210 miles and includes Clayton, Henry, Butts, Jasper, Jones, and Monroe Counties.

Begin at Exit 2 from Interstate 675 south of Atlanta. At the top of the ramp, go right 0.1 mile and turn right on Evans Road. Go 1 mile, then turn right on Rex Road for 0.4 mile, turn left on Colonade Drive, and immediately turn right on Mill Walk. **Rex Mill** is at the bottom of the hill, just beyond the old, one-lane bridge across Big Cotton Indian Creek.

The mill, with its small, overshot wheel, was built in 1830 by I. L. Hollingsworth and named after his dog. It probably closed in the 1940s, although no one seems to know for sure. Older residents of the area remember farmers bringing wagonloads of grain to be ground at the mill. (The bridge is closed to traffic at this time. Check current status with county officials.)

On the other side of the bridge, looking for all the world like someplace deep in rural Georgia, are the now-empty storefronts of old Rex Village, a little hamlet from the 19th century less than 15 miles from the State Capitol building in downtown Atlanta. Rex Road used to run through here, across the little bridge and past the mill and once-busy stores, but all that changed when a new bridge was built that now carries Rex Road high above the mill, the storefronts, and the creek.

Leaving Rex Mill, go back to Rex Road, turn left, and go east about 3 miles. Turn left on Thurman Road for one block, then turn right onto Fairview Road for 3.6 miles. At the traffic circle, take the third exit onto GA 155 north, go 1 mile, and turn right into **Panola Mountain State Park.**

LEFT: CONSTRUCTION OF THE HENRY COUNTY COURTHOUSE IN MCDONOUGH COST $13,000 IN 1897

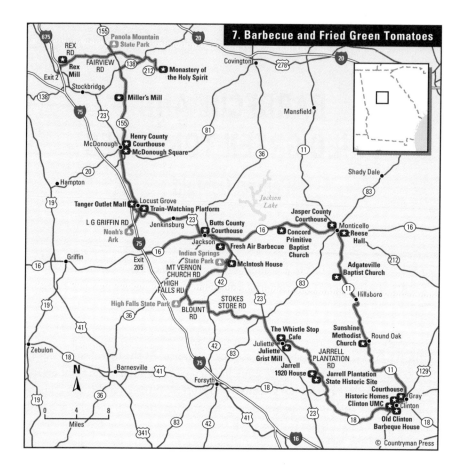

Panola Mountain is a 100-acre granite outcrop similar to Stone Mountain, but smaller and more pristine, with a rare ecosystem. Park rangers lead educational hikes where visitors can learn about the plants and animals found here.

The park also offers archery; boating (with boat rentals); fishing; hiking and running on forested fitness trails; and paved trails for biking, roller-blading, and dog-walking.

From the park, go left (south) on GA 155 for 1 mile to the traffic circle. Take the third exit, East Fairview Road, and go 4 miles, then turn left on GA 138. In a half-mile, turn right on Tucker Mill Road, go 1.4 miles, turn right on GA 212, and the **Monastery of the Holy Spirit** will be on your left in about a mile.

Founded by Trappist monks in 1944, it took 15 years to build the Abbey Church and other buildings, while the monks lived in a barn on a nearby plantation. A harmonious blend of tradition and modernity, the simple yet dignified architecture of the church reflects the lifestyle of the monastic community.

Today, the monastery is not only a home for the monks, but also a retreat

REX MILL WAS A CENTER OF ACTIVITY IN REX VILLAGE FOR MORE THAN A HUNDRED YEARS

center and a place where anyone can come for an hour, a day, or longer to rest and meditate.

Exhibits and films in the visitor center introduce the lives of the monks. You can see the stained-glass windows in the Abbey Church, learn about bonsai at the Monastery Garden Center, shop the Abbey Store, take a prayer walk, or follow the lakeside Stations of the Cross.

Leaving the monastery, go back on GA 212 to Tucker Mill Road. Turn left, then go 1.4 miles to GA 138, turn left for 3.6 miles, and turn left again on GA 155. Go 3.8 miles to Miller's Store, on the right. **Miller's Mill**, also known as McDonough Mill, is on the right just before the bridge over Big Cotton Indian Creek.

Built around 1890, it has been out of operation since at least 1960 and is in poor condition. Foliage makes it very hard to see, except in winter, but it you're a totally serious mill buff, you can see it by parking at Miller's Store and walking down the hill along the fenceline. Don't forget that it's on private property, so stay outside the fence. A better view can be obtained from the other side of the creek, especially in winter.

From the mill area, continue south on GA 155 for about 6 miles. GA 155 becomes Sims Street as you enter McDonough. Turn right at John Frank

IT TOOK THE MONKS 15 YEARS TO BUILD THE ABBEY CHURCH

Ward Blvd./GA 20/81 and go 0.3 mile to **McDonough Square**. The old Romanesque Revival **Henry County Courthouse**, built in 1897, will be on your right and the beautifully landscaped park will be on your left. You can park on three sides of the square, but not on the north (courthouse) side. Visit the McDonough Welcome Center, housed in a restored 1920s Standard Oil service station at 5 Griffin Street on McDonough Square, and pick up brochures and guides to the city.

From McDonough Square, take Griffin Street/US 23/GA 42 south for 7 miles to Locust Grove. The old Locust Grove downtown will be on the right, lined up across from the railroad tracks, and on the left is a covered pavilion, the **Train-Watching Platform**, where you can watch in comfort as up to fifty Norfolk Southern trains roll through Locust Grove every day. It's open all day every day, it's free, and the parking is free. The covered platform is also the setting for a farmers' market featuring locally grown produce on Saturday mornings, 8 a.m. to noon, June through September.

From the Train-Watching Platform, continue 0.5 mile on US 23/GA 42, then turn right onto Martin Luther King, Jr. Blvd. Go 0.6 mile to Tanger Blvd. Cross it and continue onto L G Griffin Road for 2.5 miles to **Noah's Ark**, a unique, non-profit sanctuary for animals founded in 1978.

A 250-acre park-like habitat, the sanctuary is home to more than 1,500 abused, unwanted, and neglected animals of all kinds, both domestic and exotic.

In 2001, Noah's Ark became home to a remarkable animal trio: a bear, a lion, and a tiger, found together as cubs in terrible conditions in the basement of a house in Atlanta during a drug raid. The three were taken to Noah's Ark, where they were nursed back to health and lived together as inseparable companions until the death of Leo the lion from liver cancer in 2016. Shere Khan the tiger followed in 2018, so now only Baloo the bear survives as a witness to their amazing story.

Check their website (noahs-ark.org) for up-to-date information about hours and tours. There is no admission charge, but your donation will be appreciated and put to good use.

If you have money left after making a substantial donation to Noah's Ark, go back on L G Griffin Road to Tanger Blvd. and turn left for 1.7 miles to the main entrance to **Tanger Outlet Mall**. With seventy stores featuring just about every well-known brand imaginable, they're open 9 a.m.–9 p.m. Monday–Saturday and 10 a.m.–7 p.m. on Sunday.

From Tanger Outlets, go back on Tanger Boulevard to the intersection with Martin Luther King, Jr. Blvd. and L G Griffin Road, and continue south on Tanger Blvd. for 1.7 miles, then turn right on US 23/GA 42 for about 8 miles to the intersection with GA 16 in Jackson.

Bear left and follow US 23/GA 42/GA 16 through downtown Jackson for about a mile. You will pass through the town square, with the 1898 Victorian Eclectic **Butts County Courthouse** on your left. When US 23 and GA 42 slant right, stay straight (left fork) and continue on GA 16. From that point, it's about 8.5 miles to **Concord Primitive Baptist Church**, built circa 1808, on the right, about 1.5 miles east of the Ocmulgee River bridge.

Although it's been many years since the church has had an active congregation, it appears to be reasonably well cared for and is probably used for occasional special services. Like many structures of its time, the floor joists are laid on stacked stone pillars; however, the stone has been replaced with

UP TO 50 TRAINS ROLL BY THE TRAIN-WATCHING PLATFORM IN LOCUST GROVE EVERY DAY

BALOO THE BEAR IS THE ONLY SURVIVOR OF A TRIO OF ANIMAL CUBS RESCUED DURING A DRUG RAID IN ATLANTA

bricks on one side and the steps and railings appear to have been replaced since my last visit 5 years ago.

From Concord Primitive Baptist Church, continue east on GA 16 for 7.7 miles to **Monticello**.

The Neoclassical Revival **Jasper County Courthouse**, built in 1908, sits across from the northeast corner of a pretty town square that is the setting for a May-through-September Saturday morning farmers' market. Also on the square at 119 West Washington Street is the visitor center, where you can pick up information about Monticello and the many natural attractions of Jasper County. Hunters will be interested to know that Jasper County bills itself as the deer capital of Georgia.

From the courthouse, go east 0.2 mile on East Greene Street to **Reese Hall**, at Number 421, on the corner of East Greene and Blue Ruin Streets. Dr. David Addison Reese, the son of a Revolutionary War soldier, moved to Monticello as a young man, where he married Mary Gaines Merriweather and, in 1820, built Reese Hall. A member of the State Senate for many years, he was also a trustee of the University of Georgia and later was a US Congressman.

Backtrack to the courthouse, stay on Greene Street for one block, go left on Forsyth Street for a block, then go left again on Washington Street. In two or three blocks, bear right on Macon Road/GA 11 for 6 miles to **Adgateville Baptist Church** on the right, at the intersection with Clay Tillman Road.

Founded as Hebron Primitive Baptist Church in 1812, the church was reorganized as Adgateville Baptist in 1915, and the present building was erected. The church is still in active use.

From the church, continue south on GA 11 for 3.7 miles to Hillsboro. Once a thriving community, Hillsboro owed its existence to the vision and hard work of a farmer named John Hill, who also founded the Methodist Church in 1808. Now there's not much left except John Hill's **Methodist Church**, which was closed for some years, but now has reopened for three Sundays a month; there are also a pair of Baptist Churches, the 1915 Ben Hill School, now the community center, and the old two-story **Masonic Lodge**, probably built in the 1880s.

Continue on GA 11 for about 6 miles to the Round Oak community and **Sunshine Methodist Church**. Turn right at the historical marker and church sign.

The original church on this site was a log structure built by a Baptist congregation. It was the scene of one of the few battles won by Rebel forces

CONCORD PRIMITIVE BAPTIST CHURCH WAS BUILT IN 1808

REESE HALL, BUILT IN 1820, HAS BEEN COMPLETELY RENOVATED

during the Atlanta Campaign, when Stoneman's Raiders (Union) ran into three Confederate brigades under General Alfred Iverson in July 1864. However, four months later, Sherman's men burned the church on their way to Savannah. The Methodists acquired the site and erected a building in 1880.

Continue on GA 11 for about 10 miles to Gray (continue straight when GA 11 turns right). At the intersection with US 129/GA 22, turn right for 0.1 mile and the 1905 Romanesque Revival **Jones County Courthouse** will be on your left.

From the courthouse, continue on GA 22 West/US 129 South 1.2 miles to Lite-N-Tie Road. Turn right and go one block, at which point the road becomes Randolph Street in the **Old Clinton Historic District**. Cross Pulaski Street, go one block, and turn left on Madison Street. On the right at No. 412 is the 1810 Parrish-Billue House. At the corner, turn left onto Washington Street and the **Barron Blair House** on your left. Clinton was settled in 1808. When Captain John Mitchell built this house in 1820, Clinton had a population of 841 souls, making it the fourth largest city in Georgia. However, in November 1864, Sherman's terrible March to the Sea destroyed two-thirds of Clinton. Today, only 13 of the original buildings remain.

Continue on Washington Street and turn right on Pulaski. The small house on the left is the **McCarthy-Pope House**. Built in 1809, it is believed to be the oldest house in Old Clinton. Turn around in the gravel drive across from the house and go back to Washington Street. Turn left, and then left again on Madison for one block to Hawkins Street. The house on the corner, at No. 438, is the **Clower-Gaultney House**, built circa 1816–19.

Turn right, continue on Hawkins Street for about 0.2 mile, and cross Green Settlement Road to the **Clinton United Methodist Church**, built circa 1821. The church is still in use and is very well maintained. It's just across the street from **Cedar Ridge Cemetery**, which contains many examples of quarried stone work by Jacob P. Hutchings, a former slave and granite mason of unusual skill. The cemetery is also the final resting place of many Civil War soldiers.

Leaving the church and cemetery, go right (west) on Green Settlement Road for about 0.3 mile to the intersection with US 129/GA 18 and the **Old Clinton Barbecue House** just across the highway. Open since 1958, the fame of Old Clinton Barbecue has spread far beyond the little town of Gray—it has been featured in *Southern Living, USA Today, The Washington Post,* and many other publications and internet blogs.

From the Barbeque House take US 129 South/GA 22 & 18 West for about a half-mile. Turn right on the bypass, then left on GA 18 West and follow it for about 10 miles. Turn right on Jarrell Plantation Road for 2.9 miles, turn left, then turn left again into the parking lot at **Jarrell Plantation State Historic**

WHEN THE BARRON BLAIR HOUSE WAS BUILT IN 1820, CLINTON HAD A POPULATION OF 841

Site, an 1847 cotton plantation in the rolling, red clay hills of Middle Georgia. Originally settled by John Fitz Jarrell, the farm was owned by the same family for 140 years and eventually included a steam-powered grist mill, a sawmill, cotton gin, barns, and various other workshops and buildings. In 1974, the Jarrell descendants donated the buildings to the state to establish the Jarrell Plantation Historic Site.

The plantation is open Thursday–Saturday 9 a.m.–5 p.m. and is closed Thanksgiving, Christmas, and New Year's Day. Admission is $6.50 for adults, $6 for seniors, and $4 for ages 6–17. Children under six are admitted free.

Adjacent to the plantation, but not part of the Historic Site, is the third and last Jarrell home— an 1850s-style plantation house built in 1920, with walls and ceilings of heart pine felled, milled, and assembled by Dick Jarrell and his sons.

THE OLD CLINTON UNITED METHODIST CHURCH HAS BEEN IN CONTINUOUS USE SINCE 1821

The Jarrell 1920 House is now a lovely bed and breakfast inn, operated by Philip Haynes, a grandson of Dick Jarrell, and his wife Amelia.

From the plantation, go back to Jarrell Plantation Road and turn left.

THE JARRELL HOMESTEAD AT THE JARRELL PLANTATION STATE HISTORIC SITE

Go a bit more than 3.6 miles, then turn left onto Round Oak Juliette Road for 3.5 miles, cross the railroad tracks and turn left on McCrackin Street to **Juliette, Georgia**, the tiny village made famous by the movie *Fried Green Tomatoes*. The town has survived by making a cottage industry of itself, with a number of small shops and the **Whistle Stop Cafe**, featuring good country cookin' and—what else? *Fried Green Tomatoes!*

Across the railroad tracks from the Whistle Stop Cafe is the **Juliette Grist Mill** on the Ocmulgee River. Built in the 1920s, it is believed to have been the largest water-powered grist mill in the US at one time.

Leaving Juliette, go back to Juliette Road and turn left for 0.7 mile, then right on US 23 north for 3.6 miles to GA 83. Turn left, go about 0.2 mile, and slant right on Old Stewart Road. In about 0.2 mile bear right onto Stokes Store Road. Go about 4 miles, then turn left at the stop sign to continue on Stokes Store Road for 3 more miles to an unmarked T intersection with GA 42. Go right for about 1 mile, then left on Blount Road for 3.5 miles to another unmarked T intersection (High Falls Road). Turn left and go about a mile to the entrance to **High Falls State Park**.

Encompassing a 650-acre lake within its 1,050 acres, High Falls Park is noted for excellent hybrid and white bass fishing. It also offers camping facilities, 4.3 miles of hiking trails, boating and boat rentals, canoeing, and swimming. However, the park's best-known feature is the highest waterfall in Middle Georgia, as the Towaliga River plunges more than 135 feet in a series of falls and cascades.

From the High Falls parking lot, go back left (north) on High Falls Road for 3.1 miles, then turn right on Mt. Vernon Church Road for 4.3 miles. Turn left on GA 42 and go north for about a mile to **Indian Springs State Park** and the **McIntosh House/Indian Springs Hotel**.

Indian Springs State Park is the oldest state park in the United States,

FAMOUS FOR *FRIED GREEN TOMATOES*, THE WHISTLE STOP CAFE IS A BUSY PLACE ON WEEKENDS. NOTHING FANCY ABOUT THE WHISTLE STOP CAFE, JUST A DOWN-HOME PLACE

having been operated continuously as a public park by the state of Georgia since 1825, although it was not actually given the title of "state park" until 1931. The original attraction at the park was the spring water, believed to possess healing qualities. Visitors can still sample the water, flowing from inside the stone Spring House.

The 528-acre park offers 10 cottages and 60 campsites. There is boating, fishing, and swimming in 105-acre Lake McIntosh, biking, and 4 miles of hiking trails.

Across GA 42 from the park is the McIntosh House, built in 1823 by Chief William McIntosh as an inn. It was known for many years as the Indian Springs Hotel. McIntosh, a descendant of a prominent Savannah family, was the son of a Creek Indian mother and became a chief in the Creek Nation. In 1825, he sold a large portion of the Creek lands to the United States in violation of Creek law. He was executed by his fellow Creek chiefs for his offense.

The McIntosh House is now a museum of early 19th-century life. It is open for tours on weekends from Memorial Day to Labor Day.

From Indian Springs, continue north on GA 42 for about 1.5 miles, then

THE HIGH FALLS ON THE TOWALIGA RIVER DROP 135 FEET IN A SERIES OF FALLS AND CASCADES

THE MCINTOSH HOUSE, BUILT BY CREEK INDIAN CHIEF WILLIAM MCINTOSH, WAS A POPULAR RESORT FOR MANY YEARS AS THE INDIAN SPRINGS HOTEL

merge left onto US 23 North for 1.3 miles to **Fresh Air Barbecue** at 1164 GA 42. Serving their own recipe of tangy, slow-cooked pit barbecue since 1929, Fresh Air Barbecue has been recognized as one of Georgia's premier barbecue restaurants. In fact, *Esquire* magazine named it one of the "Best Heritage BBQ Joints in America."

From Fresh Air Barbecue, continue north for 2 more miles to the intersection with GA 16 and turn left (west) on 16 for 9 miles to Interstate 75 and the end of this tour.

IN THE AREA

Accommodations

BEST WESTERN, 805 Industrial Boulevard, McDonough. 770-898-1006.

THE JARRELL 1920 HOUSE, 715 Jarrell Plantation Road, Juliette. 478-986-3972. www.jarrellhouse.com

RAMADA INN, 197 Stanley K. Tanger Boulevard, Locust Grove. 770-898-1216.

Dining

CRAVINGS HOME COOKING, 2180 GA 20, McDonough. 678-432-4888. www.cravingshc.com.

FRESH AIR BARBECUE, 1164 GA 42, Jackson. 770-775-3182. freshair barbecue.com.

MARTHA JANE'S SOUTHERN COOKIN', 114 Frobel Street, Monticello. 706-435-7188.

OLD CLINTON BARBECUE HOUSE, 4214 Gray Highway, Gray. 478-986-3225. oldclintonbbq.com.

TAQUERIA LA ESKINA, 107 West Washington Street, Monticello. 762-435-7156.

THE WHISTLE STOP CAFE, 443 McCrackin Street, Juliette. 478-992-8886. www.thewhistlestopcafe.com.

Attractions and Recreation

JARRELL PLANTATION HISTORIC SITE, 711 Jarrell Plantation Road, Juliette. 478-986-5172.

HIGH FALLS STATE PARK, 76 High Falls Park Drive, Jackson. 478-993-3053.

INDIAN SPRINGS STATE PARK, 678 Lake Clark Road, Flovilla. 770-504-2277.

McINTOSH HOUSE/INDIAN SPRINGS HOTEL MUSEUM, 1834 GA 42 South, Flovilla. 770-775-5350. thevillageatindiansprings.com/indian _spring_hotel_museum.

NOAH'S ARK, 712 L G Griffin Road, Locust Grove. 770-957-0888. www .noahs-ark.org.

PANOLA MOUNTAIN STATE PARK, 2620 GA 155 Southwest, Stockbridge. 770-389-7801.

TANGER OUTLETS, 1000 Tanger Drive, Locust Grove. 770-957-5310. www.tangeroutlet.com/locustgrove.

Events

Jasper County
Deer Festival, November.
Farmers' Market on the Square, Saturday mornings, May–September.

Jones County
Old Clinton War Days and Reenactment, May.
Daylily Festival, June.
Syrup Making & Story Telling, Jarrell Plantation, November.

8

A PLACE OF BEGINNINGS

East Central Georgia

This tour is approximately 130 miles in length and covers some of east central Georgia's richest historic areas, including Greene, Oglethorpe, Madison, Wilkes, and McDuffie Counties.

Begin at Greensboro, halfway between Atlanta and Augusta. If you're traveling Interstate 20, take Exit 130 and follow US 278/GA 44/Main Street for 2.7 miles to downtown.

Founded in 1786, Greensboro is the county seat of Greene County and is the doorway to **Lake Oconee**, with 400 miles of shoreline and ten championship golf courses.

The downtown business section centers around the intersection of Main and Broad Streets. Cross Broad, and go one block to the **Greene County Courthouse**, on the right. Built in 1848, it is the eighth-oldest courthouse in Georgia and the second-oldest still in use. It is considered to be one of the finest examples of Greek Revival architecture in the state. The upper floor was designed to house the Masonic Lodge, which it does to this day.

Just around the corner, on East Greene Street, is the oldest public building in Greensboro—the **Old Rock Gaol** (*gaol* is the way the English spell jail) was built in 1807, with granite walls 2 feet thick. Patterned after the Bastille in Paris, the original cells and gallows are all still in place. You can arrange a tour by calling 706-453-7592.

Turn right just beyond the Rock Gaol and the old **Sheriff L. L. Wyatt Jail** will be on the right. Built in 1895, it is named for the legendary lawman who was sheriff of Greene County for 37 years.

The Wyatt Jail is now the home of the Chamber of Commerce, where you

LEFT: HAWTHORNE HEIGHTS WAS NAMED FOR THE HAWTHORN HEDGE AROUND ITS 8-ACRE GARDEN

The map shows locations including Comer, Colbert, Collier Church Rd, Chandler-Silver Rd, Watson Mill Bridge State Park, Watson Mill Covered Bridge, Howard's Covered Bridge, Lexington, Church Street Houses, Goodness Grows Nursery, Oglethorpe County Courthouse, Salem Baptist Church, Maxeys, Philomath Rd, Historic Homes, Walker Rd, Philomath, Philomath Presbyterian Church, Penfield Baptist Church, Penfield, Woodville, Bethesda Baptist Church, Peachtree Ave, Hawthorne Heights, McCommons Big Store, Union Point, Greensboro, Old Rock Gaol, Courthouse, Exit 130, Siloam, White Plains, Rayle, Callaway Plantation, Washington, Historic Homes and Churches, Courthouse, Washington Historical Museum, Crawfordville, Sharon, Norwood, Tignall, Lincolnton, Clarks Hill L., Log Cabin & General Store, Wrightsboro Methodist Church, Wrightsboro Rd, Exit 172, Thomson. © Countryman Press

can pick up a walking tour brochure. There are quite a few interesting things to see in Greensboro, but it's so compact that a walking tour is a very practical way to explore the town.

Returning to the intersection of Main and Broad, **McCommons Big Store** is at 103 South Main. Built in 1858, it was the largest store between Atlanta and Augusta in its day and boasted of "selling everything from the cradle to the grave." It has housed many businesses in its history, including a blacksmith shop and a funeral home, and now it is home to the **Greensboro Antique Mall**, among other shops.

Just up the street from McCommons, and across from the courthouse at 114 North Main, is a good place to start your tour, or perhaps an even better place to finish it—**The Yesterday Cafe**, famous for buttermilk pie and other good things. Country music star Carrie Underwood ordered 300 of the buttermilk pies for her wedding reception.

Other points of interest in Greensboro that I especially liked were the 1854 **Davis-Evans House** on West Broad Street, about a block from the Main Street intersection, the 1824 **Happy Times House** at 205 West Broad Street, and the pre-1846 **Spinks-Kanitra House** at 201 West Greene Street.

The Davis-Evans House is next to the Methodist Church and was the parsonage for many years. It is now the parish house. Happy Times was a dormitory for the Greensboro Female College. Tradition says that Louisa May Alcott, the author of *Little Women*, was once a teacher there.

A don't-miss location is the **Ripe Thing Market** at 112 West Broad Street. Featuring fresh, locally grown fruits and vegetables as well as grass-fed, hormone-free meat, poultry, and lamb, they also serve outstanding home-made soups, deli sandwiches, and fresh-baked desserts.

Leaving Greensboro, continue on US 278/ GA 44 about 7 miles to Union Point. Go about three blocks past the intersection with GA 77 and turn left on Scott Street, cross the railroad tracks, and turn left on Carleton Street for another block. **Hawthorne Heights** is on the corner of Carleton and Thornton, at 607 Carleton Street. Originally a cottage built in 1848 by James Brook Hart, it was named for the haw-thorn hedge around its 8-acre garden. In 1900

THE OLD ROCK GAOL IN GREENSBORO WAS PATTERNED AFTER THE BASTILLE IN PARIS

the porch was removed and the columns added. This is private property, so you will have to be content with a look from the entrance. But there's almost no traffic, so you can take your time.

From Hawthorne Heights, go back about 0.3 mile to US 278/GA 44/77 and turn right on GA 44/77. Stay right on GA 44 for 4.5 miles to Bethesda Church Road, then turn left and go about a mile to **Bethesda Baptist Church**. The church was organized in 1785, and in 1818 this building was erected after two years of making bricks by hand on the property. The church is alive and active to this day, more than 230 years after its founding.

Leaving Bethesda Church, go back on GA 44 to the junction with GA 77 and turn right for 3.7 miles to Woodville. Turn left on West Peachtree Avenue and go 4 miles to **Penfield Baptist Church** on the right in the Penfield Community. Mercer University was founded here in 1833 as a manual labor school. Erected in 1846 as the college chapel, Penfield Church is a striking example of Greek Revival architecture that looks remarkably contemporary even today, more than 170 years later.

Return to Woodville and go left (north) on GA 77 for 17 miles to the T inter-section with US 78/GA 22 in Lexington. Turn left, then right to follow GA 22 toward Comer for 11 miles to Watson Mill Road. Turn right and go 3 miles to **Watson Mill Covered Bridge** and **Watson Mill Bridge State Park**.

THE 1848 GREENE COUNTY COURTHOUSE IS THE EIGHTH-OLDEST IN GEORGIA

Spanning 229 feet across the South Fork of the Broad River, the Watson Mill bridge is the longest covered bridge in Georgia. Built in 1885 by W. W. King, son of the freed slave and master bridge-builder Horace King, the bridge is constructed with a Town lattice truss system held together by wooden pegs and is in daily use by visitors to the state park.

One of the most picturesque of Georgia's state parks, 1,118-acre Watson Mill Bridge Park offers camping, horseback riding, hiking, bike riding, and

THE GALLERY OF THE SPINKS-KINITRA HOUSE IN GREENSBORO

water fun in the shoals below the covered bridge. Open 7 a.m.–10 p.m. daily, there is no admission charge, but a $5 parking pass is required.

From Watson Mill Covered Bridge, return to GA 22 and cross it onto Collier Church Road. Go 1 mile, then turn left on Chandler-Silver Road for 2 miles (the last mile or so is gravel) to **Howard's Covered Bridge**. Built in 1904 across Big Cloud Creek in a now-isolated part of Oglethorpe County, Howard's Covered Bridge is 164 feet long and of Town lattice truss construction, with planks

PENFIELD BAPTIST CHURCH WAS BUILT TO BE THE CHAPEL ON THE FIRST CAMPUS OF MERCER UNIVERSITY

fastened together with wooden pegs. The original builder was probably J. M. "Pink" Hunt. It is truly the bridge to nowhere, given that whatever road was at the other end of the bridge has long since been obliterated.

From the bridge, go back on Chandler-Silver Road to Collier Road and GA 22. Turn right and return to the intersection of US 78/GA 22. Go left, and in 0.4 mile the old jail will be on the right. Built in 1879, it was in use until 2007. Turn right into the parking lot beside the jail if you'd like to pick up a tour brochure at City Hall.

One block further along is the 1887 Romanesque Revival **Oglethorpe County Courthouse**.

For a tiny town, Lexington has an amazing number of really old, really fine houses, many of them concentrated in a few blocks of Church Street, which was once the main drag through town.

You will have your own favorites, but some I especially liked, going from west to east, are:

- the 1832 **Willingham Watkins House** at 222 West Church
- the 1827–36 **Platt Brooks House** at 102 East Church
- the late 1700s **Bray House** at 103 East Church Street
- the circa 1812 **Presbyterian Manse** at 211 East Church, which was

TOP: OGLETHORPE COUNTY COURTHOUSE, LEXINGTON
BOTTOM: THE AARON-MCGEHEE HOUSE IN LEXINGTON APPEARS TO HAVE AN ARCHITECTURAL STYLE ALL ITS OWN

WATSON MILL COVERED BRIDGE IN MADISON COUNTY IS THE LONGEST REMAINING COVERED BRIDGE IN GEORGIA

the original home of Columbia Theological Seminary, now located in Decatur

- Beth-Salem **Presbyterian Church** is across the street. With only three remaining members, the congregation was dissolved in 2015, 230 years after its founding.

Not on Church Street, but behind the courthouse at 206 South Gilmer, displaying delightfully different vernacular architecture, is the circa 1800 **Aaron-McGehee House**.

Gardening enthusiasts should be sure to check out the **Goodness Grows Nursery**. Turn right at the east end of Church Street and return to US 78/GA 22. Turn left and go a short distance to the intersection with Elberton Road. Go left again. Goodness Grows is about a half-mile down on the left.

Started in 1977 by two friends at the University of Georgia, today Goodness Grows is more than six acres of plants for the wholesale market and a 1-acre retail location. About seventy percent of the plants are herbaceous perennials; the rest are flowering shrubs, trees, and other species.

Return to US 78/GA 22 and go left. Stay on GA 22 for about 5 miles to **Salem Baptist Church**, built in 1828, on the left. Although founded more than 225 years ago, the church is still in use with an active congregation.

From Salem Church, continue 7 more miles to Philomath. As soon as you see the Philomath town limit sign on the right, look left to see the **James V. Drake House** on the left at No. 2235. An imposing Greek Revival plantation house, it was built in 1844 by a descendant of Sir Francis Drake.

A short distance farther, on the left, is the **Philomath Presbyterian Church**, erected in 1848. President Woodrow Wilson's father, the Rev. Joseph Wilson, was a frequent guest minister here. *Philomath*, by the way, is a Greek word meaning "lover of learning." A little farther along on the right is the **Bryant House** at No. 2334, whose owner told me, when I stopped to ask about another location, that her house was built in 1802.

From the church, continue south on GA 22 just over a mile to Walker Road. Turn left and continue for 7 miles (Walker Road will become Philomath Road after 2.5 miles) to a T intersection with US 78 (unmarked at this point). Go right for about 5.5 miles to **Callaway Plantation** on the right, across from the airport.

The plantation began in 1785, with the Callaway family living in a log cabin (the original cabin burned, but a replica stands in its place), and ultimately grew to 3,000 acres. In 1790, Jacob Callaway built the **Grey House**, a fine example of Federal Plain Style architecture, where the family lived until building the Greek Revival **Manor House** in 1869 using bricks made of Georgia red clay.

Other structures on the Callaway Plantation include a circa 1840 slave

HOWARD'S COVERED BRIDGE OVER BIG CLOUD CREEK IS THE "BRIDGE TO NOWHERE"

TOP: PRESIDENT WOODROW WILSON'S FATHER WAS A FREQUENT GUEST MINISTER AT PHILOMATH
PRESBYTERIAN CHURCH
BOTTOM: THE CALLAWAY FAMILY LIVED IN THE FEDERAL PLAIN STYLE GREY HOUSE FROM 1790 UNTIL 1869

cabin, a circa 1871 one-room school, and a circa 1930 general store. All the buildings are open for guided tours Tuesday through Saturday from 10 a.m. to 5 p.m. In the 1980s, the plantation was given as a gift by the Callaway Family to the City of Washington.

From Callaway Plantation, continue on US 78 east and slant right on Busi-

THE WILKES COUNTY COURTHOUSE IN WASHINGTON WAS BUILT IN A PLAYFULLY ORNATE STYLE CALLED RICHARDSONIAN ROMANESQUE

ness 78/GA 10 to downtown Washington, a small city with a very distinguished history. The final cabinet meeting of Jefferson Davis' Confederate government took place in Washington, and it was here that the Confederacy was officially dissolved.

Washington and Wilkes County also have the most antebellum homes in Georgia—more than a hundred. Stop by the visitor center at 22B West Square near the funky Richardsonian Romanesque 1904 **Wilkes County Courthouse** and pick up a map to guide you on a fascinating walking or driving tour. You could easily spend a lot of time in Washington!

A good place to start is the **Washington Historical Museum**, located in the 1835 Semmes-Barnett House at 308 East Robert Toombs Avenue. But before you leave the square, check out the 1898 **Fitzpatrick Hotel**. Closed for more than 50 years, it has been fully restored and features 17 luxurious rooms furnished in Victorian period furniture.

Also, be sure to see the 1814 **Robert Toombs House Historical Site** at 216 East Robert Toombs Avenue. The mansion is open for tours Tuesday through Saturday, 10 a.m.–4 p.m. **The Presbyterian Church**, built in 1825, is nearby at 206 East Robert Toombs Avenue. **The 1793 Liberty Inn**, at 108 West Liberty Street, is believed to be the oldest original house in Washington. **Jackson Chapel African Methodist Episcopal Church** at

318 Whitehall Street was built in 1867 by newly freed slaves and remains active to this day.

For a taste of the more recent but rapidly disappearing past, visit the soda fountain/lunch counter at **the Fievet Pharmacy** at 115 East Robert Toombs Avenue. They're open 8 a.m.–4:40 p.m. Monday through Friday and 8 a.m.–2 p.m. on Saturday, serving breakfast, burgers, sandwiches, salads, milkshakes, and sodas.

Leaving Washington, take US 78 south for a bit over 19 miles to Stagecoach Road on the right. Go 2.5 miles to the stop sign, stay to the right, and continue on Wrightsboro Road for 1.3 miles to the **Wrightsboro Methodist Church**, on the left.

Wrightsboro was first settled by Quakers in 1754, and the original town was named Brandon. However, it was renamed after Royal Governor James Wright and incorporated as Wrightsboro in 1799. The church was built at public expense in 1810–12 for use by all Christian denominations. The Methodists apparently used it most, and in 1877 the property was deeded to them;

THE FITZPATRICK HOTEL ON THE SQUARE IN WASHINGTON WAS CLOSED FOR 50 YEARS BUT HAS NOW BEEN FULLY RENOVATED

THE CONGREGATION OF THE WRIGHTSBORO METHODIST CHURCH DISBANDED IN 1964. THE CHURCH AND CEMETERY ARE MAINTAINED BY MCDUFFIE COUNTY

but by 1964 the Methodists had disbanded and ownership reverted back to McDuffie County. Graves in the adjacent cemetery date back to 1800.

Across Wrightsboro Road from the church is a reconstructed 1840 log cabin and the 1918 Hawes General Store, which is original to the site.

Leaving Wrightsboro Methodist Church, go back east on Wrightsboro Road to Stagecoach Road and US 78. Turn right and go south to Interstate 20. Exit 172 at Thomson and the end of this tour.

IN THE AREA

Accommodations

THE FITZPATRICK HOTEL, 16 West Washington Square, Washington. 706-678-5900. thefitzpatrickhotel.com.

GOODWIN MANOR BED AND BREAKFAST INN, 306 South Main Street, Greensboro. 706-453-6218. goodwinmanor.com.

WHITE COLUMNS INN, 1890 Washington Road (US 78), Thomson. 888-347-2319. www.whitecolumnsinn.com. The White Columns Inn is clean, comfortable, and inexpensive, and it serves the best breakfast I have ever had at a non-bed and breakfast hotel/motel.

Dining

BLAZERS HOT WINGS, 640 Washington Road, Lexington. 706-743-0036. blazerslexington.com.

FIEVET PHARMACY, 115 East Robert Toombs Avenue, Washington. 706-678-2260.

THE PIG & BULL GRILL, 714 East Robert Toombs Avenue, Washington. 706-678-7637.

THE ROWDY ROOSTER, 123 East Main Street, Lexington.

THE SQUARE CAFE, 22 West Square, Washington. 706-678-5908. Breakfast and lunch.

THE YESTERDAY CAFE, 114 North Main Street, Greensboro. 706-453-0800. theyesterdaycafe.com.

Attractions and Recreation

GOODNESS GROWS NURSERY, 332 Elberton Road, Lexington. 706-743-5055. goodnessgrows.com.

RIPE THING MARKET, 112 West Broad Street, Greensboro. 706-454-2155. www.facebook.com/RipeThingMarket.

ROBERT TOOMBS HOUSE HISTORIC SITE, 216 East Robert Toombs Avenue, Washington. 706-678-2226.

WATSON MILL BRIDGE STATE PARK, 650 Watson Mill Road, Comer. 706-783-5349.

For more information on any Georgia State Park or Historic Site, visit the state parks website: www.georgiastateparks.org.

Events

Wilkes County

Reenactment of Revolutionary War Battle of Kettle Creek, second weekend in February.

Spring Tour of Homes, first weekend in April.

Cruise-in on the Square Antique Car Show, Second Saturday of May and September.

Mule Day Southern Heritage Festival, second Saturday in October.

9

HISTORIC CHURCH ROW

East Central Georgia

This tour is about 130 miles in length and includes McDuffie, Columbia, Warren, Washington, Hancock, and Taliaferro Counties.

Take Exit 169 from Interstate 20 and go south on 3 Points Road for about a half-mile. After crossing Cedar Rock Road, 3 Points Road becomes West Bypass Road. Continue on West Bypass for 1.3 miles, then turn right onto Rock House Road (if there's a sign there, I didn't see it). **The Rock House** is about a quarter-mile on your right at 1455 Rock House Road, Thomson.

Dating from 1785, the house was built by Thomas Ansley, an ancestor of 39th President Jimmy Carter. It is the oldest stone house in Georgia and among the oldest documented buildings in the state. With three levels, including a full basement (albeit with a dirt floor) and several fireplaces, the house is surprisingly roomy and livable, even by today's standards. Ansley built very well, although it does seem a little short on bathrooms. I found this to be one of the most interesting buildings on this tour.

Leaving the Rock House, go back east on Rock House Road toward West Bypass Road and turn right for 2 miles. Turn left onto Mesena Road for 0.4 mile, turn right onto Vigortone Road for 0.3 mile, then left (east) on US 278 for about 14.5 miles. Turn left on North Louisville Street in Harlem. **The Laurel and Hardy Museum** is on your immediate right in the Columbia theater.

The great comedian Oliver Hardy was born in Harlem, and the museum is dedicated to Hardy and his partner Stan Laurel, who together formed one of the world's most famous comedy teams. The museum contains artifacts, memorabilia, and a theatre to watch any of the 106 movies they made.

LEFT: THE POWELTON METHODIST CHURCH WAS BUILT IN 1830

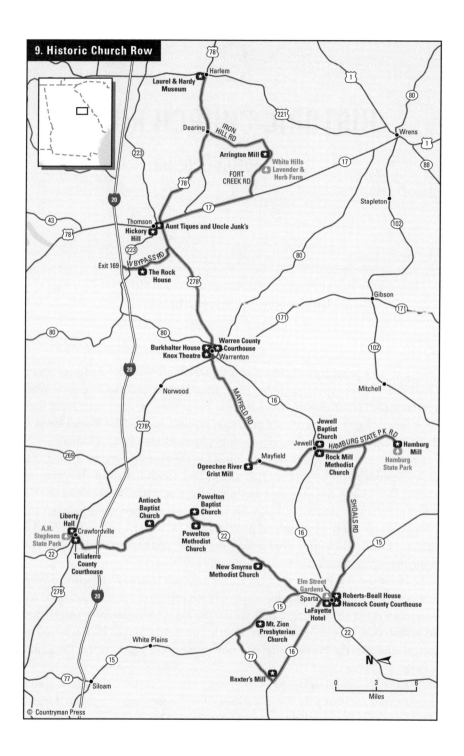

9. Historic Church Row

Harlem
Laurel & Hardy Museum
Dearing
IRON HILL RD
Arrington Mill
White Hills Lavender & Herb Farm
FORT CREEK RD
Wrens
Stapleton
Thomson
Aunt Tiques and Uncle Junk's
Hickory Hill
Exit 169
W BYPASS RD
The Rock House
Gibson
Warren County Courthouse
Burkhalter House
Knox Theatre
Warrenton
Norwood
Mitchell
MAYFIELD RD
Jewell Baptist Church
Jewell
HAMBURG STATE PK RD
Hamburg Mill
Rock Mill Methodist Church
Hamburg State Park
Mayfield
Ogeechee River Grist Mill
Antioch Baptist Church
Powelton Baptist Church
Liberty Hall
A.H. Stephens State Park
Crawfordville
Powelton Methodist Church
SHOALS RD
Taliaferro County Courthouse
New Smyrna Methodist Church
Elm Street Gardens
Sparta
Roberts-Beall House
Hancock County Courthouse
LaFayette Hotel
White Plains
Mt. Zion Presbyterian Church
Siloam
Baxter's Mill

N

0   3   6
Miles

© Countryman Press

TOP: THE ROCK HOUSE NEAR THOMSON WAS BUILT BY AN ANCESTOR OF PRESIDENT JIMMY CARTER
BOTTOM: THE INTERIOR OF THE ROCK HOUSE IS SURPRISINGLY ROOMY

Admission is free, and patrons are encouraged to stay and watch a movie or two. The museum is open 10 a.m.–4 p.m., Tuesday through Saturday.

From Harlem, go west on US 78/278 for 4.5 miles to Dearing. Turn left on South Main Street, which will become Iron Mill Road. After 2 miles, keep left on Luckey's Bridge Road for 2 miles and turn right on Fort Creek Road Ext. Go 0.2 mile and turn right on Fort Creek Road for about a mile to **Arrington Mill** on the right, a lovely, small mill that is no longer in operation. The setting is beautiful and peaceful.

From Arrington Mill, continue on Fort Creek Road for 1.1 miles to **White Hills Lavender and Herb Farm** on the left. The herb gardener, of course, will find the place fascinating, but so also will many others who would never have given the matter a second thought. White Hills features instructions and demonstrations on cooking with herbs and offers tea parties and luncheons in season. They're open on Fridays, 10 a.m.–6 p.m., and other days for special occasions. Call them at 706-595-5081 or check their website at (www .whitehillsherbs.com) to see what's cooking. It's a working farm, so if you don't get an answer, leave a message. They will call you back.

From the herb farm, continue on Fort Creek Road 2.4 miles to GA 17 (Happy Valley Store will be across the road). Turn right (north) and continue for 7 miles to the junction with US/78/278 in Thomson.

Hickory Hill, a National Historic Landmark at 502 Hickory Hill Drive in

THE ARRINGTON MILL IN MCDUFFIE COUNTY IS TYPICAL OF MANY SMALL MILLS AROUND GEORGIA THAT ONCE GROUND GRAIN FOR LOCAL FARMERS

THE OGEECHEE RIVER MILL IN HANCOCK COUNTY HAS BEEN COMPLETELY RENOVATED AND IS OPEN FOR TOURS

Thomson, was the home of Thomas E. Watson. Known as the "sage of Hickory Hill," he was a leader of the Populist Party, served in the US House of Representatives and Senate, and also published a magazine for many years. Although originally built in 1864, Hickory Hill was acquired by Watson in 1900 and extensively renovated. The Greek Revival mansion now serves as a house museum and is open for tours by appointment. Call 706-595-7777.

Aunt Tiques and Uncle Junk's, at 201 First Avenue in Thomson, is a picker's delight. They specialize in unusual antiques, stained glass, iron fencing, and lots more. Check out their Facebook page (m.facebook.com/unclejunksthomson) to see what's new in old stuff.

Leaving Thomson, take US 278 west about 10 miles to Warrenton. From the intersection of US 278 and Business 278, go 0.3 mile on US 278/East Main Street. Turn right on North Gibson, then take the first right. The **Jacob Burkhalter House** is the third on the left, at 69 Davis Street. Built in 1778 by Revolutionary War soldier Jacob Burkhalter, the Burkhalter House was the first recorded home to be built in Warrenton and is one of the oldest houses I know of in East Central Georgia. The Marquis de LaFayette stayed at the house for two weeks in March 1825 after falling sick while traveling by stagecoach from Augusta to Milledgeville. A grand ball was held in his honor before he left.

From the Burkhalter House, go to the end of the block, turn right, then right again on East Main Street. The **Warren County Courthouse**, built in 1909, contains an impressive collection of paintings of historical landmarks by local painters. The **Knox Theatre**, dating from 1937, is currently being renovated. Pick up a tour map and brochures at the Depot Welcome Center, 46 South Norwood Street.

From the courthouse in Warrenton, continue west on US 278 for about a half-mile to the bypass. Turn right, go one block, and turn left on Mayfield

WITH SEVERAL SETS OF MILLSTONES, THE OGEECHEE RIVER MILL CAN DO MORE THAN ONE GRINDING OPERATION AT A TIME

HAMBURG MILL, BUILT IN 1921, STILL OPERATES ON SPECIAL OCCASIONS

Road. After about 8 miles, and just after crossing the river, turn right at the **Ogeechee River Grist Mill** sign and go back about a quarter-mile to the mill entrance.

The first mill at this location was built in 1847 on the other side of the river, but was rebuilt on its present site in 1933 to avoid flooding. The original wooden dam was replaced by a concrete dam at that time.

The mill is unusually beautiful and well-preserved and is in regular service with a number of clients for its products. It's a good idea to call well in advance to arrange a tour because the mill is located on a working cattle farm and owners Missy Garner and her son Alex Broward are busy people. Call them at 706-464-2195 or 706-831-1432 and leave a message if you don't get an answer. The cost of the tour is $10 for adults; schoolchildren get in free. I assure you that you will get your money's worth.

Southern-style grits are a specialty, and if the mill isn't grinding grits when you visit, you can buy a bag or two at the IGA grocery store in Warrenton.

Leaving the mill, continue on Mayfield Road for about 0.8 mile, turn left, cross the railroad tracks, and go south on Hamburg State Park Road for 4.5 miles to the Jewell Historic Community. Cross GA 16 and continue on Hamburg State Park Road. **Rock Mill Methodist Church**, circa 1840, will be on your immediate right. This beautifully restored church was spared by Sherman because of the Masonic affiliation of Daniel Ashley Jewell. **Jewell Baptist Church**, built in 1869–70 of locally handmade bricks, is on the left.

Continue about 6.5 miles to **Hamburg State Park** and **Hamburg Mill**.

Built in 1921 on the Little Ogeechee River, the mill was in operation for more than 40 years until it was put out of business by large-scale competitors. The property was deeded over to the state in the late 1960s and Hamburg State Park was created. The mill still operates on special occasions, including the third Saturday of September each year at the park's Fall Harvest Festival. Corn meal ground at the mill is for sale in the park's Country Store.

Hamburg State Park also features fishing and boating and boat rentals on the 225-acre millpond, as well as camping, hiking, and picnicking sites on its 741 acres. Like most Georgia state parks, Hamburg Mill is open 7 a.m.–10 p.m. daily. Admission is free, but a $5 parking pass is required.

From the state park, go back on Hamburg State Park Road about 3 miles and turn left on Shoals Road (unmarked) for 10 miles to GA 15. Go right for 2 miles to downtown Sparta, where the two most prominent buildings on Broad Street are the **Hancock County Courthouse** and the **Lafayette Hotel**, also known as the **Eagle Tavern**.

Built 1881–83, the courthouse is an unusually fine example of Second Empire architecture. Although it was gutted by fire in August 2014, leav-

THE LAFAYETTE HOTEL WAS BUILT IN 1840 ON THE SITE OF THE LATE 1700S EAGLE TAVERN

THE HANCOCK COUNTY COURTHOUSE WAS GUTTED BY FIRE IN 2014, BUT HAS BEEN COMPLETELY REBUILT

ing only the exterior brick walls standing, it has now been completely restored.

On the east side of the courthouse is the Lafayette Hotel, built on the site of the old Eagle Tavern. Dating from the late 1700s, the Tavern was a stagecoach inn and was the scene of a grand ball for the Marquis de Lafayette in 1825. After it burned in the late 1830s, the Lafayette Hotel, originally named the Edwards' House, replaced it in 1840. In 1897, the name was changed to Drummer's Home (a "drummer" was a traveling salesman), and the hotel became one of the most popular in Georgia for many years. The name was changed to Lafayette Hotel in 1941, but locals still call it the Eagle Tavern. It now provides housing for senior citizens.

Sparta has many other interesting old buildings. Two that I especially like are the circa 1845 **Roberts-Beall House** on Monument Square, across from the courthouse, a grand old home looking for an owner who will love and restore it; and the distinctive 1834 **Bird-Pierce-Campbell House** at 12530 Broad Street.

Drop by the visitor information center on Elm Street and pick up a self-guided tour brochure. And while you're in the neighborhood, check out the **Elm Street Gardens**, a gardener's paradise located behind an historic 1840s house at 15 Elm Street. Completely organic, they grow vegetables year-round, using a no-till method.

From Sparta, take GA 16 west for 10 miles to the intersection of GA 77 and **Baxter's Mill** on Shoulderbone Creek. It has also been known by many other names through the years—Millmore Mill, Eatonton Mill, and Sparta Mill are some—and is known locally as Shoulderbone Mill.

The mill was probably built around 1800, although no one seems to know for certain. It was mentioned in the Hancock County chronicles in 1814, confirming that it was in existence by that time. Although it is no longer in operation, it appears to be in excellent condition and is a very picturesque sight.

From the mill, go right (north) 4.5 miles on GA 77 to the intersection with GA 15 and turn right (south) on 15 for 1.5 miles to **Mt. Zion Presbyterian Church**, on the right. The beautiful old structure, which cost its parishioners $700 to build in 1814, is all that survives of a once-thriving community with an academy that was one of Georgia's most celebrated institutions. Famous educators and writers were associated with Mt. Zion, which is said to have narrowly lost to Athens as the location for the University of Georgia.

Continue south on GA 15 for 3.8 miles to the intersection of GA 22 and go left (north). This stretch of GA 22 is truly old church row! First up, in 3.7 miles, is **New Smyrna Methodist**. In fact, it is the second-oldest Methodist church in

POWELTON BAPTIST CHURCH IS THE SECOND-OLDEST BAPTIST CHURCH IN GEORGIA

TOP: EVEN IN NEGLECT AND ABANDONMENT, THE ANTIOCH BAPTIST CHURCH HAS GREAT DIGNITY
BOTTOM: THE PULPIT AREA OF ANTIOCH BAPTIST CHURCH APPEARS TO BE JUST AS IT WAS AFTER THE FINAL SERVICE

THE TALIAFERRO COUNTY COURTHOUSE PRESIDES OVER THE LEAST POPULOUS COUNTY IN GEORGIA

Georgia, founded sometime before 1790. A building was erected in 1800 and remodeled in 1878 on the original frame, foundation, and hewn log floor joists of the 1800 building. It is listed on the National Register of Historic Places. The church is no longer active but has been lovingly maintained by the Hill family for many years. It is the setting for an annual homecoming celebration.

Go another 6 miles on GA 22, and at the point where Powelton Church Road intersects from the right, slant left onto a dirt road appropriately named Quiet Lane. **Powelton Methodist Church** will be on your immediate left. Built in 1830, it has not been maintained recently and looks every one of its 190-plus years, although it appears to still be structurally sound.

Leaving Powelton Methodist, continue north on GA 22 for half a mile to **Powelton Baptist Church** on your right at Jones Bridge Road. Erected in 1798, Powelton Baptist is the second-oldest Baptist church building in the state and can in many ways be considered the mother church of the Baptist denomination in Georgia, since the Georgia Baptist Convention was organized there in 1822. The bell tower and covered porch were added in 1822. It is still in service with an active congregation.

From Powelton Baptist, continue north on GA 22 for 3 miles to **Antioch Baptist Church**, built in 1899 by the sons and daughters of former slaves. It has been abandoned for years and is now in need of major repairs, although occasional services are still held there. Even in its deteriorated state, it exudes a presence of patient nobility.

From Antioch, continue on GA 22 for about 7.5 miles to Crawfordville, the county seat of Taliaferro (pronounced "Tolliver"—don't ask me why) County. With 1,462 residents in 2020, Taliaferro is the least populous county in Georgia and has the second smallest of any county population east of the Mississippi River. Nonetheless, Crawfordville and Taliaferro County have become very popular locations for movie-making. Thirteen movies, including *Get Low* (2009), *Pushing up Daisies* (2007), *Sweet Home Alabama* (2001), *Neon Bible* (1994), *Stars and Bars* (1987), *GORP* (1979), and *Summer of my German Soldier* (1978), have been filmed in whole or in part in Crawfordville. Perhaps it has something to do with the fact that Crawfordville's downtown has hardly changed since the early 1900s, making it a perfect movie set. Many of those downtown storefronts are empty these days, but one is alive and cooking. **Nick's Place** serves excellent food three times a day at reasonable prices. I also like Taliaferro County's funky High Victorian Eclectic, one-turret **Courthouse**, built in 1902.

If you're up for one more stop on historic church row for a very special church, go east on Crawfordville's main street (actually named Broad Street) and turn left on GA 47/East Sharon Street. Go 5.7 miles and turn right on Barnett Road SE, then quickly turn left onto Davidson Road. Davidson will turn slightly right and become Locust Grove Road SE. On your left will be the very first Roman Catholic church in Georgia, **Locust Grove Catholic**

Church, established in 1792, 10 years before the first Catholic church in Savannah. The present building was built in 1884.

Return to Crawfordville, and for a final stop on our tour, visit **A.H. Stephens State Park** and **Liberty Hall**. Built in 1875, Liberty Hall was the home of Confederate Vice-President and Georgia governor Alexander Hamilton Stephens. It has been fully restored and houses one of Georgia's largest collections of Civil War artifacts.

The park offers facilities for camping, boating, hiking, and picnicking on its 1,177 acres; however, it's best known for its 21 miles of horseback riding trails. From the park, go back to Interstate 20 and the end of this tour.

IN THE AREA

Accommodations

WHITE COLUMNS INN, 1890 Washington Road (US 78), Thomson. 888-347-2319. www.whitecolumnsinn.com. Clean, comfortable, inexpensive, and serves the best breakfast I have ever had at a hotel/motel.

There are several chain hotels near the I-20 intersection in Thomson. The Comfort Inn, Econolodge, and Hampton Inn all have about the same rating as the White Columns Inn. I recommend the White Columns, as stated above, because of its great breakfast.

Dining

BORDEAUX STEAK & SEAFOOD, 250 254 Seymour Drive North, Thomson. 706-244-1715.

DOWN SOUTH SEAFOOD, 972 Sparta Highway, Sparta (actually south of Sparta on the way to Milledgeville). 478-452-2100.

IVERY'S RESTAURANT, 112 Railroad Street, Thompson. 706-595-2666.

MAMA CHUCHA'S CAFE, 114 Monument Street Southeast, Crawfordville. 706-456-1160.

MISS JANE'S RESTAURANT, 542 Main Street, Warrenton. 706-465-3882. www.facebook.com/pages/Miss-Janes-Restaurant/117352058325046.

NICK'S PLACE, 115 Broad Street, Crawfordville. 706-456-1160.

Attractions and Recreation

A.H. STEPHENS STATE PARK, 456 Alexander Street Northwest, Crawford-ville. 706-456-2602.

ELM STREET GARDEN, 15 Elm Street, Sparta. elmstreetgardens.com.

HAMBURG STATE PARK, 6071 Hamburg State Park Road, Mitchell. 478-552-2393.

HICKORY HILL, 502 Hickory Hill Drive, Thomson. 706-595-7777. www.hickory-hill.org/#hickory-hill.

LAUREL AND HARDY MUSEUM, 250 North Louisville Street, Harlem. 888-288-9108. laurelandhardymuseum.org

WHITE HILLS LAVENDER AND HERB FARM, 1419 Fort Creek Road, Dearing. 706-595-5081. whitehillsherbs.com.

For more information on any Georgia State Park or Historic Site, visit the state parks website: www.georgiastateparks.org.

Events

Columbia County
Laurel and Hardy Festival, Harlem, first Saturday in October.

McDuffie County
Belle Meade Hunt Opening Meet, November.
Camelia City Festival, Downtown Thomson, October.

Warren County
March Hare 5K Fun Run, March.
Art on Main Fine Art Festival, June.
Fiddles & Vittles Music and Food Festival, October.

Washington County
Fall Harvest Festival, Hamburg State Park, third Saturday in September.

10

THE GREAT SOUTHWEST

Southwest Georgia

This tour is about 290 miles in length and includes Dooly, Sumter, Webster, Stewart, Randolph, Clay, Early, Calhoun, Dougherty, Worth, and Crisp Counties.

Beginning at Interstate 75, Exit 109 in Vienna, take GA 215/East Union Street a quarter-mile west to our first stop—the **Georgia Cotton Museum**, at 1321 East Union.

Located in a small, circa 1890, school building, the Cotton Museum tells the story of cotton and cotton production in Georgia through video, displays, photographs, and artifacts. It's open Thursday and Friday 9 a.m.–4 p.m. and Saturday 10 a.m.–2 p.m. There's no admission charge, but naturally, donations are accepted.

As you continue west on GA 215/East Union toward downtown Vienna, GA 215 will merge into GA 27. Continue on GA 27/Union Street to the town square, occupied by a shady park. Just beyond it is the Romanesque Revival **Dooly County Courthouse**, built in 1892—definitely a banner year for Georgia courthouses.

From the courthouse, continue on GA 27/Union Street west for 0.8 mile and bear left to stay on GA 27. It's about 25 miles through beautiful South Georgia countryside to downtown Americus. GA 27 merges with US 280 and becomes Forsyth Street one-way west through town. Turn left on Jackson Street, go to the end of the block, and the **Windsor Hotel** will be on the left.

One of America's great historic hotels, the Windsor was built in 1892 and has been an icon of the city of Americus ever since. It was closed in 1972, but was renovated and reopened in 1991. Since 2010, it has been part of the Best

LEFT: PROVIDENCE CANYON IN STEWART COUNTY IS ONE OF GEORGIA'S SEVEN NATURAL WONDERS

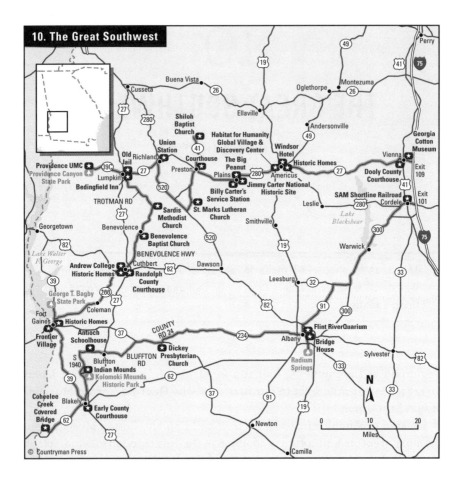

Western chain. It's a great place to stay, and rates are surprisingly reasonable. But if you're just passing through without staying over and would like to tour the building, call 229-924-1555 for information or visit their website (www.windsor-americus.com).

Just down the block from the Windsor on Lamar Street, which is one-way east through town, is the Welcome Center, on the left. Parking is easy to find—Americus is one of those few intelligent towns that hasn't driven everyone out to suburban malls with parking meters. Chattanooga, Tennessee, which I consider my home town, made that mistake many years ago, to the detriment of all.

Pick up a tour guide to the city and county from the helpful folks at the Welcome Center and set off to see the sights.

Just down the hill from the Windsor, at 111 Jackson Street, is the old **Carnegie Library**, designed by the T.F. Lockwood firm of architects and built in 1908 with a $20,000 grant from the Carnegie Foundation.

And just down the hill from the library is the Queen Anne–style **Ameri-**

cus Presbyterian Church, built in 1884 and still very much in active ministry.

When you look at the driving tour map of the historic houses in Americus, the first thing you will notice is that there are many of them. I didn't try to visit them all, but here are a few I liked.

The cottage at 144 Taylor Street was built in the 1850s. It has an unusual nine panes over six panes front window design. The original front porch has been removed and a pediment door casing has been added.

The Taylor-Felder-Lanier House at 201 Taylor Street was built by early Americus resident Seth Kellum Taylor in the 1850s and remodeled to Classical Revival style in 1906–07, adding the tall Corinthian Columns, two-storied portico, plate-glass windows, and fanlight entrance.

The Greek Revival Herschel Smith House at 217 Taylor Street was built circa 1856. Beautifully landscaped, it is considered one of the finest surviving antebellum homes in Americus.

THE WINDSOR HOTEL IN AMERICUS IS NOW PART OF THE BEST WESTERN CHAIN

The James K. Daniel House, at 504 Rees Park, was built in 1847 and enlarged in the 1880s. It is now a bed and breakfast, the very highly rated Garden Inn.

Before you leave Americus, be sure to go to the Habitat for Humanity Global Village and Discovery Center at 721 West Church Street. Learn about Habitat's worldwide mission to see people adequately housed, and experience what Habitat houses are like all around the world. The center is open for tours 9 a.m. to 5 p.m., Monday through Friday, and 10 a.m.–2 p.m. on Saturday, at no charge. Call 800-422-4828, extension 7937, for information, or visit their website at (www.habitat.org/gvdc).

From Americus, take US 280 west for about 10 miles to Plains, the home town of 39th President Jimmy Carter. The Plains Visitor Center is on the left about a mile before you get to town. Continue past ranks of large metal peanut and grain storage buildings to the main intersection in Plains at US 280 and Bond Street.

Turn right on North Bond Street and go about 0.1 mile to the Jimmy Carter National Historic Site Museum & Visitor Center on the right at the old Plains High School, 300 North Bond, where he and Rosalynn Smith were students. A visit to the site provides an insight into rural southern culture and its influence in molding the character and political policies of Jimmy Carter.

The museum and visitor center are open daily 9 a.m.–5 p.m. Admission is free.

Just beyond the visitor center, on the left, is **Plains Baptist Church**, organized in 1848. This building is the fourth in their history and was built in 1906. Jimmy Carter attended here earlier in life.

Continue on North Bond Street from the church for about a hundred yards and slant right on GA 45 for about 0.3 mile to **"The Big Peanut,"** a 13-foot-tall peanut effigy with the famous, toothy Jimmy Carter grin. Originally created for a political rally in Indiana in 1976, it stood beside the Plains railroad depot for many years, where it was vandalized by souvenir hunters. It has now been moved to the Davis E-Z Mart on GA 45. The people there keep an eye on it and say it's probably "the most-photographed thing in Plains."

EXCEPT FOR THE SIGNS, NOT MUCH HAS CHANGED IN DOWNTOWN PLAINS OVER THE YEARS

Another 0.1 mile along GA 45 is Maranatha Baptist Church, which the Carters attend when in Plains. Mr. Carter teaches Sunday School here several months each year. Anyone who wishes to attend will be welcomed.

Go back to US 280 and turn right. Partway down the block on the right is **Billy Carter's Service Station**, where the "First Brother," who was somewhat of a local character, held forth about (among other things) the virtues of Billy Beer. His service station is now a museum of memorabilia of the life and times of the outspoken and individualistic man whose brother was president. The museum is open 9a.m.–5 p.m. every day, but like Billy himself, the hours tend to be a little erratic, so it's a good idea to call ahead. 229-824-5373.

Continue to the end of the block, turn left, cross the railroad tracks, and the **Jimmy Carter Campaign Headquarters** in the old

THE BIG PEANUT IS SAID TO BE THE MOST POPULAR PHOTO SUBJECT IN PLAINS

Plains railroad depot will be on the right. Also a part of the Jimmy Carter National Historic Site, the **Train Depot Museum** is open daily 9 a.m. to 4:30 p.m., with no admission charge.

Turn left and the block of storefronts, which is downtown Plains, will be on the right. The first floor of the building at 106 West Main Street is an interesting antique mall with 20 display booths, and the second floor is the **Plains Historic Inn**, a bed and breakfast with seven suites with authentic period furnishings from the '20s to the '80s.

Go the end of the block and turn right on South Bond Street. Continue for about 0.3 mile to Number 219, the modest home where **First Lady Rosalynn Smith Carter** grew up. There are historic plaques marking the site.

From Plains, take US 280 west for 9 miles to Preston and turn right (north) on GA 41 for one block, then right again at the next intersection, where the two previous **Webster County Jails** stand side by side. The wooden building was built in 1856 and served until 1910, when the brick jail was built. It was used until the 1990s.

From the jails, go back to GA 41, turn right, and go 6.5 miles to **Shiloh Baptist Church**. Built in 1835 by a congregation organized in 1812, the church appears to have been repainted recently, and according to a prominent sign, services are being held regularly. The church sits behind its cemetery, on the right side of GA 41 just south of Enterprise Church Road.

BILLY CARTER'S SERVICE STATION WAS A POPULAR GATHERING PLACE FOR THE MEDIA DURING HIS BROTHER'S PRESIDENCY

The area, called Church Hill, is mostly deserted these days but once was a substantial community with five churches of different denominations in close proximity. Hence the name "Church Hill."

From Shiloh Church, go back to Preston and turn right on US 280 for one block. The 1915 Neoclassical Revival **Webster County Courthouse** will be on the right. At one point during World War II, the belvedere on top of the courthouse was used as an observation post to warn of enemy planes headed for Fort Benning.

From the courthouse, turn left (south) on GA 41 and continue for about 3.5 miles to Ben Williams Road (CR 129). Turn left, go approximately another 3.5 miles, and turn left on Mill Pond Road (sign missing). In 1 mile, **St. Marks Lutheran Church** will be on your left.

In 2016, I spent at least an hour and a half looking for this church at its original location 5 miles west of Plains in the now-extinct community of Botsford, only to find that in 2010, it had been moved by Ernie Guilford a short distance to a new site across the county line into Webster County, south of Preston. The church, which had been allowed to deteriorate, has been restored by Guilford and looks very good. The interior walls and floors are made of heart-pine planks, 6 to 12 inches wide. Very beautiful.

Founded in the 1860s by immigrants of German descent who came from South Carolina, St. Mark's has historical ties to Mt. Zion-St. Luke's Lutheran Church in Oglethorpe, Macon County.

TOP: HANDMADE PEWS AND HEART PINE FLOORS IN ST. MARK'S LUTHERAN CHURCH
BOTTOM: THE RICHLAND HOTEL WAS BUILT IN 1899 AND HAS BEEN RECENTLY RENOVATED

From St. Mark's Church, go back to Ben Williams Road, turn right, and go 2 miles, then turn left on East Centerpoint Road for about 8.5 miles. Turn left on Nicholson Street for about a mile to the traffic light, turn right on Wall Street, and go one block to East Broad Street. Turn right to the two blocks of downtown Richland, where citizens have been hard at work restoring and revitalizing. The unique 1890 **Richland Hotel and Bank** was the most extensive project. It sits on the left at the end of the second block, and just beyond, on the right, is the restored **Union Station**, built in 1913, which is now the City Hall and Museum.

Lovers of barbecue should not miss the annual **Pigfest**, a community event held on the second weekend of November since 1997.

From Richland, stay on GA 27 for about 8.5 miles to Lumpkin (town, not county). As you approach the town square, the **Old Stewart County Jail** (now retired to more pleasant occupations—it was a Halloween fun house when last seen) will be on the right. Just beyond is the town square, with the Neoclassical Revival **Stewart County Courthouse**, built in 1923.

Just past the courthouse, on the corner of Broad and Cotton Streets, is the **Bedingfield Inn**, built by Dr. Bryan N. Bedingfield in 1836 as a stagecoach inn and family residence. It continued to serve as a hotel or boarding house into the 1930s, was purchased by the Stewart County Historical Commission in 1965, and is now a house museum depicting West Georgia life in the 1830s and 1840s.

At the back of the garden behind the inn is a "dogtrot-style" log cabin dating from the 1830s—the **Cornelius Lynch House**, which was moved to this site from another location in the county.

The Bedingfield Inn is open Friday and Saturday, noon to 4 p.m. Admission is $5 for adults, $2 for children. The tour also includes the log cabin and **Dr. Hatchett's Drug Store Museum**, with its old-time soda fountain. Check their website (bedingfieldinn.wordpress.com/about) for more information.

From the Bedingfield Inn, go to the end of the block on Cotton Street and turn right on Main Street. The first house on the left is the **Erasmus Beall House**, built around 1836. Continue on Main Street to near its end, cross Chestnut Street, and turn left. The third house on the right, built around 1835, was the **boyhood home of General Clement Evans**, one of Georgia's most distinguished citizens of his era. He was an attorney, judge, and state senator, and yet he enlisted in the Confederate army as a private. He ended the war as a general. After the war he was ordained as a Methodist minister and served congregations in North Georgia for 26 years.

From the Evans boyhood home, go back to Chestnut Street, turn left and go one block to Broad Street/GA 27. Turn left again for a half-mile to US 27. Go right (north) for 0.3 mile, then left on GA 39C for 6 miles to **Providence Canyon State Park**.

Entering the park, the canyon will be on the left, and on the right, about a

SARDIS METHODIST CHURCH WAS BUILT IN 1848 AND RESTORED IN THE 1970S

half-mile back and within the park grounds, is the 1859 **Providence United Methodist Church** and cemetery.

Providence Canyon, Georgia's "Little Grand Canyon," ranked as one of the state's Seven Natural Wonders, is actually the result of poor farming practices and unchecked erosion. It simply has to be seen to be believed. Perhaps even more difficult to believe is that in 1859, when Providence Church was built, the canyon was only a gully about five feet deep!

There are several overlooks from which to view the canyon, most of which require some walking. One of the best, though, requires relatively little walking and is one of the first you come to, just beyond the restrooms. The state parks people, who should know, say the canyon is 150 feet deep. But it looks much deeper.

In addition to viewing the canyon, which is certainly worth the trip, the 1003-acre park also offers picnic shelters, pioneer campsites, backcountry campsites, 3 miles of hiking trails, and a 7-mile backcountry backpacking trail. It's open daily 7 a.m.–6 p.m. September 15–April 14, and 7 a.m.–9 p.m. April 15–September 14. As with most Georgia state parks, there's no admission fee but a $5 parking pass is required.

When Providence Methodist Church was organized, around 1832, the congregation met in a log building on a site that is now between two of the canyons. The present building was erected in 1859, fortunately on a different site. The church is not locked. You can go inside, but be respectful. Unfortunately, the state, which owns the land, has not done a good job of upkeep on the cemetery, where many Stewart County pioneer families are buried.

From Providence Canyon, go back to Lumpkin and turn right on Martin Luther King, Jr. Drive, the first street beyond the courthouse. MLK will become Trotman Road/County Road 148 as you leave the city limits. Go 2.6 miles and bear left at the fork to continue on Trotman Road. Go 7 more miles to Sardis Road, turn left, and go 0.3 mile to **Sardis Methodist Church**, built around 1848. In the 1970s, when the structure had serious dry rot and termite damage, the congregation had to decide whether to renovate the building or build a new one. Fortunately for lovers of history, they chose renovation. The church continues to be very nicely maintained, and according to the sign in front, it still has services once a month. The cemetery across the road is also well maintained.

From the Sardis church, go back to Trotman Road/CO 148, turn left, and continue south for 6 miles to the Benevolence community and **Benevolence Baptist Church**. The congregation was established in 1840 and the present building was erected in 1906. The unusual steeple has elements of Victorian Chapel/Carpenter Gothic design.

Trotman Road becomes Benevolence Highway after you cross into Randolph County. After 7 more miles, Benevolence Highway will cross US 27 and continue on for 1 more mile into Cuthbert as North Webster Street. Turn right on Broad Street, by the water tower—which, by the way, was erected in 1895 and has the distinction of being the only water tower in the middle of a US highway—and go to the town square, which is a park with storefronts all around.

The classic 1885 Dutch Romanesque **Randolph County Courthouse** is a block off the square on Court Street/GA 216. Go to the end of the block past

THE JOHN M. GUNN HOUSE IN CUTHBERT WAS CALLED A "WIFE-KILLER" BECAUSE IT WAS SO HARD TO HEAT

the courthouse and turn left on East Church Street. Go one block and the "Front Square" style **John M. Gunn House** will be on the right on the corner of East Church and Lumpkin.

John McKenzie Gunn, eighth son of Scottish immigrants of the Clan Gunn, came to Cuthbert as a young man and established one of the most successful general merchandise businesses in Southwest Georgia. He built the house for his bride in 1853, and their descendants lived in it until 1940. The house fell on hard times after that but has now been successfully restored.

Turn right on Lumpkin and go one block to number 279, the handsome, six-columned Greek Revival mansion on the left named **Boxwood**, built in 1846 by Judge William Taylor, first judge of the Southwestern Circuit. Boxwood is just across from the end of Douglas Street.

Go back south on Lumpkin to College Street/US 82. On your way, you will pass the recently renovated 1917 **Carnegie Library**, at 122 Lumpkin Street.

Turn right (west) on College Street. If Cuthbert seems just a bit more cosmopolitan than some of the other small southwest Georgia towns, there's a reason for that—Cuthbert is a college town—the home of **Andrew College**, founded in 1854 as Andrew Female College, the second-oldest college in the US to grant degrees, rather than certificates, to women.

OLD MAIN, THE ANDREW COLLEGE ADMINISTRATION BUILDING, WAS BUILT IN 1892

In 1917, Andrew became a junior college, and in 1956, it became a co-educational institution granting Associate degrees. It is affiliated with the United Methodist Church.

When the school's buildings burned to the ground in 1892, the Cuthbert community raised enough money to build **Old Main**, the school's signature building, that very same year. Old Main is at 493 College Street, on the right going west—you can't miss it—and is the school's Administration Building.

Continuing west on College Street, the **Moye-Goode-Lay House** at Number 313 was built by Seaborn H. Smith around 1860 for the Reynolds family. It was later owned by Robert Leiden Moye, who was mayor of Cuthbert for 30 years. Four generations of the Moye family lived in this home and it is now owned by a descendant. Most of the original furnishings are still there.

Andrew College was not the only women's college to be founded in Cuthbert in the 1850s. Rev. Thomas Muse, a very influential Baptist minister, founded the Baptist Female College of Southwest Georgia, also known as Cuthbert Female College, in 1852. The school eventually died in the 1870s but left as evidence of its existence the Greek Revival **Baptist Female College**

Dormitory, with six square columns across the front, built the same year the school was founded.

Since the college's demise, the building, known locally as the **Muse-Dews-Gay-Martin-Blaskow House**, has been a private residence. It is currently unoccupied and, while still beautiful, could use some maintenance. It is located at 235 College Street, on the right at the intersection of College and Villa Nova Streets, about four blocks from Andrew College.

On the left, going west, is the **King Stapleton House** at 212 College. It was built in 1856 for Dr. Clayton Thornton and restored in 1917 by Walter E. King, later mayor of Cuthbert. The original floors, woodwork, plastered walls, and elliptical staircase have all been preserved.

Also on the left at 152 College is **Janes Hall**, a Greek Revival mansion built in 1840 by plantation owner William Janes, who was one of the original trustees of the Baptist Female College. The windows, moldings, heart pine floors, and hand-planed doors are all original.

Cuthbert is an interesting old town with many more points of interest than we can cover here. I highly recommend you go by the Chamber of Commerce at 51 Court Street and pick up a driving tour brochure. They also have one for Randolph County and another for the town of Shellman.

From downtown Cuthbert, take College Street/US 82 west for about 2 miles, then turn left on GA 266. It's about 18 miles to Fort Gaines. Merge

JOHN DILL USED HIS WIFE'S MONEY TO BUILD HER "THE FINEST HOME ON THE FRONTIER"

left onto GA 39 and go about 1 mile. GA 39 becomes Hancock Street in Fort Gaines.

If you were to turn right instead of left on GA 39, in about 4 miles you would come to **George T. Bagby State Park** on 48,000-acre Lake Walter F. George (also known as Lake Eufaula). The park itself is 770 acres, with a 60-room lodge and conference center and five cottages plus a group cottage. The park offers fishing, boating with boat rentals, a marina, gas dock, and boat ramp, and the **Pilot House Grill Restaurant**. There are also 3 miles of hiking trails, a swimming pool and a swimming beach, a picnic shelter, and much more.

The park is open 7 a.m.–10 p.m. daily. There's no admission charge, but you will need a $5 parking pass. Call 229-768-2571 for information, 877-591-5575 for lodge reservations, or visit the lodge website (www.george tbagbylodge.com).

Continuing on Hancock for now, go to the T intersection with GA 37/Hartford Street (the street sign may say Martin Luther King, Jr. Blvd.), go left for one block, and turn left on Washington Street. The 1873 **Clay County Courthouse**, vernacular with Greek Revival influences, will be on your right at the corner of Washington and Thomas.

JOHN SUTLIVE BOUGHT THIS BUILDING FROM JOHN DILL TO USE AS A TOLL HOUSE FOR HIS FERRY ACROSS THE CHATTAHOOCHEE RIVER

Continue on Washington Street to #102—the **John Dill House**. Dill was the commander of the fort at Fort Gaines for a time, as well as being a successful businessman.

Elizabeth Stewart, the woman who later became John Dill's wife, was captured by Seminole and Creek Indians in 1817. During her time as a slave of the Indians, she picked up paper money from the ground where it had been discarded by Indian raiding parties because it had no value to them, and by the time she was rescued in 1818 she was a wealthy woman. She married Dill in the early 1820s and with her money he built her "the finest home on the frontier" around 1827.

On the right side of the house is a large live oak tree, with a trunk 16 feet in circumference. It was brought from Florida and planted here by General Edmund P. Gaines, who built the original fort at Fort Gaines.

Just across Commerce Street, at 106 Washington, is the **Brown House**, built in 1830.

Turn left on Commerce Street. About

halfway down the block on the left is the **Wayside Inn**, built in the 1850s. It served as a Confederate hospital in 1863. Continue to the corner and on the left will be the **Coleman Opera House**, dating from 1880, fronting on Hancock Street.

Turn right on Hancock and go one block, then turn left on Jefferson Street. On the right near the end of the block at 103 West Jefferson is the **McRae House**, built in 1844.

Turn left on Troupe street and go one block, then turn right on Commerce and follow it to its end at Bluff Street. Turn left on Bluff. Just before the pavement ends, notice on your right a log cabin. Just behind it is a smallish, two-story white building that was built by John Dill. In the 1820s John Sutlive bought it and used it as the **Toll House**, where he collected tolls from passengers taking the ferry across the Chattahoochee River. It was also used for Methodist church services.

THE BENEVOLENCE BAPTIST CHURCH HAS AN UNUSUAL VICTORIAN CHAPEL/ CARPENTER GOTHIC DESIGN

Go on beyond the end of the pavement to the replica blockhouse. It was here, on this bluff 130 feet above the Chattahoochee, that **Fort Gaines** was built in 1816 for defense against the Indians. The fort was square, one hundred feet to a side, and enclosed by an eight-foot stockade with two blockhouses.

Go past the blockhouse and down a short but steep slope to the **Frontier Village**, made up of ancient log buildings relocated from various places around the area and restored.

Take the dirt road out the back of the village, turn left on Jackson, and then right on Carroll Street. Go back to Hancock, turn right, then left at GA 37/MLK for a block, and then right on GA 39/Washington Street for about 18 miles.

On the outskirts of Blakely, merge left onto GA 62. At the traffic light at North Main Street/GA 62 in Blakely, turn right and go about a mile to the imposing Neoclassical Revival **Early County Courthouse**, built 1904–05, in the Blakely town square. From the square, continue on GA 62 about 9.5 miles and take the first right after the Coheelee Creek Park sign.

Go 0.4 mile to the T intersection, go right, and continue for about 1.2 miles. After crossing the highway bridge, turn left on a dirt road and go down to the 121-foot-long **Coheelee Creek Covered Bridge**, set in a park with a picnic area. Built in 1891 by J.W. Baughman and using a modification of the queen post truss design, it is the southernmost bridge in the United

THE COHEELEE CREEK COVERED BRIDGE IN EARLY COUNTY IS THE SOUTHERNMOST COVERED BRIDGE IN THE US

States. Just below the bridge is a small waterfall, which may possibly be the southernmost waterfall in Georgia.

From the covered bridge, go back to GA 62, turn left, and go back to downtown Blakely. From the courthouse, take Main Street north for about 2 miles. Turn left on 1st Kolomokee Road north for about 5 miles to **Kolomoki Mounds Historic Park**.

The oldest and largest Woodland Indian site in the Southeast, the Kolomoki Historic Site consists of nine mounds of varying sizes. The 57-foot-high Great Temple Mound overlooks two smaller burial mounds and several ceremonial mounds. The park museum is actually built around an excavated mound.

The 1,293-acre park has two lakes of 50 and 80 acres, 24 campsites, picnic shelters, group shelters, pioneer campgrounds, and a dining hall. You can also find a swimming beach, fishing dock, boat ramp, canoe, kayak, and pedal boat rentals, and 5 miles of hiking trails.

The park is open daily 7 a.m.–10 p.m. There's no admission charge, but a $5 parking pass is required. The museum and historic site is open 8 a.m.–5 p.m. Admission is $5 for adults, $4 for seniors, and $3.50 for ages 6–17. Children under six are free.

Leaving Kolomoki, turn right (the road is unmarked) and go 4.9 miles to a T intersection, which is Bluffton Road, although it's also not marked.

Turn right for about 5.5 miles (by which point Bluffton Road will be marked as Fort Gaines Road), to the intersection with North Broad Street and turn right for about a half-mile to Bluffton Baptist Church.

In 1922, the pastor, H.M. Melton, challenged his congregation to set aside 1 acre of farmland and devote the proceeds to support the cash-poor church. Seven farmers agreed. The "Lords Acres" thrived and the movement, which began at a modest country church in an obscure place, spread and became an international phenomenon that continues to this day.

From the church go back to Fort Gaines Road and turn right onto Pine Street. Cross Pine, and in a quarter-mile or so, cross US 27 (a four-lane, divided highway) and continue on County Road 130/Fort Gaines Road for 3.4 miles. Meanwhile, Fort Gaines Road will change its name again, back to Bluffton Road! Bear left on Bluffton Road as it continues onto County Road 150, go 4.9 miles, and merge right on GA 37/Hartford Street in Edison. Stay on GA 37 for about 5 miles, then turn right on County Road 23 (dirt). Watch carefully, because the sign is easy to miss. Go 0.2 mile to **Dickey Presbyterian Church** on the right at 1625 County Road 23. A lovely old church in a serene setting, Dickey Presbyterian was built in 1871 and served the people of the area until 1998, when the congregation became too small to continue. Since then, the building has been lovingly maintained through the devotion of the Whitney and Dickey families.

From the church, go back to GA 37, turn right, and go about 0.2 mile to County Road 24/Dickey Bypass Road. Turn left, and in about 3.8 miles you will come to an intersection with GA 41. Turn left, and in about one city block, turn right on County Road 25/Charles Cheney Road. Go 1.1 miles, turn left on GA 45, and after 2.5 miles, keep right to continue onto GA 234 when GA 45 goes left.

From that point, it's about 22 miles to the intersection with Pine Street in Albany. Go right on Pine for 1.5 miles to downtown Albany.

Since this book is about the backroads and byways of Georgia, I have avoided writing about the larger towns. However, there are many worthwhile things to see in Albany, and it would be remiss not to mention some of them. It would be easy to spend an enjoyable weekend here.

First among the sights, if you've taken some of the other tours in this book and have seen covered bridges built or designed by the freed slave and master bridge builder Horace King, is **The Bridge House** on Front Street, which King built in 1858, along with a bridge over the Flint River. The bridge was swept away by a flood in 1897, but the Bridge House still stands and is now the centerpiece of Riverfront Park and serves as Albany's Welcome Center. Hours are Monday–Friday, 9 a.m. to 5 p.m., Saturdays 10 a.m. to 4 p.m., and Sundays noon to 4 p.m.

The Bridge House is at 112 Front Street on the riverfront, between the

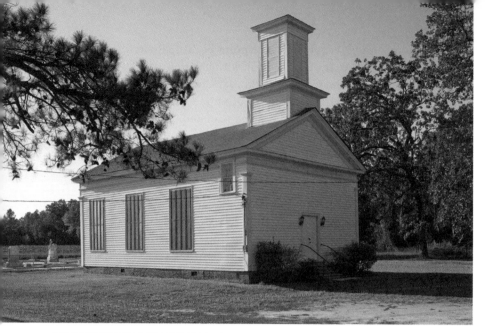

THE LAST SERVICE AT DICKEY PRESBYTERIAN CHURCH IN CALHOUN COUNTY WAS HELD IN 1998

Flint RiverQuarium and the **Ray Charles Memorial**. The **Horace King Overlook** is also adjacent to the Bridge House.

The Flint RiverQuarium, at 101 Pine Avenue, offers a unique look into the life of a Georgia river. Its most unusual feature is a 175,000-gallon, 22-foot-deep Blue Hole Spring, with more than 120 species of fish, turtles, and alligators swimming in its clear water. The RiverQuarium is open 9 a.m. to 5 p.m., Monday through Friday; 10 a.m. to 6 p.m. on Saturday, and 1 p.m. to 5 p.m. on Sunday. Admission is $9 for adults, $8 for seniors, and $6.50 for ages 4–12. Children three and under are free.

Radium Springs, Georgia's largest natural spring, is about 4 miles south of the riverfront area via Radium Springs Road. With a flow of 70,000 gallons of fresh, clear water per minute, Radium is listed as one of the Seven Natural Wonders of Georgia. Traces of radium in the water give the spring its name. The spring is surrounded by a 95-acre botanical park that includes the ruins of an early 20th-century casino and resort. Open Tuesday through Saturday, 9 a.m.–5 p.m. and 1 p.m.–5 p.m. on Sunday, admission is free.

Leaving Albany, take North Jefferson Street north for about 2 miles to GA 91 north. Turn right and go 10.5 miles to GA 32. Turn right again and go 3.5 miles, then turn left on GA 300 for 16.8 miles. Turn left onto GA 300 Connector for 3.3 miles, make a slight right onto US 280 east for 1.6 miles, then turn left onto South 7th Street for 0.5 mile. Turn right onto 9th Avenue East and the **SAM Shortline Railroad** Depot will be on your left.

The SAM (Savannah, Americus, and Montgomery) Railroad is an excursion line operated by the Georgia State Park system. Passengers ride in air-conditioned, 1949-vintage railroad cars on all-day, round-trip excursions through Southwest Georgia, stopping at various small towns along the way. It's a great way to cap off your tour, retracing some of the points you've already covered, but in a different, more relaxing way.

The SAM Shortline Railroad operates Monday through Saturday, 8:30 a.m. to 4:30 p.m. Basic fees are $39.99 plus tax for adults and $29.99 plus tax for children. Lounge and Premium seating are also available—check the SAM website (samshortline.com) for schedules and other information.

From the railroad depot, go back south to US 280, turn left (east) and follow it to Interstate 75 Exit 101 at Cordele and the end of this tour.

IN THE AREA

One thing to keep in mind as you tour the Southwest Georgia back country is that food is where you find it. It will probably be country cooking, and it will most probably be good. But it probably won't be haute cuisine. There are likewise very few places to stay in the hinterlands.

Accommodations

BEST WESTERN PLUS WINDSOR HOTEL, 125 West Lamar Street, Americus. 229-924-1555. www.windsor-americus.com.

GARDEN INN BED AND BREAKFAST, 504 Rees Park, Americus. 229-931-0122. www.americusgardeninn.com.

HAMPTON INN AND SUITES, 2628 Dawson Road, Albany. 229-405-2000.

THE LODGE AT GEORGE T. BAGBY STATE PARK, 330 Bagby Parkway, Fort Gaines. 877-591-5575. www.GeorgeTBagbyLodge.com.

PLAINS HISTORIC INN, 106 West Main Street, Plains. 229-824-4517. www .pinn@sowega.net.

WILLIS COUNTRY HOME BED & BREAKFAST, 1753 Colomokee Church Road, Blakely. 229-308-0691. www.williscountryhome.com.

Dining

LILY'S SOUTHERN CAFE, 223 Main Street, Lumpkin. 229-838-5309.

PEARLY'S FAMOUS COUNTRY COOKING, 814 North Slappey Drive, Albany. 229-432-0141. www.pearlysfamouscountrycooking.com.

PILOT HOUSE GRILL, George T. Bagby State Park, 330 Bagby Parkway, Fort Gaines.

ROSEMARY & THYME RESTAURANT, 125 West Lamar Street, Americus. 229-924-1455.

Attractions and Recreation

FLINT RIVERQUARIUM, 101 Pine Avenue, Albany. 229-639-2650. www .flintriverquarium.com.

GEORGE T. BAGBY STATE PARK, 330 Bagby Parkway, Fort Gaines. 229-768-2571. gastateparks.org/georgetbagby.

HABITAT FOR HUMANITY GLOBAL VILLAGE AND DISCOVERY CENTER, 721 West Church Street, Americus. 800-422-4828, extension 7937. www.habitat.org/gvdc.

JIMMY CARTER NATIONAL HISTORIC SITE MUSEUM & VISITOR CENTER, 300 North Bond Street, Plains. 229-824-4104. www.nps.gov/jica/index.htm

KOLOMOKI MOUNDS STATE PARK, 205 Indian Mounds Road, Blakely. 229-724-2150.

PROVIDENCE CANYON STATE PARK, 8930 Canyon Road, Lumpkin. 229-838-6870.

RADIUM SPRINGS GARDENS, 2501 Radium Springs Road, Albany. 229-430-6120. visitalbanyga.com/attraction/radium-springs-gardens.

SAM SHORTLINE RAILROAD, 105 East 9th Avenue, Cordele. 229-276-0755. samshortline.com.

Events

Dooly County

Big Pig Jig, Vienna. www.doolychamber.com.

Stewart County

Pigfest, Richland. www.facebook.com/RichlandGeorgiasAnnualPigFest.

11

ALL AROUND SAVANNAH

The Georgia Coast

The length of this tour is approximately 185 miles and includes Effingham, Chatham, Bryan, and Liberty Counties.

Beginning at Exit 109 from Interstate 95, take GA 21/30/Augusta Road north for 3.4 miles. Turn right on Old Augusta Road for about 8.5 miles. Continue straight through the first roundabout, and at the second roundabout take the first exit and go right on GA 275 for about 3 miles. **Jerusalem Lutheran Church**, the oldest church building in Georgia, will be on your right at 2966 Ebenezer Road, Rincon.

The church was originally organized in Augsburg, Germany in 1733, by a group of Protestants who had been exiled from their homes by the Catholic Archbishop of Salzburg, Austria. An English mission society sponsored their passage to America and the first settlers arrived in Savannah on March 12, 1734. They soon founded the town of Ebenezer on Ebenezer Creek in present-day Effingham County, but the location was not healthy, so they moved to the present site at New Ebenezer on the Savannah River.

The German pioneers established the first Sunday School in Georgia in 1734 and the first orphanage in 1737. The church building itself was completed in 1769, with brick walls 21 inches thick. Some of the windows still have their original glass panes. Not only is it the oldest church and oldest public building in Georgia, it is also the earliest Lutheran church still in service in America.

Affiliated with the Evangelical Lutheran Church, Jerusalem Church has Sunday School and worship weekly. The bells, brought from Europe, still ring before each service.

From the church, go back east on GA 275 for 3 miles to the roundabout,

LEFT: A DRIFT FENCE HELPS PREVENT EROSION OF THE DUNES AT TYBEE ISLAND BEACH

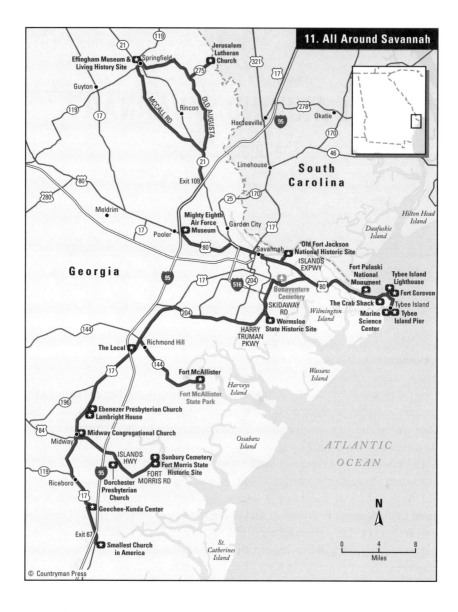

then right on Long Bridge Road, which becomes Third Street, which becomes Long Bridge Road again, for 2.7 miles, then turn left on Stillwell Road for 3.2 miles. Turn right on South Ash Street for a mile, then left on Early Street for 0.2 mile, and right on North Pine Street to the **Effingham Museum and Living History Site** on the right in the old jail at 1002 North Pine Street, Springfield.

The site is open 9 a.m.–12 p.m. on Monday and 9 a.m.–1 p.m. Tuesday through Friday, with docents who portray life in colonial Georgia. Call 912-754-2170 for admission fees and to arrange tours.

From the Living History Museum, go back southeast on North Pine Street for about one block. The old Effingham County Courthouse, completed in 1909, will be on your left. Turn right on Rabun Street for another block, then left on North Laurel Street for 0.2 mile. Turn right on GA 119/West Madison Street for 0.4 mile, then left on GA 21 for about 16 miles to Interstate 95 and turn right onto the south ramp.

(If you decide to skip the Effingham History Museum, leave the church and go back east on GA 275 for 3 miles, then left onto Rincon-Stillwell Road for 1.4 miles, then continue straight onto Old Augusta Road south for 7.2 miles. Turn left onto GA 21 South for 3.4 miles, then turn right onto the Interstate 95 south ramp.)

Go about 6 miles on I-95 and take exit 102 to Louisville Road/US 80 East. Turn left at the bottom of the ramp for 0.2 mile, then turn left on Bourne Avenue for 0.2 mile to the **Mighty Eighth Air Force Museum** at 175 Bourne Avenue in Pooler.

Formed in Savannah in January 1942 in response to Pearl Harbor and the urgent threat of Nazi Germany, the Eighth Air Force of the United States Army Air Corps became the premier fighting air force in the world and played a major part in air operations in the European theater of World War II.

Using graphics, memorabilia, movies, photographs, exhibits, and interactive features, the museum's galleries tell a powerful story of World War II, the events leading up to it, and the Eighth Air Force's role in it. Flying and World War II history buffs will especially like the Combat Gallery, where planes used by the Eighth Air Force and enemy forces are displayed, including a Boeing B-17 "Flying Fortress" bomber, one of only about 50 surviving of the 12,731 built between 1935 and 1945. It has been fully restored by a group of dedicated volunteers.

Other fighting planes on exhibit include a B-47 Stratocruiser bomber, an F-4 Phantom II fighter, and a Russian Mig-17A. Actor Jimmy Stewart, by the way, flew 25 missions as a pilot with the Mighty Eighth Air Force.

The museum is open Tuesday-Saturday, 10 a.m.–5 p.m. and Sunday 12 p.m.–5 p.m. Tickets may be purchased at the door, but are less expensive if purchased online (www.mightyeighth.org).

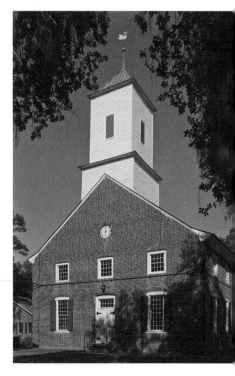

JERUSALEM LUTHERAN CHURCH IS THE OLDEST CHURCH BUILDING IN GEORGIA

From the museum, go back to US 80 and go left for 7 miles. Since this book is about backroads and byways, I don't usually write about cities. However, I would be remiss if I failed to point out that for about the last mile or two of this segment of the tour along West Bay Street, the buildings on the left were part of the old Factor's Walk. Now it's lined with various kinds of shops, but in the early 1800s the Walk was the place where cotton was bought and sold, exported and imported. It's well worth your while to stop for a bit, pick up a brochure or two, and check out the old buildings.

When US 80 turns right, continue straight on West Bay Street for 2.7 miles. Turn right on East Broad Street for 0.2 mile, then turn left on East President Street for 2.1 miles. Turn left on Woodcock Drive (the sign is easy to miss, but fortunately there's a handy turnaround a block farther along if you miss it). Go 0.5 mile on Woodcock, then right on Fort Jackson Road for 0.7 mile to **Old Fort Jackson National Historic Site**.

The oldest standing brick fort in Georgia, Fort Jackson was built in 1808 at a strategic location on the Savannah River about 2 miles east of the city as part of President Thomas Jefferson's coastal defense system. After the fall of Fort Pulaski in 1862, Fort Jackson became the headquarters for all the river defenses protecting Savannah during the Civil War. However, it fell to Federal forces in 1864, as General Sherman culminated his March to the Sea by taking Savannah. The US War Department abandoned the fort in 1905, and

A WORLD WAR II B-17 "FLYING FORTRESS" BOMBER AT THE MIGHTY EIGHTH AIR FORCE MUSEUM, POOLER

PREPARING TO FIRE THE CANNON, FORT JACKSON

it is now operated by the Coastal Heritage Society as a museum dedicated to education and military history.

The fort, named after Revolutionary War Colonel James Jackson, who accepted the surrender of the British at Savannah at the close of the war, is open seven days a week from 9 a.m. to 5 p.m. A demonstration of muzzle-loading cannon firing is given at 11 a.m. and 2 p.m. daily and there are interactive programs for kids, adults, and families. The admission charge is $7 for adults and $4 for children ages 2–12.

Leaving Fort Jackson, go back to US 80, turn left, and go 10 miles to the entrance to **Fort Pulaski National Monument** on the left. It is 1 mile back to the fort.

Built on Cockspur Island in the mouth of the Savannah River over a period of eighteen years, using 25 million bricks and costing a million dollars, the fort was completed in 1847. Its seven-and-a-half-foot solid brick walls, backed up by concrete piers and earthworks, were considered impregnable.

However, by the onset of the Civil War, it had not yet been garrisoned and was seized by the State of Georgia, which then transferred the fort to the Confederate States of America. In November 1861, Federal forces established a beachhead at Hilton Head Island, causing Confederate forces to abandon nearby Tybee Island. The Federals brought in something new: rifled cannon capable of far greater range and power than anything previously known and,

INSIDE THE WALLS OF FORT PULASKI

in April 1862, set up batteries on the northwest shore of Tybee and swiftly proceeded to breach the "impregnable" walls of Fort Pulaski. Colonel Olmstead, the Confederate commander, surrendered in just 30 hours. It was a turning point; the beginning of a new era in warfare.

Fort Pulaski is part of the National Park System and is open every day except Thanksgiving and Christmas from 9 a.m. to 5 p.m., with extended hours in summer. Admission is $10 per person, and those under 15 are admitted free. Annual passes are $35, and lifetime passes to all national parks and historic sites for seniors 62 and over are $80.

Leaving Fort Pulaski, turn left again on US 80 for 1.8 miles and turn right on Catalina Drive, then immediately left on Estill Hammock Road to the **Crab Shack**, 0.4 mile on the left at 40 Estill Hammock Road. Voted Savannah's best seafood since 1998, the super-casual atmosphere at the Crab Shack might make you think you've stumbled upon a pirates' hangout, but the food and service are worth walking the plank for. If you've never had their low-country shrimp boil, you are going to hate yourself for all the years you've wasted.

From the Crab Shack, go back to US 80 and continue east toward Tybee Island. In 1.1 miles, turn left on Polk Street, go 0.2 mile, then turn right on Fort Avenue. In 0.2 mile, continue onto Taylor Street for 0.3 mile and then continue onto Meddin Drive to **Tybee Island Lighthouse** and **Fort Screven**. Or, just follow the green "turtle" signs to the lighthouse and fort. Completed in 1867, the lighthouse is 154 feet in height and is the fourth on this site, going back to 1736. The first two were wooden and did not survive long. The third tower was built of brick in 1773. When the Confederates abandoned Tybee Island, they attempted to blow it up with a keg of gunpowder, but its brick shell, 12 feet thick at the base, survived and forms the first 60 feet of the present lighthouse. The beacon, still with its original lens, continues to guide maritime traffic at the mouth of the Savannah River. The lighthouse keeper's house was built in 1881. The lighthouse is open for sunset tours on a lim-

SHRIMP BOATS DOCK IN LAZARETTO CREEK ON THE CAUSEWAY TO TYBEE ISLAND

THE TYBEE ISLAND LIGHTHOUSE GUIDES SHIPS AT THE MOUTH OF THE SAVANNAH RIVER

ited basis, including climbing all 178 steps to the top. Call 912-786-5801 for information and reservations.

Fort Screven, the fortification adjacent to the lighthouse, was mandated by the state of Georgia in 1786, but construction did not actually begin until 1897, after the federal government took over the site. Completed in 1905, it was used as a coastal defense artillery fort and an infantry post and was decommissioned in 1947. Today, Battery Garland, one of six remaining batteries at Fort Screven, houses the Tybee Museum which, along with the Tybee Island Light Station, is operated by the non-profit Tybee Island Historical Society.

The museum is open daily except Tuesday, 9 a.m.–4:30 p.m. Admission is $12 for adults and $10 for seniors and children 6–17. Children 5 and under are admitted free.

Also at Fort Screven is **Officer's Row**, a group of houses with sweeping ocean views that were built as officer's residences around 1900.

There is an abundance of places to stay on Tybee Island, most of them expensive to very expensive, but if you enjoyed the lighthouse area you can actually stay on Officer's Row at the 1910 **Lighthouse Inn Bed and Breakfast**, highly rated and quiet yet relatively moderately priced and only 300 yards from the beach.

After visiting the lighthouse and fort, take some time to explore **Tybee Island**. It has a great beach, one of the best on the Georgia coast and probably the most accessible.

The **Tybee Island pier** juts out into the Atlantic just off US 80 at Tybrisa Street. It's a place for fishing, walking, and people-watching, and the pavilion at the end is available to rent for weddings, receptions, and other social functions.

Also, while you're near the pier, visit the **Marine Science Center**, located off the 14th Street parking lot near the pier. Their mission is "to cultivate a responsible stewardship of coastal Georgia's natural resources through education, conservation, and research." They offer walks, talks, and treks, maintain a gallery of exhibits of coastal Georgia flora, fauna, and habitats, and operate week-long sea camp ocean adventures for kids 6–11 each summer. They're open Thursday–Sunday from 10 a.m.–4 p.m. Admission is $10, kids 4 and under are free.

You could easily spend days or weeks at Tybee Island, and many do. But if you're ready to move on (with a mental resolution to come back), take US 80 West toward Savannah for about 13 miles. Turn right on River Drive, the leftmost of the two streets which turn right off US 80 at that point. River Drive becomes Bonaventure Road. Continue for about a mile, then turn right on Greenwich Road into **Bonaventure Cemetery**.

Made famous by the book *Midnight in the Garden of Good and Evil* by John Berendt, the cemetery is located on the site of a 1760 plantation named from the Italian words *buona ventura*, "good fortune."

Open to the public daily 8 a.m. to 5 p.m., Bonaventure Cemetery is a natural cathedral filled with hauntingly beautiful cemetery sculptures. The small, so-called "Bird Girl" statuette photographed by the late, distinguished photographer Jack Leigh for the cover of *Midnight in the Garden of Good and Evil* has been moved to protect it from vandalism and is on public display at the nearby Jepson Center for the Arts.

Leaving the cemetery, go back on Bonaventure Road and turn right on US 80/Victory Drive. Turn left on Skidaway Road for about 4.5 miles to **Wormsloe State Historic Site**. The entrance is on the right at 7601 Skidaway Road, and is difficult to see unless you're watching very carefully.

Noble Jones, one of the original group of colonists who came to Georgia with General James Oglethorpe in 1733, acquired property on the Hope River in 1736 and began a plantation to grow silk, rice, cotton, and cattle. He named it "Wormslow" and built a manor house of tabby, a durable mixture of oyster shells, lime, sand, and water—ingredients abundantly available on the Georgia coast and used for a great many colonial-era structures.

One of the most impressive features of Wormsloe is the entranceway: a 1.5-mile-long avenue under an archway of live oak trees, planted in 1890. At the end of the archway is the visitor center, from which you can take a pleasant walk of a half-mile or so back to the ruins of Jones's tabby home, the oldest structure in Georgia.

Wormsloe also features a museum with a short film about the site and the founding of Georgia, and an interpretive nature trail along the coastal marsh to the Colonial Life Area where docents in period dress demonstrate the tools and skills of colonial Georgia during the programs and special events which are held throughout the year.

The park is open every day 9 a.m.–4:45 p.m. Admission to the historic site is $10 for adults, $9 for seniors, $4.50 for ages 6–17, and $2 for children under 6. Guided tours are available at 10 a.m., 11 a.m., 2 p.m., and 3 p.m.

OPEN AIR LUNCH ON THE DECK AT THE CRAB SHACK

Leaving Wormsloe, turn left and go back northwest on Skidaway Road for 0.8 mile, then turn left onto East Montgomery Cross Road for 0.5 mile. Turn left onto the Harry S. Truman Parkway ramp south and continue on Truman Parkway for 3.7 miles, then turn left onto Abercorn St/Abercorn Extension and continue for about 6.5 miles. Take the exit for US 17 and go south for 5.5 miles. Turn left onto GA 144 East for 5 miles, then turn left onto GA 144 Spur East for 3.7 miles to **Fort McAllister State Park**, 3894 Fort McAllister Road, Richmond Hill.

Fort McAllister, with its massive earthworks guarding the mouth of the Ogeechee River south of Savannah, is the Confederacy's best-preserved fort of its kind. Built in 1861 and attacked unsuccessfully seven times by Union gunships, including ironclads, it was nonetheless vulnerable to attack by land. On December 13, 1864, near the end of General William T. Sherman's "March to the Sea," the Confederate garrison of only 230 troops was quickly overrun by a land force of 4,000 under Union Major General Oliver Otis Howard, thus clearing the river for Sherman's siege and capture of Savannah.

Visitors can roam the grounds, where cannon, a furnace to heat cannon balls red hot to set wooden ships ablaze, powder magazines, barracks, palisades, and a Civil War museum bring the past to life. There are daily programs on topics such as soldier life, weapons, wildlife, and crafts, and also a guided tour at 2 p.m. each day.

The 1,725-acre park offers facilities for camping, fishing, boating, and picnicking, as well as seven cabins on stilts near the marsh. There are also boat ramps, a dock and pier, and canoe, kayak, paddleboard, and bike rentals available. Admission to the park is free but requires a $5 parking pass. Admission to the historic site is $9 for adults, $8 for seniors, and $5 for ages 6–17. The park is open 7 a.m. to 10 p.m. daily.

If you're hungry from all that walking, take GA 144 Spur and GA 144 back to US 17 and go left (south) 1.8 miles to **The Local on 17**, on the left at 4040 US 17. My wife and I stayed two nights in Richmond Hill and ate at the Local twice. Great shrimp, and we enjoyed talking to genial host Jay Yancey. Check their website (thelocalon17.com) for hours and current menu.

I should mention that my wife and I have this idea that when we go to the coast, we should eat seafood at every opportunity (though maybe not for breakfast). We enjoy barbecue, we enjoy country cooking, we enjoy steaks, Italian, Mexican—but when we go to the coast we want fresh seafood!

From the Local on 17, it's about 8 miles south on US 17 to **Ebenezer Presbyterian Church** on the left at Limerick Road in Freedmen's Grove, so called because of the many freed slaves who settled in the area after the Civil War. An historic African-American church, Ebenezer was built in 1880 by the Reverend Joseph Williams, who had organized a large Presbyterian con-

THE TABBY RUINS OF WORMSLOE MANOR HOUSE ARE ALL THAT REMAINS OF GEORGIA'S OLDEST BUILDING

gregation of black people at the Midway Church in 1868. As it says on his gravestone, which is across US 17 from the church: *Rev. Joseph Williams—Founder of Presbyterianism among the colored people of Georgia.*

Born on Providence Island in the West Indies in 1805, Rev. Williams lived to be 94 years old.

Turn left on Limerick and go about 0.2 mile to the **Lambright House** on the left. The weathered, two-story, Plantain Plain structure was the home of Rosa Lambright, a beloved elementary teacher in the black community for nearly fifty years and a faithful member of Ebenezer Presbyterian Church. Her home, a landmark of late-1800s Coastal Georgia, unfortunately appears to be in need of restoration.

Go back to US 17 and turn left (south) 2.7 miles to **Midway Congregational Church** on the left.

An elegant example of colonial architecture and the second-oldest church in Georgia, the Midway Church was built in 1792 to replace the original church on the same site, built in 1752 by Congregationalist Puritans from New England by way of Dorchester in South Carolina. That building was burned by the British in 1778 in retaliation for the Midway settlers' strong pro-independence sentiments.

The influence of the church as a center of both religious and political power in colonial Georgia can hardly be overstated. Two of Georgia's three

CANNON STILL GUARD THE MOUTH OF THE OGEECHEE RIVER AT FORT MCALLISTER STATE PARK, RICHMOND HILL

EBENEZER PRESBYTERIAN CHURCH AT FREEDMEN'S GROVE WAS BUILT BY GEORGIA'S FIRST CONGREGATION OF BLACK PRESBYTERIANS

signers of the Declaration of Independence, Lyman Hall and Button Gwinnett, were members of the Midway Church, as were Revolutionary War Generals James Screven and Daniel Stewart. Other members in ensuing years included governors, congressmen, and US Senators.

However, as the population of the coastal area pushed westward in the first half of the 19th century, things began to wind down at the Midway Church. The last regular minister left in 1867, and the trustees leased the church to the Reverend Joseph Williams' congregation of black Presbyterians, who used it until they built their own church at Freedmen's Grove in 1880.

The Midway Cemetery is just west of the church, on the other side of GA 17. Both the church and the cemetery are lovingly maintained by the people of the Midway community.

From Midway Church, continue south for about 0.2 mile and turn left on US 84. In about 4 miles US 84 ends, but the highway continues as Islands Expressway. In 1.8 miles turn right on Brigdon for 0.2 mile to **Dorchester Presbyterian Church** on the left.

In the 1840s, some families from Midway and others from the dying town of Sunbury began to build summer homes on the higher, healthier ground of an area between the two towns that they at first called "The Village" but soon renamed Dorchester. In 1854, they built a church and placed the 1799 Sunbury town bell in the steeple. Only summer services were held at first, but by the outbreak of the Civil War, regular weekly services were held. In 1871, the congregation was accepted into the Savannah Presbytery as Dorchester Presbyterian Church.

MIDWAY CONGREGATIONAL CHURCH NUMBERED TWO SIGNERS OF THE DECLARATION OF INDEPENDENCE AMONG ITS MEMBERS

This church is obviously well maintained and, to me, is one of the most beautiful churches I've photographed for this book. It is still used for annual gatherings of descendants of the original members and for other special occasions.

From Dorchester Church, go back to Islands Expressway and turn right for 2.1 miles. At Fort Morris Road, turn left and go 2.5 miles. The entrance to **Fort Morris State Historic Site** will be on the right, just beyond Marshview Drive.

Built in 1777 to protect the port city of Sunbury at the mouth of the Medway River, Fort Morris was an earthworks and wood fortification encompassing about an acre and bristling with cannon. When the British attacked the fort in November 1778 with a force of about 750 troops, their commander, Lieutenant Colonel L. V. Fuser, sent a letter demanding the surrender of the fort. American commander Colonel John McIntosh informed him, in one of the great moments in American history, that if he wanted the fort, he could "Come and take it."

The British declined to do so, and withdrew. Unfortunately, they returned with a superior force in January 1779 and captured the fort after a brief but intense bombardment.

In addition to the fort, the 67-acre park has picnic facilities and a 1-mile nature trail. Bird-watching visitors can borrow binoculars and a field guide to look for downy and pileated woodpeckers, goldfinches, wood storks, painted buntings, great egrets, and the many other coastal species that inhabit the area. Check the website (gastateparks.org/FortMorris) for hours and current entrance fees to the historic site and museum.

Leaving Fort Morris, turn right on Fort Morris Road and go 0.4 mile. Continue straight through the Y intersection onto Brigantine-Dunmore Road. At the stop sign, turn left on Sunbury Road, go 0.1 mile, and turn right on Dutchman's Cove Road for 0.1 mile to **Sunbury Cemetery**, on the right at the curve near 127 Dutchman's Cove Road, if you're using GPS.

The cemetery was established in 1758 as a public burying ground for the town of Sunbury, once a thriving port city rivaling Savannah. However, Sunbury was destroyed by the British in the Revolutionary War and never recovered, gradually dwindling down to a ghost town, alone with its ghosts and its cemetery. It is the final resting place of many prominent citizens of Sunbury and Midway, but only 34 grave markers still stand, the oldest dated 1788.

From the cemetery, take Fort Morris Road back to Islands Expressway, turn right, and go back to Midway via the Expressway and US 84. Turn left (south) on US 17 and go 12 miles to Christ's Chapel, the **"Smallest Church in America,"** which will be on your left, set back from the road in a grove of sturdy pine trees.

Mrs. Agnes Harper, who operated a grocery store in the area, built Christ's Chapel in 1949 and "deeded it to Jesus Christ" to serve as a place of rest and meditation for travelers.

Is it really the smallest church in America? Hard to say, because that cat-

THE CEMETERY AT SUNBURY WAS ESTABLISHED IN 1758; ONLY 34 GRAVE MARKERS REMAIN

egory is more competitive than you might imagine. But at 10 feet by 20 feet, it's just big enough to seat a dozen people plus a preacher. Sadly, vandals burned the church in November 2015 but donations began pouring in and it was rebuilt in less than a year, including a very beautiful stained-glass window depicting Jesus with his arms open wide.

The church is open all day, every day, and local ministers hold services there the third Sunday of each month. Thousands of travelers have found the little church a welcome and welcoming place for a few minutes of rest and meditation. And admission is free! Certainly one of the best deals on the Georgia coast. But remember: Close the door on your way out, so the automatic lights will go off!

From the smallest church, go back north on US 17 for 1.2 miles to Interstate 95 Exit 67 and the end of this tour.

As you go, consider that much of this tour has been through areas that not so long ago were part of the Gullah Geechee culture. Developed by enslaved people, mostly of West African descent, who labored on the plantations of the sea islands and coasts of South Carolina and Georgia, they lived in isolation from the larger world. They developed their own language, based on English with African elements, and a culture based on working hard and making do with extremely limited resources. Their religion was Christianity with the addition of African elements. Pat Conroy wrote of this culture in his book *The Water Is Wide*. The 1974 movie *Conrack* was based on the book.

TOP: IS THIS AMERICA'S SMALLEST CHURCH?
BOTTOM: THE STAINED-GLASS WINDOW IN "THE WORLD'S SMALLEST CHURCH"

IN THE AREA

Accommodations

BEST WESTERN PLUS, 4564 US 17, Richmond Hill. 912-756-7070. Pet-friendly.

LA QUINTA INN AND SUITES, 414 Gray Street, Pooler. 912-748-3771. Pet-friendly and 100% non-smoking.

LIGHTHOUSE INN BED AND BREAKFAST, 16 Meddin Drive, Tybee Island. 912-786-0901. www.tybeebb.com.

TYBEE ISLAND INN, 24 Van Horne Avenue, Tybee Island. 912-786-9255. visittybee.com/profile/tybee-island-inn/13991.

Dining

CAPTAIN JOE'S SEAFOOD, 3217 South Coastal Highway, Midway. 912-884-5118. www.captainjoesseafood.com/Locations_Midway.shtml.

THE CRAB SHACK, 40 Estill Hammock Road, Tybee Island. 912-786-9857. thecrabshack.com.

THE LOCAL ON 17, 4040 US 17, Richmond Hill. 912-980-7811. www.thelocalon17.com.

Attractions and Recreation

BONAVENTURE CEMETERY, 330 Bonaventure Cemetery Road, Savannah. 912-651-6843. bonaventurehistorical.org.

FORT JACKSON NATIONAL HISTORIC LANDMARK, 1 Fort Jackson Road, Savannah. 912-232-3945. www.chsgeorgia.org.

FORT McALLISTER STATE PARK, 3894 Fort McAllister Road, Richmond Hill. 912-727-2339.

FORT MORRIS STATE HISTORIC SITE, 2559 Fort Morris Road, Midway. 912-884-5999.

FORT PULASKI NATIONAL MONUMENT, US 80 East, Savannah. 912-786-5787. www.nps.gov/fopu/index.htm.

HISTORIC EFFINGHAM SOCIETY MUSEUM AND LIVING HISTORY SITE, 1002 Pine Street, Springfield. 912-754-2170. historiceffingham society.org.

MUSEUM OF THE MIGHTY EIGHTH AIR FORCE, 175 Bourne Avenue, Pooler. 912-748-888. www.mightyeighth.org.

TYBEE ISLAND LIGHTHOUSE AND MUSEUM, 30 Meddin Drive, Tybee Island. 912-786-5801. www.tybeelighthouse.org.

WORMSLOE STATE HISTORIC SITE, 7601 Skidaway Road, Savannah. 912-353-3023.

For more information on any Georgia State Park or Historic Site, visit the state parks website: georgiastateparks.org.

Events

Effingham County
Salzburger Heritage Festival, each Labor Day at Jerusalem Lutheran Church.
Effingham Oktoberfest, the last weekend in September, Springfield.

Liberty County
Liberty Food Truck Festival, March and October.
Blues, Brews & BBQ Festival, September

12

DARIEN TO ST. MARYS AND POINTS WEST

The Georgia Coast

This tour is approximately 200 miles in length and includes McIntosh, Glynn, Camden, and Charlton Counties.

From Interstate 95, Exit 49, take GA 251 east for about a mile to US 17/GA 25. Turn right (south) toward **Darien**.

Founded in 1736 when James Oglethorpe settled a band of 177 Scottish highlanders at the mouth of the Altamaha River to serve as a restraining presence against the Spanish in north Florida, Darien was Georgia's second planned city, laid out in squares according to Oglethorpe's Savannah plan.

The town was looted on June 11, 1863, by Union troops stationed on St. Simon's Island, in a senseless action more than a year before Sherman's March to the Sea. Most of the buildings in Darien were burned, including all but one of the churches.

Go right (south) for about 1 mile on US 17/GA 25, and just before the **McIntosh County Courthouse**, built in 1872, turn left on GA 99. Go 1.4 miles to St. Andrews Cemetery Road, turn right and go less than 0.2 mile to the cemetery. The dirt road on the left leads to the **Ashantilly Historic Site**.

The original house on this site, known as "Old Tabby," was built circa 1820 as the mainland home of prominent planter and legislator Thomas Spalding. It burned in 1937 and was rebuilt and restored as an ongoing project by William G. Haynes, Jr., an artist, letterpress printer, and environmentalist. Mr. Haynes passed away in 2001, but in 1993, he donated the property to the Ashantilly Center, which carries on his legacy through cultural and educational events and workshops "to provide a vehicle for continuing education,

LEFT: THE ST. SIMONS ISLAND LIGHTHOUSE AND MUSEUM

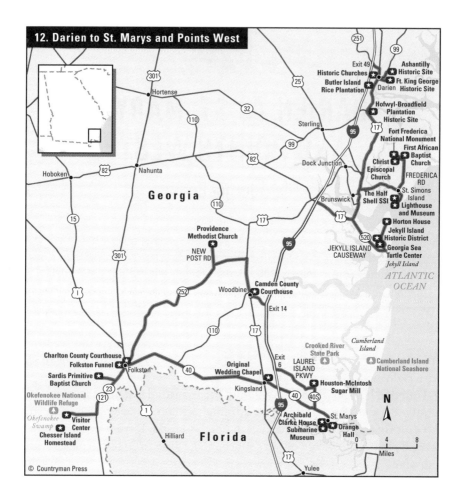

12. Darien to St. Marys and Points West

scientific advancement and charitable endeavor which focus on the natural and built environments integral to the Georgia Coast."

Ashantilly board members and volunteers have reclaimed the old garden, which is now used as a demonstration environment for experimental and organic gardening practices. Mr. Haynes's **Ashantilly Press**, where he produced fine letterpress printing, is available for printing projects by qualified artists.

Visitors are welcome at Ashantilly. Call 912-437-4473 to arrange a tour of the house and beautiful grounds.

Leaving Ashantilly, go back on GA 99 to Market Street, which is the cross street one block before the intersection with US 17, turn right, and go about two blocks to the **First African Baptist Church**, at 500 Market Street, the oldest African-American congregation in McIntosh County. The original church building, erected in 1834, was torched along with other churches in Darien in 1863. The present edifice was built in 1868 as a replica of the 1834 church.

ASHANTILLY WAS THE HOME OF ARTIST AND ENVIRONMENTALIST WILLIAM G. HAYNES, JR

Take Jefferson Street west to US 17 from the First African Baptist Church and turn left (south) for about 0.3 mile. Turn left on Fort King George Drive (just before the bridge) and go 0.2 mile to **St. Cyprian's Episcopal Church,** on the right, built of tabby in 1876 by freed slaves. It is thought to be one of the largest tabby structures still in use in Georgia and is one of the few black Episcopal congregations in the state.

Leaving St. Cyprian's, take the street directly across from the church (Rittenhouse Street) and go two short blocks to Washington Street. Turn left and go one block to Vernon Square (which is actually a circle, but who's counting?). **St. Andrew's Episcopal Church** is on the east side of the square. The congregation was organized in 1841 and built a wooden sanctuary in 1844, which was burned in the 1863 attack. The present building was erected in 1879, with classic 14th-century architecture copied from a village church in England.

Today, St. Andrew's and St. Cyprian's function as one Episcopal community, sharing a pastor and parish hall and participating jointly in Sunday School.

In the northwest quadrant of Vernon Square is the Darien United Methodist Church, at 201 Franklin Street.

John Wesley visited Darien in January 1737, but it was not until 1836 that a Methodist church was organized. The cornerstone for a church building was laid in 1841, and it was the only church to survive the 1863 attack, even though the Federal troops tried twice to set it ablaze. It was finally destroyed by a hurricane in 1881 and was replaced by the present sanctuary in 1883.

From Vernon Square, go south one block and then left on Fort King George Drive. Follow the signs for about 1 mile to **Fort King George Historic Site**, at 302 McIntosh Road. The route is well-marked with signs.

Built by the British in 1721 as a defense against the Spanish forces in Florida, the fort had a blockhouse, barracks, and other buildings, and earthwork walls with wooden palisades. The fort was abandoned in 1727, after 140 officers and men died of diseases such as dysentery and malaria—but none died from war.

Using old records and drawings, the state of Georgia has reconstructed the site and opened it to the public as an historic site. The park is open Tuesday through Sunday, 9 a.m.–5 p.m. Admission is $7.50 for adults, $7 for seniors, and $4.50 for ages 6–17. Children under six are admitted free.

In addition to the fort, there's a museum which focuses on the 18th-century cultural history of the Darien area, picnic facilities, a nature trail, canoe and kayak rentals, and birding along the Colonial Coast Birding Trail.

ST. ANDREW'S EPISCOPAL CHURCH IN DARIEN WAS MODELED AFTER A 14TH-CENTURY ENGLISH VILLAGE CHURCH

Leaving the fort, go back on Fort King George Drive to the intersection with US 17. Cross 17 and continue on Broad Street for one block to the **Adam Strain Building** at number 109, on the left at the corner of Broad and Screven Streets. A two-story stuccoed-tabby cotton warehouse built on the bluff above the Altamaha River about 1813, it was the only building other than the Methodist Church to survive the 1863 raid. At the time of writing this edition, it is apparently being restored.

If you're hungry for seafood, go down the hill toward the waterfront on Screven Street to **Skipper's Fish Camp**, on the right. My wife and I enjoyed some really good shrimp on their covered deck.

From the Strain Building, go north on Screven Street to the corner of Third Street, then left for two blocks to the Kenan-Fox House, built in 1865. It is believed to be the oldest house in Darien.

THE ADAM STRAIN BUILDING WAS ONE OF ONLY TWO BUILDINGS TO SURVIVE THE 1863 YANKEE RAID ON DARIEN

Go back east on Third Street to US 17 and go right (south) to the bridge over the Altamaha River. As you cross the bridge, look to your left to see the **fleet of shrimp boats** anchored at the docks.

Also, as you cross the river, look for **"The Monster of the Altamaha!"** Or, as locals call it, the "Altamahaha" (www.exploresouthernhistory.com/altamahaha.html).

On the south end of the bridge, about a mile from Darien, is the historic **Butler Island Rice Plantation**, on the right side of the highway.

The plantation at Butler Island began in the 1790s, when Revolutionary War hero Major Pierce Butler began planting rice in the Altamaha Delta, a location that provided perfect growing conditions for the crop. When he died in 1822, his grandson and namesake Captain Pierce Butler took over the operation, and by the 1850s it was one of the largest plantations in the South, with more than 500 slaves.

In 1834, Captain Butler, who lived mostly in Philadelphia, met and married Fanny Kemble, a famous British stage actress. She did not visit Butler Island until 1838, and when she did, she was appalled by the practice of slavery and the living and working conditions of the slaves. The ultimate result of her visit was a divorce and the writing of a book, *A Journal of a Residence on a Georgian Plantation in 1838–1839*, which was very influential in the abolition of slavery. Not as well-known now as *Uncle Tom's Cabin*, but possibly

SHRIMP BOATS IN THE ALTAMAHA RIVER AT DARIEN

just as influential in its day, it may also have helped keep England from coming into the war on the side of the Confederacy.

Today, all that's left of Butler Plantation is the 75-foot **Smokestack** of the steam-powered **Rice Mill**, dating from 1820, and the nearby **Grist Mill**, powered by the incoming and outgoing tides.

The property is now owned by the Nature Conservancy and is part of the Altamaha Waterfowl Management Area. It is open all day, seven days a week, and admission is free. The house on the property is not original and is not open to the public.

Please be advised that this is snake and 'gator country, so watch where you step! Did you ever notice that country people usually look down when they walk? It's because they're in the habit of watching where they put their feet!

In a side note, Owen Wister, author of *The Virginian* and other novels, was the son of Pierce's and Fanny's daughter Sarah and frequently visited the plantation.

From Butler Island, continue south for about 3.5 miles to the entrance to the **Hofwyl-Broadfield Plantation Historic Site** on the left at 5556 US 17. It's just past the intersection of US 17 and GA 99.

The plantation began in 1806, when William Brailsford began acquiring land in the swamps of the Altamaha River. One of his purchases was an estate called Broadface, which he renamed Broadfield. The plantation eventually grew to hold 7,300 acres of land and house as many as 357 slaves.

When slavery ended with the Civil War, labor-intensive rice farming became much less profitable. However, Brailsford's descendants continued growing rice until 1913, driving the plantation deeper and deeper into debt. They converted it into a dairy farm and were able to pay off all their obligations before closing the dairy in 1942.

The plantation house was built in the 1850s by Brailsford's granddaughter Ophelia and her husband George Dent and named **Hofwyl House** after a school he had attended in Switzerland. Ophelia Dent's granddaughter (also named Ophelia) willed the property to the state of Georgia in 1973. The house is as she left it, with furniture and possessions from five generations of Brailsford's descendants.

Hofwyl-Broadfield is open Wednesday–Sunday, 9 a.m.–5 p.m. Admission is $8 for adults, $7 for seniors, and $5 for ages 6–17. Children under six are free. Facilities include a museum and gift shop, picnic facilities, a nature trail, and bird-watching. The estate's 1,268 acres of land and 696 acres of freshwater marshes are managed by the Georgia Department of Natural Resources.

A 75-FOOT SMOKESTACK FROM THE STEAM-POWERED RICE MILL AND A TIDE-POWERED GRIST MILL ARE ALL THAT REMAIN OF THE GREAT BUTLER ISLAND PLANTATION

Leaving the plantation, turn left (south) on US 17 and continue toward Brunswick. After 10.5 miles, turn left onto the J.F. Torras Causeway to St. Simons Island. At the end of the causeway, bear left, then right onto DeMere Road for 1.1 miles to the traffic circle. Take the third exit, Frederica Road, and go about 4 miles to a second traffic circle. Take the second exit—Frederica Road—and go 0.8 mile. **Christ Episcopal Church** will be on your left. Pass it for now—we'll come back—and continue about 0.1 mile to the entrance to **Fort Frederica National Monument**, also on the left.

In 1736, only three years after founding Savannah, James Oglethorpe led a group of 44 men and 72 women and children to build a fort and a town at a strategic location on

ONLY A SMALL PART OF FORT FREDERICA STILL GUARDS ST. SIMON'S ISLAND

St. Simon's Island on Georgia's southern coast. He named it Frederica, after Crown Prince Frederick, son of George II.

It was only an earthworks at first, but under Oglethorpe's leadership and inspiration, a substantial fort of tabby was built within a few years, and inland, behind the fort, a village with walls and a moat, laid out in 84 plots, most of them 60 by 90 feet, with broad streets lined with orange trees and substantial homes of brick, wood, and tabby, housing a population of as many as 500.

After being routed by the British in the Battle of Bloody Marsh on St. Simons in 1742, the Spanish were no longer a serious threat to Georgia, and the garrison at Frederica was disbanded in 1749. Without the economic input of several hundred soldiers, the town withered and died, becoming effectively a ghost town by 1755.

Today, all that remains of Frederica is a small piece of the fort, although that piece is in very good condition, along with the many house foundations, excavated by archaeologists, that line the streets.

Fort Frederica is open daily 8:30 a.m.–5 p.m. and admission is free. The visitor center has an interesting 23-minute film about Fort Frederica and an exhibit of objects unearthed from the ruins of the town.

From Fort Frederica, go back to Christ Episcopal Church at 6329 Frederica Road. Founded in 1808 on a site where both John and Charles Wesley had preached to the settlers at Frederica in the 1730s, Christ Church did not have a permanent building until 1820. That first structure was severely damaged during the Civil War by Union troops stationed on St. Simons.

The present sanctuary was erected in 1884, built in the shape of a cross, with beautiful stained-glass windows throughout, including one by Tiffany, and another depicting John Wesley preaching to the settlers. The woodwork is also unusually fine.

Best-selling author Eugenia Price, who made Christ Church nationally known through her historical novels, is buried among the live oaks in the church's cemetery.

The church is frequently, but not always, open, so it's a good idea to call before your visit if you would like to tour the church and grounds. The number is 912-638-8683.

On the left as you go back to the roundabout is the **First African Baptist**

THE INTERIOR OF CHRIST CHURCH EPISCOPAL ON ST. SIMONS ISLAND

ONE OF THE STAINED-GLASS WINDOWS AT CHRIST CHURCH DEPICTS JOHN WESLEY PREACHING TO THE SETTLERS

Church. Although the current building only dates from 1929, the church was first organized in 1859, when most of the members were still slaves, worshipping at that time in a little tabby church at West Point Plantation.

Go back to the traffic circle and continue south on Frederica Road through the traffic light on to the DeMere Road traffic circle. Take the third exit— Demere Road east—and go 2.1 miles to a stop sign. After the stop sign, continue on DeMere for about two blocks. It will curve around to the right and become Beachview. Go two more blocks and look for the entrance to the parking lot at **St. Simons Island Lighthouse and Museum** on the left.

Dating from 1872, the St. Simons light replaced one built in 1810 that was destroyed by the Confederates during the Civil War to make navigation more difficult for Yankee ships.

The original light was 75 feet high and made of tabby taken from the ruins of Fort Frederica, in case you were wondering why so little is left of that fort. Some of it probably went into other building projects on the island as well. The use of tabby was the idea of James Gould, who, after building the lighthouse, became its keeper for 27 years. Eugenia Price wrote about Gould in her historical novel *Lighthouse*, the first book in her St. Simons trilogy.

Congress authorized building a new lighthouse in 1867, but the project was delayed because of unhealthy living conditions. Stagnant ponds near the site bred mosquitoes, and two contractors died of fever before the light-house and Victorian-style keeper's residence were completed in 1872.

Now owned and managed by the Coastal Georgia Historical Society, the lighthouse and keeper's residence, currently a museum, are open for tours, including climbing the 129 steps to the top of the 104-foot tower. Hours are 10 a.m.–5 p.m. Monday through Saturday and 1:30 p.m.–5 p.m. on Sunday. Admission is $12 for adults and $5 for ages 6–12. Children five and under are free. Call 912-638-4666 for more information.

From the lighthouse, you can either go back to DeMere Road and follow it back to the causeway, or, if you would like to do a bit more exploration of a very interesting place, continue on Beachview for a few blocks to a shopping area with some very good restaurants. My wife and I have eaten seafood several times at **The Half Shell SSI**, 504 Beachview Drive and always found it excellent.

Leaving St. Simons, turn left at the west end of the Torras Causeway onto US 17/Glynn Avenue for 4.2 miles. Be sure to notice the beautiful and grace-ful Sydney Lanier suspension bridge that carries you across the Brunswick River. At the end of the bridge, turn left on US 520/Jekyll Island Causeway for 6.3 miles. In about 4 miles, you will come to a toll booth. A daily pass is $6, and a weekly pass is $28. Annual passes are also available.

Once the playground of the rich and famous, now one of Georgia's premier vacation spots, **Jekyll Island** is owned by the state but is not a state park. It is managed by the Jekyll Island Authority, whose mission is to maintain the delicate balance between nature and mankind on the island.

Continue on from the toll booth and take the first left toward Riverview Drive. Go 0.4 mile on Riverview, turn right on Stable Road for 0.8 mile, then continue on Riverview Drive for 2.7 miles to the **Horton House** ruin on the right.

Major William Horton, who was second in command of Oglethorpe's regi-ment, settled on Jekyll Island in 1738 and began to build roads and clear land

BUILT IN 1740, THE HORTON HOUSE ON JEKYLL ISLAND IS ONE OF THE OLDEST BUILDINGS IN GEORGIA

for planting, as well as building for himself a two-story plantation house of tabby. Completed in 1740, it is one of the oldest buildings in Georgia. The house was gutted by fire in the Spanish invasion of 1742, but was rebuilt. After 1886, when the island was sold to the Jekyll Island Club, the house unfortunately was allowed to deteriorate until only the sturdy tabby walls remain. The site is open daily, and there is no admission charge other than the entrance toll to the island.

In addition to other crops, Horton grew hops and barley on his plantation and operated Georgia's first brewery.

You might also like to check out the rest of the **Jekyll Island Historic District**, where the clubhouse built by the millionaires of the Jekyll Island Club is now a surprisingly affordable historic hotel, and where many of their "cottages" have been restored and are open to the public. Jekyll Island also has 10 miles of beaches, four golf courses, a water park, and the **Georgia Sea Turtle Center**, plus hotels, cottages, and campgrounds.

From the Horton House, backtrack to GA 520 and go west to the junction with US 17. Go left and continue on US 17/GA 25 for 5.6 miles to the intersection with Interstate 95 and go south about 23 miles to Exit 6, Laurel

Island Parkway. Take the parkway east approximately 5 miles (it becomes Colerain Road as you go) to Kings Bay Road. Turn left and go 1.2 miles to GA 40 Spur/Charlie Smith Sr. Parkway. At that point you will be in front of the entrance to the Kings Bay Naval Submarine Base. Turn left and go about a hundred yards to the **Houston McIntosh Sugar Mill**, known locally as the Tabby Sugar Works. The site is on the left, set back about a hundred yards from the road in a publicly accessible park open all day, every day with no admission charge.

After the War of 1812, during which John Houston McIntosh led an unsuccessful effort to annex East Florida to the United States, he settled in Camden County, Georgia, acquired two plantations, and began growing rice and sugar cane.

One of the plantations, which he named New Canaan, was located near St. Marys, and it was there that he built, around 1825, a large, two-story mill with thick walls of tabby to process the cane into sugar. It was believed at the time that thick walls were necessary to maintain the heat needed for production of superior sugar. The mill that squeezed the sweet juice out of the cane was a new design, purchased from the West Point Foundry in New York, and was powered by yoked cattle.

The mill was in use at least through the Civil War, during which it was

THE HOUSTON MCINTOSH SUGAR MILL NEAR ST. MARYS WAS ONCE THOUGHT TO BE THE RUINS OF A SPANISH MISSION

also used to produce large quantities of arrowroot starch. As time passed, the history of the mill was forgotten and local residents thought the ruins were an old Spanish mission, because they seemed to be too large to have been used for any agricultural purpose.

If you turn left from the Tabby Sugar Works and go about 4 miles, you will come to **Crooked River State Park**, a 500-acre facility featuring eleven cottages, 62 campsites, saltwater fishing, pontoon boat tours, boat, kayak, and bike rentals, plus 4 miles of hiking trails and birding along the Colonial Coast Birding Trail.

But if you want to go to St. Marys, go right (south) from the sugar mill ruins on GA 40 Spur/Charlie Smith Sr. Parkway for 2.7 miles to the intersection with GA 40, turn left, and go about 3 miles to downtown **St. Marys**. Although the town was officially founded in 1787, it had originally been settled by the Spanish in 1566—just one year after the founding of St. Augustine, Florida. That would make St. Marys the second-oldest continuously inhabited city in the United States, or so claim many residents.

Stop first at the welcome center on the left at 400 Osborne Street, at the intersection of Osborne and Conyers Streets, and pick up a brochure for the walking tour of historic buildings, of which St. Marys has many in a fairly small area, most of them beautifully preserved or restored.

That intersection of Osborne and Conyers Streets, by the way, is to me the most interesting in St. Marys. On the northeast corner is the welcome center, as noted, and across Osborne Street on the northwest corner is the **First Presbyterian Church** at 100 West Conyers Street.

A picture-perfect piece of architecture dating from 1808, it is one of the oldest Presbyterian church buildings in Georgia. The church was non-denominational until a young Presbyterian missionary named Horace Pratt came from New Jersey to St. Marys in 1821. Through his influence, the church was incorporated as the First Presbyterian Church of St. Marys in 1828 and remains in active service to this day.

On the southwest corner, at 311 Osborne Street, is **Orange Hall**. Built circa 1830 in the Doric temple style of Greek Revival architecture, some consider it to be the first, and certainly one of the finest, examples of Greek Revival in the antebellum South. It was built for Rev. Pratt by his wife's family and named for the orange trees that grew around it.

Orange Hall is now a house museum open for tours 10 a.m.–3 p.m. Monday through Friday; 10 a.m.–4 p.m. on Saturday; and 1 p.m.–4 p.m. on Sunday. Admission is $5 for adults, $4 for seniors and military, and $3 for ages 6–12. Call 912-882-4000 for more information.

Across the street, on the southeast corner of the intersection, is the **Archibald Clarke House**, at 314 Osborne Street. Probably the oldest surviving house in St. Marys, it was built in 1801 or 1802. Legend has it that Aaron Burr was given refuge here by the owner, General Archibald Clark,

BUILT IN 1808, THE FIRST PRESBYTERIAN CHURCH OF ST. MARYS IS STILL IN USE

in 1804 as he was fleeing to avoid arrest after killing Alexander Hamilton in a duel. The house has been extensively renovated by its present owners.

And in the traffic island near the middle of the intersection is the stump of the last **Washington Oak**, one of four planted in honor of President George Washington on the day of his burial. The wooden post nearby marks the well dug that same year, known as the **Washington Pump**. It was one of six wells that provided St. Marys with pure water until the tidal wave of 1818.

Working our way toward the waterfront, we come to the **General John Floyd House** at 213 Osborne Street. A Brigadier General in the Georgia Militia, Floyd served in the War of 1812 and in the Creek Indian Wars of 1813–1815. He later served in the Georgia House of Representatives. He built this house in 1830.

Just down the street and on the same side is **Our Lady Star of the Sea Catholic Chapel**, at 201 Osborne Street. Unlikely as it may seem, this small but lovely church began life in 1840 as a bank. It was purchased sometime after 1847 by Lewis and Marie Ponce DeFour and given to the Catholic diocese, which it served until a larger church was built in 1957. It is still in use as a chapel and for special services. The steeple probably was added around 1952–54.

Just east of the welcome center on Conyers Street is **St. Marys Method-**

LEGEND SAYS AARON BURR ONCE SOUGHT REFUGE AT THE ARCHIBALD CLARKE HOUSE IN ST. MARYS

ist Church, at 105 East Conyers. The Methodist congregation, established in 1799, is the oldest in St. Marys. This building was erected in 1858 and served until the adjacent modern building was completed in 1964. It was until recently used as a chapel.

Back on Osborne Street at Number 126 is the **Stotesbury-Johnson House**, at the corner of Osborne and Bryant Streets. Built in 1821, it was until recently the Blue Goose Wine and Coffee Shoppe, but is now a private home.

If you don't feel like walking, the **Historic District Tram Tour** leaves from the **Waterfront Pavilion** at the end of Osborne Street at 11 a.m. and 2 p.m. Monday through Saturday. The tour takes about an hour and costs $5 for adults, $3 for age 12 and under. Call 912-882-4000 for more information.

The Waterfront Pavilion, by the way, is also the setting for a **Community Market** every Saturday, 9 a.m.–1 p.m., featuring locally grown and organic produce and hand-made items for sale.

The waterfront at St. Marys is also the gateway to **Cumberland Island National Seashore**, with 17 miles of beaches and 9,800 acres of Congressionally designated wilderness. The ferry, which operates every day March through November, leaves St. Marys at 9 and 11:45 a.m. and returns at 10:15 a.m. and 2:45 and 4:45 p.m. The winter schedule, from December 1 through February 28, has departures at 9 and 11:45 a.m. and returns at 10:15 a.m. and 4:45 p.m. There is no ferry service on Tuesdays and Wednesdays in winter.

Another of the many places worth a visit in downtown St. Marys is the **Submarine Museum**, at 102 W. St. Marys Street. It's open 10 a.m.–5 p.m. Tuesday through Saturday and noon until 5 p.m. on Sunday. Admission is $5 for adults, $4 for active duty military, veterans, seniors, and students age 13 and up, and $3 for ages 6–12. Children under six are admitted free. Call 912-882-2782 for more information.

Leaving the St. Marys waterfront district, take GA 40 west 10.8 miles to the intersection with US 17 in Kingsland. On my way, I stopped at **St. Marys Seafood & More** at 1837 Osborne Road/GA 40 and enjoyed some great shrimp.

In the not-too-distant past, the little burg of Kingsland was quite well known to certain segments of the population. Back then, the State of Florida required a blood test and a three-day waiting period before a marriage could take place. But just up US 17, a few miles over the state line in Georgia, was a place where you could get a blood test, a license, and a marriage ceremony right then and there! No waiting! I suspect quite a few people in those days woke up from a good drunk and found themselves in bed with—and married to—someone they couldn't remember ever having met.

With a number of places providing this package deal, Kingsland called itself the "Marriage Capital of the South," a claim that probably would have been disputed by Ringgold, in North Georgia, just a few minutes down US 41 from Tennessee, which had laws similar to Florida's.

From Kingsland, continue about 20 miles to downtown Folkston. As the highway turns right, the Neoclassical Revival **Charlton County Courthouse**, built in 1928, will be on the right.

Follow the highway as it turns left in front of the courthouse and continue to the **Folkston Funnel** train-watching station, about a block down on the left just before the railroad tracks. It's a wooden pavilion with the Folkston name on the roof and seats so you can watch in comfort while up to 70 trains, including eight Amtrak trains, roll through Folkston every 24 hours, going and coming from Atlanta and Savannah and points north to or from Florida. There's even wi-fi and a scanner to allow visitors to listen to train engineers as they pass through.

From the funnel, continue through downtown Folkston and turn left on GA 121—The Okefenokee Trail. Follow 121 for 2.3 miles to Sardis Road. Turn right and go 2.3 miles to **Sardis Primitive Baptist Church**. It's on a dirt road on the right behind Sardis Cemetery.

Sardis is an excellent example of the meeting houses used by the Crawfordite faction of the Primitive Baptist Church, a group unique to the "Wiregrass" area of South Georgia. Named after Elder Reuben Crawford, they follow an especially rigid and austere form of Calvinism. They do not believe in Sunday Schools or sending out missionaries, nor will they wear neckties or allow radios or television in their homes.

Their meeting houses reflect their philosophy, made as they are of rough, unpainted pine with neither heat nor electric lights—nothing that, in their view, would distract them from worship. However, one aspect of modernization has reached them: instead of outhouses, all their churches now have separate, outdoor restrooms with running water, in accord with public health regulations.

Organized in 1821, the Sardis congregation is the oldest of any denomination in Charlton County. The present church was probably built around 1840, although the pulpit is thought to be from an earlier structure. The cemetery is large and has many interesting pieces of statuary. The Sardis Church does not appear to be in current use, as there is evidence of deterioration. Some boards need replacing, and the grass has not been mowed recently.

From Sardis Church, go left and return to GA 121. Turn right and continue for about 5 miles to the sign marking the turn-off to **Okefenokee National Wildlife Refuge**. Turn right and go 4 miles to the park entrance.

Known to the Creek Indians as "the land of trembling earth" (although some linguists say it means "shaking water"), the Okefenokee is a more-than-500,000-acre swamp lying mostly in southeastern Georgia; a vast bog covering an immense, saucer-like depression in the earth more than a hundred feet above sea level. About 400,000 acres are included in the wildlife refuge. It is drained by the Suwannee River flowing southwest to the Gulf,

THE AUSTERITY OF THE SARDIS PRIMITIVE BAPTIST CHURCH REFLECTS THE PHILOSOPHY OF ITS PARISHIONERS

CHESSER ISLAND PIONEER HOMESTEAD IN THE OKEEFENOKEE NATIONAL WILDLIFE REFUGE

and the St. Marys River flowing eastward, forming the boundary between Georgia and Florida as it makes its way to the Atlantic. There are three main entrances to the refuge: the Folkston entrance on the east side, which is considered the main entrance; **Stephen Foster State Park**, on the west, which opens to an area that looks more like what I picture when I think of a swamp; and a commercial entrance at the north end near Waycross.

There's something for just about everyone who loves the outdoors to do in Okefenokee: the 7.5-mile Swamp Island (wildlife) Drive, hiking trails, canoe/kayak trails, boat trails (in fact, there are 120 miles of water trails), guided boat tours, the **Chesser Island Homestead** (where you can see how a swamp family lived in the late 1800s), and the Chesser Island Boardwalk.

The hours at the Richard S. Bolt Visitor Center vary by season, so it's best to call 912-496-7836 or visit their website (www.fws.gov/refuge/Okeefenokee) as you plan your visit. A pass to the Refuge costs $5 and is good for seven days.

The Swamp Island Drive, hiking trails, Chesser Island Boardwalk, and Okefenokee Adventures are open a half-hour before sunrise. They close at 7:30 p.m. March through October, and at 5:30 p.m. November through February.

A word of warning: They lock the gates at closing time, and although you may not be planning to stay overnight, you may find yourself doing so if you're late to the gates.

Leaving the park, go back to Folkston and and turn left on US 1/23/301/ GA 15 for 0.8 mile. Turn right on GA 40 Connector East for about a half-mile to the flashing red lights, then go left on GA 252 for approximately 18 miles

UNLIKE SOME MORE MODERN CHURCHES, PROVIDENCE METHODIST CHURCH IN CAMDEN COUNTY LEANS DECIDEDLY TO THE RIGHT

to the intersection with New Post Road. Go left on New Post for 2.7 miles to the intersection with Providence Church Road and **Providence Methodist Church**, built in 1856, on the right at the corner. In 1922, a hurricane nearly blew the church over. According to a woman I met at the church, her grandfather attached rings to the building and nearby trees and used ropes and pulleys to pull it upright. However, to this day the church leans noticeably to the right, a condition not shared by some of today's other churches.

Leaving the church, go back on New Post Road and turn left on GA 252 for 4.5 miles to the intersection with US 17/GA 25. Turn right (south) and go about 4 miles to Woodbine. The **Camden County Courthouse** is about two blocks off US 17 on the left.

From the courthouse area, continue south on US 17/GA 25 for about half a mile and go left (east) on GA 25 for 2.3 miles to Interstate 95, Exit 14 and the end of this tour.

IN THE AREA

Accommodations

THE INN AT FOLKSTON BED AND BREAKFAST, 3576 Main Street, Folkston. 912-496-6256. www.innatfolkston.com/index.html.

OPEN GATES BED AND BREAKFAST INN, 301 Franklin Street on Vernon Square, Darien. 912-348-5185. www.opengatesbnb.com/.

SPENCER HOUSE INN BED AND BREAKFAST, 200 Osborne Street, St. Marys. 912-882-1872. spencerhouseinn.com.

VILLAGE INN AND PUB, 500 Mallery Street, St. Simons Island. 912-623-4000. www.villageinnandpub.com.

Dining

B & J'S STEAKS AND SEAFOOD, 900 North Way, Darien. 912-437-2122. bandjssteaksandseafood.com.

THE HALF SHELL SSI, 504 Beachview Drive, St. Simons Island. 912-268-4241. www.thehalfshellssi.com.

OKEFENOKEE RESTAURANT, 1507 Third Street, Folkston. 912-496-3263. www.facebook.com/pages/Okefenokee-Restaurant/152407781453706.

ST. MARYS SEAFOOD & MORE, 1837 Osborne Road, St. Marys. 912-467-4217. stmarysseafoodandmore.com.

SKIPPER'S FISH CAMP, 85 Screven Street, Darien. 912-437-3474. www.skippersfishcamp.com.

Attractions and Recreation

ASHANTILLY HISTORIC SITE, 15591 GA 99, Darien. 912-437-4473. www.ashantilly.org.

CROOKED RIVER STATE PARK, 6222 GA 40 Spur/Charlie Smith Sr. Parkway, St. Marys. 912-882-5256.

CUMBERLAND ISLAND NATIONAL SEASHORE, 101 Wheeler Street, St. Marys. 912-882-4336.

FORT FREDERICA NATIONAL MONUMENT, 6515 Frederica Road, St. Simons Island. 912-638-3630. www.nps.gov/fofr.

FORT KING GEORGE HISTORIC SITE, 302 McIntosh Road SE, Darien. 912-437-4770.

HOFWYL-BROADFIELD PLANTATION HISTORIC SITE, 5556 US 17, Brunswick. 912-264-7333.

JEKYLL ISLAND VISITOR INFORMATION CENTER, 901 Downing Musgrove Causeway, Jekyll Island. 912-635-3636. www.jekyllisland.com.

OKEFENOKEE NATIONAL WILDLIFE REFUGE, 700 Suwannee Canal Road, Folkston. 912-496-7836. www.fws.gov/refuge/Okefenokee.

ST. MARYS HISTORIC DISTRICT TRAM TOUR, Waterfront Pavilion, St. Marys. 912-882-4000.

ST. MARYS SUBMARINE MUSEUM, 102 W. St. Marys Street, St. Marys. 912-882-2782.

ST. SIMONS ISLAND LIGHTHOUSE AND MUSEUM, 610 Beachview Drive, St. Simons Island. 912-638-4666. www.saintsimonslighthouse.org/index.html.

For more information on any Georgia State Park or Historic Site, visit the state parks website: www.georgiastateparks.org.

Events

Camden County
Rock Shrimp Festival and Railroad Days Festival, St. Marys, October.

Charlton County
Okenfenokee Festival, Folkston, October.

Glynn County

Ophelia's Classic Car Challenge, Hofwyl-Broadfield Plantation Historic Site, Brunswick, October.

McIntosh County

Que and Brew, Ashantilly Historic Site, Darien, October.

Darien Fall Festival, Darien, November.

13

GOLD'N APPLES

North Central Georgia

The total length of this tour is approximately 185 miles and includes Whitfield, Murray, Gilmer, Dawson, Lumpkin, Union, and Fannin Counties.

Beginning at exit 333 from Interstate 75 in Dalton, Georgia, take Walnut Avenue/US 76/GA 52 east through Dalton for about 8.5 miles. Slant right on GA 52 ALT for approximately 2 miles to the intersection of GA 225. Turn left (north) and the **Chief Vann House Historic Site** will be on your immediate right.

The Chief Vann house is an elegant, two-and-a-half-story brick mansion built in 1804 by wealthy Cherokee Indian Chief James Vann, who also owned a hundred slaves and more than a thousand acres in what is now Murray County. In 1805, Vann opened his home to Moravian missionaries to hold one of the first Christmas celebrations in the Cherokee Nation.

James Vann was murdered in 1809, and the property passed to his son Joseph, who, with other Cherokees, was forced out of the area in 1834. A bloody battle between claimants to the house ensued. The structure gradually deteriorated over the years until 1952, when it was purchased by a group of concerned citizens, given to the Georgia Historical Commission, and restored to its original grandeur.

The Vann House features beautiful hand carvings, an unusual "floating" staircase, a 12-foot mantle, and fine antiques. The plantation also included 95 log outbuildings, none of which survives; however the Cherokee Farmstead Exhibit at the site is made up of original 1800s Cherokee outbuildings moved from other locations.

The house and grounds are open for tours Thursday through Sunday,

LEFT: THE FIRE OBSERVATION TOWER ON FORT MOUNTAIN WAS BUILT IN 1934 BY THE CIVILIAN CONSERVATION CORPS

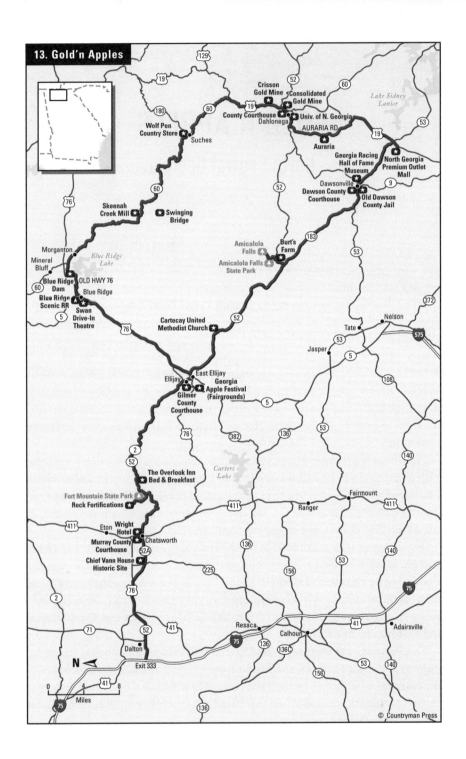

13. Gold'n Apples

129
19
180
60
52 Crisson Gold Mine
60 Lake Sidney Lanier
19 Consolidated Gold Mine
County Courthouse
Univ. of N. Georgia
Dahlonega
53
AURARIA RD
19
Wolf Pen Country Store
Suches
Auraria
Georgia Racing Hall of Fame Museum
North Georgia Premium Outlet Mall
52
Dawsonville
9
Dawson County Courthouse
Old Dawson County Jail
60
76
Skeenah Creek Mill
Swinging Bridge
183
53
Amicalola Falls
Burt's Farm
Amicalola Falls State Park
Morganton
Blue Ridge Lake
Mineral Bluff
372
Blue Ridge Dam
OLD HWY 76
60 Blue Ridge
Blue Ridge Scenic RR
Nelson
5 Swan Drive-In Theatre
Cartecay United Methodist Church
52
575
76
Tate
53
Jasper
5
East Ellijay
108
Ellijay
Georgia Apple Festival (Fairgrounds)
Gilmer County Courthouse
5
136
53
140
76
382
Carters Lake
2
52
The Overlook Inn Bed & Breakfast
Fairmount
Fort Mountain State Park
411
411
Rock Fortifications
Ranger
411 Eton
Wright Hotel
Chatsworth
136
140
Murray County Courthouse
52A
Chief Vann House Historic Site
225
156
53
2
75
76
71
52 41
Resaca
41
Adairsville
Dalton
75
Calhoun
136
136C
Exit 333
53
140
N
156
0   4   8
41
Miles
136
75
© Countryman Press

CHIEF JAMES VANN'S MANSION AT SPRING PLACE WAS THE CENTER OF A 1,000-ACRE PLANTATION

9 a.m.–5 p.m., with the last tour at 4:15 p.m. Admission is $6.50 for adults, $6 for seniors, and $5.50 for ages 6 to 17.

From the Chief Vann House, go back to GA 52 and turn left. Go 3 miles and turn left on North 3rd Avenue/US 411 for a half-mile. The Palladian influenced, Neoclassical Revival **Murray County Courthouse**, with its distinctive Jeffersonian rotunda, will be on the left, dominating downtown Chatsworth from its knoll. It was built in 1917.

From the courthouse, turn right on East Market Street for one block to the **Wright Hotel**, at 201 East Market Street, on the corner of North 2nd Avenue. Thomas Wright built the hotel in 1909, renting a brick factory for a year to make the rose-colored bricks. The heart pine lumber was cut on his farm and aged for a year. Besides being a hotel, it was also home for Wright and his wife and six children.

Historic items in the hotel include original furniture and guest registers dating back to the 1920s. The last survivor of the Wright family was a daughter, Kate Raine, who passed away in 1986, leaving the property to the Whitfield-Murray County Historical Society. The Wright Hotel is open for tours on special occasions and by appointment. Call 706-695-4416.

From the Wright Hotel, go south on North 2nd Avenue for one block and turn left on East Fort Street/GA 52. Continue on GA 52 for 7 winding but beautiful miles to the top of Fort Mountain and the entrance to **Fort Moun-**

THE ROCK FORTIFICATIONS AT FORT MOUNTAIN STATE PARK WILL PROBABLY ALWAYS BE A MYSTERY

tain State Park. There are a number of places thoughtfully provided by the road builders where you can pull off and enjoy the panoramic views.

The centerpiece of the park is an abiding mystery: an 855-foot-long wall of piled rocks which encircles the summit of the mountain, giving the park its name. Who piled the rocks, and why? And was it a fort, or was the purpose in some way ceremonial? No one knows, and it's likely no one will ever know.

Archaeologists say the wall was probably built by Indians of the Woodland Period, however, the Cherokees, who came into the area in the early 1600s, have legends of a "moon-eyed" people who built the wall for defense against intruders.

In any case, the fort at Fort Mountain is not the only one. There are similar structures in Bartow, Bibb, DeKalb, Union, and White Counties, although none is as large or as well-preserved.

More modern visitors to the 3,712-acre park will find, in addition to the stone walls, 15 cottages, more than 70 campsites, a 17-acre lake with a swimming beach, and 60 miles of trails for hiking, mountain biking, and horseback riding. And at the summit of the mountain is the restored forest fire observation tower, built by the Civilian Conservation Corps in 1934.

The park is open 7 a.m.–10 p.m. every day. There is no admission charge, but as usual, a $5 parking pass is required.

Leaving Fort Mountain State Park, turn left and continue on GA 52 for

2 miles to **The Overlook Inn Bed and Breakfast**, at 9420 GA 52. Atop the knife-like summit of the mountain, the Overlook is very appropriately named, with spectacular views from both sides. My oldest son and his wife stayed there not long ago and liked it very much.

From the Overlook Inn, continue on GA 52 for 15 miles to downtown Ellijay. The highway runs along the ridge line of the mountain, with steep slopes dropping away on both sides of the road in places. At one time, US 76 ran concurrently with GA 52 up and over Fort Mountain from Chatsworth to Ellijay. US 76 has long since been rerouted around the foot of the mountain, but it made for some interesting driving when travelers had to share Fort Mountain's steep inclines and twisting curves with semi trucks along the narrow ridge.

Like many small Georgia towns, Ellijay has a circle, rather than a square, in front of its courthouse. Built in 1898 as the Hyatt Hotel, when the county found itself in need of a new courthouse in 1934, they dressed it up with porticos and columns on two sides to give it a Neoclassical Revival look and converted it into the **Gilmer County Courthouse**.

Known as the apple capital of Georgia, Ellijay comes alive the second and third weekends of each October for the **Georgia Apple Festival**, held at the Lions Club Fairgrounds on GA 5 just south of town.

From downtown Ellijay, continue on GA 52 for about 7.5 miles, with glimpses of the beautiful Cartecay River on your right as you go, to **Cartecay United Methodist Church** on the left at 7629 GA 52.

Built in 1859, the old church has been replaced by a newer sanctuary, but is still in limited use and is well maintained. During the Civil War, it was guarded at night to protect it from the Union guerillas who roamed the area. A Sunday School has been held at this site continuously since 1851.

Leaving Cartecay Church, continue on GA 52 for 13 miles to the entrance to **Amicalola Falls State Park**. The entire route along GA 52 from Ellijay to Amicalola Falls is known as **Apple Alley.** Lined with apple orchards and sales barns, you can, if you will excuse the expression, take your pick. Seriously, many orchards will allow you to pick your own apples if you like. A large variety of other produce is also available, including, especially, pumpkins in the fall.

Burt's Farm is on the right about a half-mile before the park entrance. Growing pumpkins

A TURKEY INVITES YOU INTO HIS ORCHARD ALONG APPLE ALLEY

IN FALL, PUMPKINS AND OTHER VEGETABLES SHARE THE SPOTLIGHT WITH APPLES ALONG APPLE ALLEY

on their family's ancestral land since 1972, Johnny and Kathy Burt now grow more than 20 varieties, with customers coming from all over the Southeast, especially in the fall.

The Pumpkin Patch and Store are open 9 a.m.–6 p.m. August 27 through October 31, and 9 a.m.–5 p.m. November 1–10. Ten tractors and wagons take visitors on hayrides around the farm and to the top of a mountain overlooking Amicolola Falls every day in September and October, 10 a.m.–5 p.m., and on Saturdays and Sundays, November 1–10, 10 a.m.–4:30 p.m. Admission is free, but hayride tickets are $5, with children two and under free.

The waterfall for which Amicolola Falls State Park is named is the highest cascading waterfall in the southeastern United States, plunging 729 feet in a series of falls and cascades. You can drive to the top of the falls, or, if you're feeling vigorous, you can climb the 604-step staircase to the top. If you do, you can join the park's Canyon Climbers' Club!

The 829-acre park features a 57-room lodge and conference center atop the mountain, 14 cottages, 25 campsites, picnic facilities, and 12 miles of hiking trails. It also has Georgia's only backcountry lodge—the Len Foote Hike Inn, which can only be reached by a 5-mile hike. There is also an 8.5-mile trail to Springer Mountain, which is the southern beginning point of the 2,180-mile Appalachian Trail.

The park is open 7 a.m.–10 p.m. every day. There is no admission charge, but a $5 parking pass is required.

From Amicolola Falls Park, turn right on GA 52 and go 1.5 miles. Turn left on GA 183 and continue for 10 miles, then turn left on GA 53 for 2.5 miles to downtown Dawsonville.

The Dawson County/Dawsonville Welcome Center is in the old **Dawson County Jail**, built in 1881, at Number 54 GA 53 on the left just before the courthouse. Listed on the National Register of Historic Places, it is open for tours 8 a.m.–5 p.m., Monday through Friday. Admission is free.

All traffic coming through downtown Dawsonville circles around the old **Dawson County Courthouse**, built in 1858. The architecture is vernacular, with Greek Revival touches. No longer a working courthouse, it contains displays of historic documents, local relics, and Indian artifacts. It is also on the National Register of Historic Places. Admission is free, and the courthouse is open for tours on the same schedule as the jail.

A more recent development in Dawsonville is the **Georgia Racing Hall of Fame Museum**, which has a large display of racing memorabilia. It's located at 415 GA 53 and is open 10 a.m.–5 p.m. Monday through Saturday and 1 p.m.–5 p.m. on Sunday.

From Dawsonville, stay on GA 53 East for about 6.5 miles and turn right on US 19/GA 400 for about a half-mile to the **North Georgia Premium Outlet Mall**. With more than 140 stores featuring nationally known brands, it's one of the largest outlet malls in Georgia. Hours are 10 a.m.–9 p.m. Monday–Saturday, and 11 a.m.–7 p.m. on Sunday.

ALL THROUGH TRAFFIC IN DAWSONVILLE HAS TO CIRCLE AROUND THE OLD DAWSON COUNTY COURTHOUSE

BUILT AS A TAVERN AROUND 1830, THIS OLD STORE IS THE LAST LINK TO AURARIA'S GOLD RUSH DAYS

From the Outlet Mall, go back to US 19/GA 400. Turn left, then go 4 miles and turn left on Auraria Road for 50 yards, then turn right on GA 9/Auraria Road for 5.9 miles to **Auraria**, the first gold rush town.

In 1828, a hunter named Benjamin Parks tripped over a rock which he discovered to be full of gold. It was Cherokee Indian territory, but that did not hinder more than a thousand miners from prospecting the area by 1829. Auraria, which means "city of gold," was the county seat from 1828 to 1832 and boasted 20 saloons, five hotels, and a newspaper.

The county seat was moved to Dahlonega in 1832, and now nothing is left of Auraria except one of the taverns, which stayed in business as a general store into the 1980s. The Auraria hotel next door collapsed into a pile of rotting boards a few years ago. The store appears to be reasonably sound, but time and weather are taking their toll. Some person or organization needs to step up and do an intervention or this historically significant building eventually will be lost.

Going on from Auraria, continue on Auraria Road/GA 9 for 4.3 miles, then turn sharp right on GA 52. Go a mile, then turn left on West Main Street for about a half-mile to the Dahlonega town square. As you come into Dahlonega, you will pass the **University of North Georgia** on your right.

Founded in 1873 as North Georgia Agricultural College, the school is Georgia's second-oldest public institution of higher education and the first

PRICE MEMORIAL BUILDING AT THE UNIVERSITY OF NORTH GEORGIA IS BUILT ON THE FOUNDATION OF THE 1838 US MINT

co-ed one. It has had a military education program for many years, which continues today as the Military College of Georgia.

Price Memorial Hall, with its steeple covered in gold leaf, is the university's administration building. It was built in 1879 on the foundation of the 1838 US Mint.

Continue to the town square and the visitor center at 13 South Park Street on the right corner at the far side of the square.

In the middle of the square, of course, is the old **Lumpkin County Courthouse**, built in 1836 after the Lumpkin County seat was moved from Auraria. It is one of the oldest courthouses in the state, and now houses the **Dahlonega Gold Museum Historic Site**. The architecture is vernacular, with Classical Revival influences.

The Georgia gold rush ended in 1849, when gold was discovered in California and the miners left *en masse*, even though the Dahlonega Mint assayor Dr. M. F. Stephenson stood on the courthouse steps and tried to persuade miners to stay in Dahlonega by telling them, "There's millions in it," usually misquoted as "Thar's gold in them thar hills!"

He was no doubt correct, as the "Mother Lode" has never been found. In fact, you can still prospect for gold in the area. My wife and I spent an enjoyable afternoon with two of our grandchildren panning for gold at **Crisson's Gold Mine**, which has been in business since 1847. We did, in fact, find some gold, some of which my wife incorporated into her wedding band

THE OLD LUMPKIN COUNTY COURTHOUSE IN DAHLONEGA IS NOW THE GOLD MUSEUM

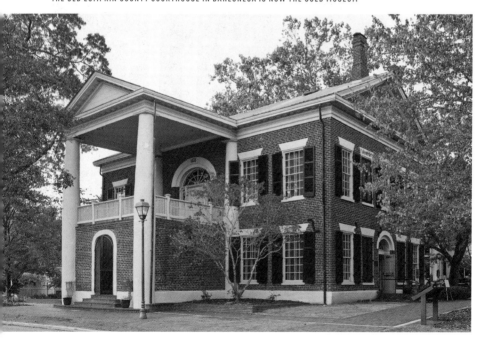

PANNING FOR GOLD AT CRISSON'S GOLD MINE, DAHLONEGA

when she had it recast. At **Consolidated Gold Mines,** you can not only pan for gold but also take a tour of the largest underground gold mine east of the Mississippi.

The Gold Museum is open Monday through Saturday from 9 a.m.–4:45 p.m., and Sunday 10 a.m.–4:45 p.m. Admission is $7.00 for adults, $6.50 for seniors, $4.50 for ages 6–17, and $2 for children under six.

DAHLONEGA'S DOWNTOWN IS NOT LARGE BUT HAS MANY INTERESTING SHOPS AND RESTAURANTS

Crisson's Gold Mine is open 10 a.m.–5 p.m. every day. Admission is $9.95 per person and includes a bucket of gold dirt to pan through.

Consolidated Gold Mine is open Monday to Friday, 10 a.m.–4 p.m. and 10 a.m.–5 p.m. on Saturday and Sunday. Admission is $16 for adults and $11 for ages 4–14, and includes a 40-minute tour of the 200-feet-deep mine and a dirt sample to pan for yourself.

You will also enjoy touring the shops and eateries in the old storefronts around the square and up the side streets. Dahlonega especially comes alive the third weekend of October for the annual **Gold Rush Days** festival, an event that floods the town with visitors.

This is Georgia wine country, with five wineries in the area, all of them offering tasting rooms. More information is available at the visitor center.

Leaving the old Courthouse in Dahlonega, continue on Main Street for two blocks to the first traffic light, turn left on Grove Street/US 19 Business/GA 60 and go north for about 9 miles. When 19 and 60 split, stay left to continue on GA 60 for 7 winding miles to remote and scenic **Suches**, at 3,000 feet, "the valley above the clouds."

There's great hiking and trout fishing around Suches, including a **Swinging Bridge** over the beautiful Toccoa River on Forest Road 816 off GA 60, so you might want to make a note to return when you have more time. Suches is also the home of the **Indian Summer Festival** on the first full weekend of October, which would be an especially good time to come back.

When you live 16 miles of mountain road from the nearest town, you need a general store that sells just about anything you might need. If the **Wolf Pen Gap Country Store** doesn't have it, you probably don't need it!

From Suches, continue on GA 60 for about 15 miles. This is mountain driving at its finest! Turn right on Skeenah Gap Road to **Skeenah Creek Mill** at the **Skeenah Creek Campground**.

In 1832, Willis Rabun Woody moved his family to the beautiful, remote valley called "Skeenah" by the Cherokees, meaning "Big Bear." Ten years later, in 1848, he built the little mill that still stands on Skeenah Creek.

NORTH GEORGIA'S MOUNTAIN ROADS INVITE THE TRAVELER TO SEE WHAT'S AROUND THE NEXT CURVE

THE SKEENAH CREEK MILL IS LOCATED IN A REMOTE BUT BEAUTIFUL PART OF FANNIN COUNTY

Although the mill is not currently in operation, it is in good condition and could be restored.

The mill is behind the campground, and even if you're not camping, the gracious people who own the property will welcome you to visit the mill. However, if you should happen to be taking this tour in a camper, you could hardly find a more delightful place to set up. Call Mark and Terry at 706-838-5500 for reservations.

Leaving the Mill/Campground, turn right and follow GA 60 for 11 miles, then merge left onto Old US 76. Continue on Old US 76/GA 60 for about 1.5 miles. When GA 60 turns right, keep straight to stay on Old 76 for 1 more mile to cross over the top of the 167-feet-high **Blue Ridge Dam**. It's a dramatic sight, with Blue Ridge Lake on your left and the Toccoa River far down on the right.

The town of Blue Ridge is somewhat of a tourist mecca these days, but it was just a remote mountain village until the four-laning of US 76/GA 5/515 opened up the region. The historic old downtown is literally wall-to-wall with all kinds of interesting shops.

Stay on Old US 76/East 1st Street for about 3.2 miles from the dam, and turn right on Depot Street. (It's a little tricky to find because the street sign is on the left at the intersection.) Cross East Main Street and proceed to the **Blue Ridge Scenic Railway** terminal, on the right at 241 Depot Street, in the old Louisville and Nashville Railroad depot, built in 1905.

The railway runs from Blue Ridge to McCaysville, GA/Copperhill, TN along the valley of the Toccoa River. The trip takes about an hour, one way, with a two-hour layover to explore McCaysville and Copperhill. If you prefer to drive, it's about a 15-minute trip up GA 5 to McCaysville, but I think the much more enjoyable way to go is via the Blue Ridge Scenic Railway.

The railway runs from March through December, but the schedule is too complex to try to reproduce here. Better you should visit their website (www .brscenic.com), where you can schedule a ride and even buy tickets online. Their phone number is 706-632-8724.

From the Blue Ridge Railway, go back on Depot Street to East 1st Street and turn right for about a half-mile to the **Swan Drive-In Theatre** on the left at the intersection with Summit Street. One of the only three remaining drive-in theaters in Georgia, the Swan has been in continuous operation since 1955.

From the Swan Theatre, continue on East 1st Street/Old US 76 for 0.8 mile. At the intersection with new US 76/GA 5/515, turn left for 14.3 miles to the intersection with US 76 at East Ellijay. Turn right and follow 76 for about 13.5 miles and turn left on Ridgeway Church Road for 0.4 mile to one of the most unusual sights on this tour: a log church built around 1865. It was in regular use until 1982, when a new church was built across the road. The interior is in quite good condition and the logs appear to be well preserved, although the building leans to the right, in keeping with the principles of most Baptists.

Leaving Ridgeway Church, turn left on US 76/GA 282 to US 411. From there, you can go left (south) on 441 to Interstate 75 at Cartersville or go right to Chatsworth and take US 76/GA 52 back through Dalton to Interstate 75.

THE SWAN DRIVE-IN THEATRE IN BLUE RIDGE IS ONE OF ONLY THREE REMAINING IN GEORGIA

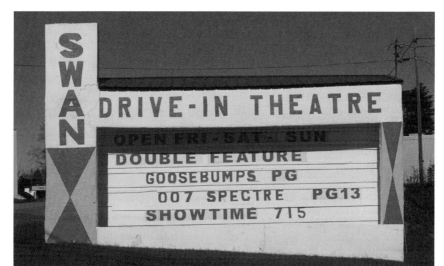

THE BLUE RIDGE SCENIC RAILWAY MAKES REGULAR RUNS BETWEEN BLUE RIDGE AND MCCAYSVILLE

IN THE AREA

Accommodations

AMICOLOLA FALLS LODGE, 418 Amicolola Falls Lodge Road, Dawsonville. 800-573-9656. www.amicalolafallslodge.com.

BLUE RIDGE INN BED AND BREAKFAST, 477 West First Street, Blue Ridge. 706-661-7575. www.blueridgeinnbandb.com.

CAMP SKEENAH CREEK CAMPGROUND & THE OLD HISTORIC MILL, 20 Skeenah Gap Road, Suches. 706-838-5500.

MOUNTAIN LAUREL CREEK INN SPA, 202 Talmer Grizzle Road, Dahlonega. 706-867-8134. www.mountainlaurelcreek.com/breakfast.html.

THE OVERLOOK INN BED AND BREAKFAST, 9420 GA 52, Chatsworth. 706-517-0300. www.theoverlookinn.com

THE SMITH HOUSE, 84 South Chestatee Street, Dahlonega. 706-725-8148. smithhouse.com/lodging.

Dining

BRATZEIT (GERMAN CUISINE), 77 Memorial Drive, Dahlonega. 706-867-7741. www.bratzeit.com.

CANTABERRY RESTAURANT BLUE RIDGE, 524 East Main Street, Blue Ridge. 706-946-7687. cantaberry.com.

CANTABERRY RESTAURANT ELLIJAY, 5 South Side Square, Ellijay. 706-636-4663. cantaberry.com.

EDNA'S RESTAURANT, 1300 US 411 South, Chatsworth. 706-695-4951. www.facebook.com/EdnasRestaurant.

THE POOL ROOM, 78 East First Street, Dawsonville. 706-265-2792.

POOLE'S BARBECUE, 164 Craig Street, East Ellijay. 706-635-4100. www.poolesbarbq.com.

THE SMITH HOUSE, 84 South Chestatee Street, Dahlonega. 706-867-7000. smithhouse.com.

SOUTHERN CHARM, 224 West Main Street, Blue Ridge. 706-632-9090. www.eatsoutherncharm.com.

Attractions and Recreation

AMICOLOLA FALLS STATE PARK AND LODGE, 280 Amicalola Falls State Park Road, Dawsonville. 706-625-4703.

BLUE RIDGE SCENIC RAILWAY, 241 Depot Street, Blue Ridge. 706-632-8724. www.brscenic.com.

CHIEF VANN HOUSE STATE HISTORIC SITE, 82 GA 225, Chatsworth. 706-695-2598.

CONSOLIDATED GOLD MINE, 185 Consolidated Gold Mine Road, Dahlonega. 706-864-8473. consolidatedgoldmine.com.

CRISSON'S GOLD MINE, 2736 Morrison Moore Parkway, Dahlonega. 706-864-6363. www.crissongoldmine.com.

DAHLONEGA GOLD MUSEUM HISTORIC SITE, 1 Public Square, Dahlonega. 706-864-2257.

FORT MOUNTAIN STATE PARK, 181 Fort Mountain Park Road, Chatsworth. 706-422-1932.

GEORGIA RACING HALL OF FAME, 415 GA 53, Dawsonville. 706-216-7223. georgiaracinghof.com.

NORTH GEORGIA PREMIUM OUTLETS, 800 GA 400 S, Dawsonville. 706-216-3609. www.premiumoutlets.com/outlet/north-georgia.

For more information on any Georgia State Park or Historic Site, visit the state parks website: www.georgiastateparks.org.

Events

Dawson County
Mountain Moonshine Festival, Dawsonville, fourth weekend in October.

Fannin County
Blue Ridge Fall Fest, Blue Ridge, third and fourth weekends in October.

Gilmer County
Georgia Apple Festival, Ellijay Lions Club Fairgrounds, October. www .georgiaapplefestival.org.
Cherry Log Festival, Cherry Log, first weekend in October.

Lumpkin County
Gold Rush Days, Dahlonega, third weekend in October.

Murray County
Black Bear Festival, Chatsworth, October.

Union County
Indian Summer Festival, Suches, October. www.suches.com/festivalinfo.htm.

14

TO HELEN BACK

The Northeast Georgia Foothills

The total length of this tour is about 110 miles and includes Hall, Banks, Habersham, and White Counties.

Beginning at the end of Interstate 285, north of Gainesville, take US 23/GA 365 north for about 4.4 miles. Turn right on Whitehall Road for 0.1 mile, then take the first left, an unmarked gravel road which is the continuation of Whitehall Road and may be marked and paved by the time you read this. Go 0.3 mile to **Healan Mill**, built by William Head in 1852, on the left at 5751 Whitehall Road. The mill has been beautifully restored and will be the centerpiece of Hall County park, which is still under development. Because of this, the site is currently closed but is available for tours. Call Becky Ruffner at Hall County Parks to see if the site has opened or to set up a tour (770-535-8280).

The lovely brook that powered the mill in its working days is actually the North Oconee River!

From the mill, go back to US 23/GA 365. Turn right for 4.3 miles, then right on Athens Street for 1.3 miles. Cross the railroad tracks in Lula and go left on GA 51 for about 2 miles and turn right on Antioch Road for 1 mile to **Lula Covered Bridge** (aka **Blind Susie Bridge**) on the right. Built in 1915 and only 34 feet long, it is said to be the shortest covered bridge in Georgia and one of the shortest in the US. It is on private property, and at this writing the owner had not bothered to clear away the undergrowth, so it may be difficult to see when the trees are in full foliage.

From the covered bridge, go back to GA 51, turn right, and go about 9 miles to Homer and the old Greek Revival **Banks County Courthouse**,

LEFT: YOU CAN ACTUALLY RENT A ROOM IN THE HELEN MOTEL AND WINDMILL SUITES

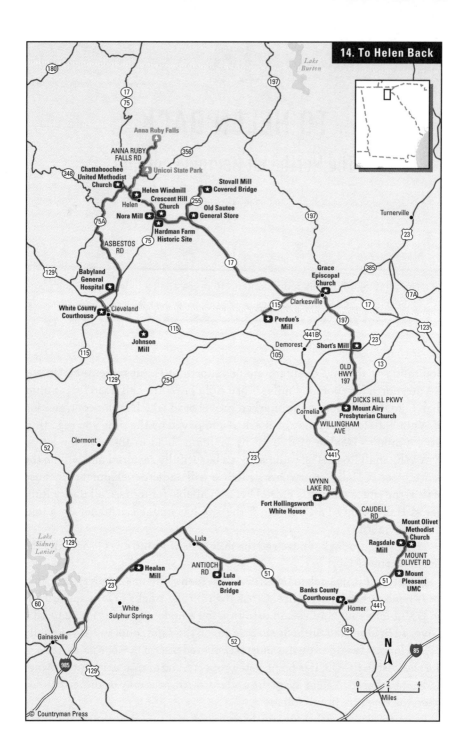

14. To Helen Back

Lake Burton

180

17
75

Anna Ruby Falls

ANNA RUBY
FALLS RD

356

Chattahoochee
United Methodist
Church

348

Unicoi State Park

197

Stovall Mill
Covered Bridge

Helen Windmill
Crescent Hill
Church

255

Helen

Old Sautee
General Store

Nora Mill

197

Turnerville

75A

Hardman Farm
Historic Site

75

ASBESTOS
RD

17

Grace
Episcopal
Church

385

17A

129

Babyland
General
Hospital

White County
Courthouse

Cleveland

115

Clarkesville

17

23

115

Perdue's
Mill

441B

123

Johnson
Mill

115

Demorest

105

Short's Mill

23

115

129

254

OLD
HWY
197

13

DICKS HILL PKWY

52

Clermont

23

Cornelia

Mount Airy
Presbyterian Church

WILLINGHAM
AVE

441

WYNN
LAKE RD

Fort Hollingsworth
White House

CAUDELL
RD

Mount Olivet
Methodist
Church

Lake
Sidney
Lanier

129

Lula

ANTIOCH
RD

Ragsdale
Mill

MOUNT
OLIVET RD

Healan
Mill

Lula
Covered
Bridge

51

51

Mount
Pleasant
UMC

60

23

White
Sulphur Springs

Banks County
Courthouse

Homer

441

Gainesville

985

129

52

164

N

85

0   2   4
Miles

© Countryman Press

THE BANKS COUNTY COURTHOUSE IN HOMER WAS BUILT 1860–63

built 1860–63. The building is open for tours on Thursdays and Fridays, 10 a.m.–4 p.m. Call 678-971-9390 for information. Admission is free.

From the courthouse, stay on GA 51 for about 4 miles and turn left on Damascus Road. About a hundred yards before the Damascus Road turnoff, **Mt. Pleasant United Methodist Church** is on the right. The congregation was organized in the 1780s and the current building dates from 1883. The church still holds regular services.

After turning left on Damascus Road, go a half-mile and slant right on Mt. Olivet Road for 1.2 miles to **Mt. Olivet Methodist Church**, built circa 1868. The church sits behind its cemetery, down a narrow paved drive on the right at 820 Mt. Olivet Road.

Although it appears not to be well known these days, not everyone in the pre-Civil War South approved of slavery. The Reverend Francis Marion Ragsdale did not, and he, his family, and some others left the Mt. Pleasant Church over the issue. In 1868, he was given a plot of ground by a neighbor and organized the Mt. Olivet Methodist Church, which he pastored for many years. The last regular service at Mt. Olivet was in 1961. It is now privately owned and is used occasionally for weddings. An annual "Old Fashioned Day" is held on the last Sunday in May, with dinner on the grounds and period clothing.

THE RAGSDALE MILL WAS BUILT BY THE REV. FRANCIS MARION RAGSDALE IN 1863

From the church, continue on Mt. Olivet Road, which becomes gravel at that point and goes down a steep hill. Go 0.2 mile, and near the bottom of the hill turn right into a gravel drive for 0.1 mile to **Ragsdale Mill**.

The first mill on Nail's Creek was built sometime before 1837. The Reverend Ragsdale, who was a man of many facets, acquired the mill site and 257 acres of land from his father in 1853 and built the mill in 1863. The millstones were imported from France and brought into Savannah by blockade runners, bypassing the US Navy guarding the port. In its heyday, the mill included a threshing machine and a sawmill.

The site includes the Ragsdale homestead and a Grange Hall, which also served as a schoolhouse. The Reverend Ragsdale was a visionary who hoped to establish a town to be called Nail's Creek, with the church, the mill, the Grange Hall, and the school as its nucleus.

The town never materialized, but perhaps it's just as well. This is one of the most serene and beautiful places to which my Georgia travels have taken me. The Sisk family, who now own the property, have thoughtfully provided picnic tables and chairs in which to sit and enjoy the peace, so please observe the sign at the entrance.

From the mill, turn right and continue northeast on Mt. Olivet Road for about a half-mile and turn left on Christmas Tree Road. Go 1 mile, turn right on Damascus Road for 0.4 mile, turn left on Caudell Road for 2.4 miles, then turn right on US 441 for 2.7 miles.

Turn left on Apple Pie Ridge Road, then immediately go left on Old US 441 for 0.4 mile and turn right on Wynn Lake Road. Go 1.2 miles to **Fort Hollingsworth-White House** on the right. Built in 1793, some believe it to be the oldest structure in North Georgia. However, the William Daniell House near Watkinsville is said to have been built in 1790. The houses are distinctive, with the Daniell house a plantation mansion while the Hollingsworth house is pioneer rustic. Each is beautiful in its own way.

Fort Hollingsworth was originally built as a two-story log fort for defense against Indian raids. That ceased to be a problem after about 1796, and the fort became a log farmhouse. During the Civil War, the fort was acquired by Joshua White and his wife Katharine, who built an addition that was connected by an open "dogtrot" passageway, making it look like many other farmhouses of the period.

In the 1980s, descendants of John and Katharine White placed the prop-

THE FORT HOLLINGSWORTH-WHITE HOUSE WAS ORIGINALLY A TWO-STORY LOG FORT

GRACE EPISCOPAL CHURCH IN CLARKESVILLE STILL HAS THE ORIGINAL BOXED PEWS

erty in a non-profit organization, Friends of the Fort. An annual Fort Day Celebration is held each May (forthollingsworth-whitehouse.com).

From Fort Hollingsworth, go back to US 441, turn left, and go about 4.3 miles.

At the traffic light, turn right on US 441 Business/Willingham Avenue (which becomes South Main Street) for 1.3 miles. At the traffic light, slant right on Wyly Street (which becomes Dicks Hill Parkway) and go 1.4 miles. At Fifth Street, turn right and then immediately left on Railroad Avenue and go about a block to number 699 and the **Mt. Airy Presbyterian Church**, built in 1907. If you miss the turn, take the next right and then jog left. The church's address is listed as 699 Grandview, but the building actually faces on Railroad Avenue.

The simple but elegant church never had a large membership, and by 1979 members were so few that those remaining were transferred to the Cornelia Presbyterian Church and the Mt. Airy church was made a chapel of the Cornelia church. The building is unchanged and still has its original furnishings.

From Mt. Airy Church, continue to the end of the block, turn left, then turn right on Dicks Hill Parkway. Go about a mile and turn left on Old GA 197 for 2.8 miles to **Short's Mill**, probably built in 1880, although some sources say the mid-1800s. Also known as Laudermilk Mill, it is set well back on the right side of the road and is difficult to see until you're almost past it. It ceased operations in 1970, although it appears to be mostly intact. The sluiceway is long gone, but the overshot wheel is still in place.

Continue on GA 197 for 4.2 miles into Clarkesville and turn right on East Green Street, which is hard to find because the sign is blocked by a lamp post. It's one block after Morgan Street and one block before the town square. Turn right opposite the yellow building on the left and go three blocks to **Grace Episcopal Church**, built in 1840. The second-oldest Episcopal church in Georgia, it is on the right at 260 East Green Street.

After more than 175 years, the church is little changed. The windows have most of their original glass, the original boxed pews with doors are still in place, and the Elben pipe organ, built in 1848, the oldest working pipe organ in Georgia, retains its 19th-century baroque tone. It was originally delivered to the church with "some assembly required" and turned out to be a foot too tall. No problem. Just create a pit for the organ in the middle of what was then the slave gallery.

From the church, go back to Washington Street/US 441/GA 17/115/197/385 and turn right for two blocks through the town square, then left on GA 17/115. Stay straight on GA 115 when 17 turns off to the right. About 4 miles from Clarkesville, turn left on Perdue Mill Road (CR 60) and go 0.4 mile to **Perdue's Mill**, sometimes spelled "Pardue." The wooden dam, which has been

PERDUE'S MILL NEAR CLARKESVILLE OPERATED FROM THE 1930S TO THE 1960S

recently rebuilt, is on top of a natural waterfall. The mill was built in the 1930s and was in operation until the mid-60s. It appears to be mostly intact, but the large wooden overshot wheel has been gone for some time.

From the mill, go back to the intersection with GA 17 and turn left for 8.9 miles to the **Old Sautee General Store**, at the intersection of GA 17 and GA 255. Built in 1872, it was a full-service country store selling food, clothing, seed, and farm equipment, and was also the post office from 1913 until 1962. The original general store interior is preserved as a museum, although in other ways the old store is quite up to date. It offers a good look at the way things were a hundred years ago.

From the store, take GA 255 north for 2.7 miles to the **Stovall Mill Covered Bridge**, at 12 Rau Road, Nacoochee. The 38-foot-long bridge was built over Chickamauga Creek (there are two Chickamauga Creeks in Georgia) in 1895 by Will Pardue, using a modified queen post truss design. It is now owned by the White County Historical Society.

From the Stovall Mill Bridge, go back to the Old Sautee Store, turn right, and go 2 miles to the **Crescent Hill Baptist Church**, on the right. Built in 1872, it was originally known as Nacoochee Presbyterian Church, but has been used by Baptists since 1921. The church currently has about 150 members, and services are held each Sunday at 11 a.m. The pulpit, pews, and stained glass are all original. This is one of the prettiest country churches I've found in my travels.

Leaving the church, turn right and go 0.2 mile. On the right will be the mansion **West End**, and in a field on the left will be the **Nacoochee Indian Mound**.

THE OLD SAUTEE GENERAL STORE IN NACOOCHEE SOLD FOOD, CLOTHING, AND FARM EQUIPMENT

ONE PART OF THE OLD SAUTEE STORE IS PRESERVED TO SHOW WHAT SHOPPING WAS LIKE AT THE TURN OF THE 20TH CENTURY

Both the house and the mound are part of the 173-acre **Hardman Farm Historic Site**.

The Nacoochee Mound is a burial site probably used by Indians of the Woodland culture. It was excavated by the Museum of the American Indian in 1915, and 75 burials were found, about a third of them with artifacts indicating high social status.

When the Cherokees came into the area, they used the mound for ceremonial purposes. The legend that two Indian lovers from the Cherokee and Chickasaw tribes committed suicide on the mound because their tribes were enemies is romantic but probably not true.

The unusual Italianate-style house on the right was built in 1870 by Captain James Nichols for his wife and named West End because it was at the west end of the Nacoochee Valley. The interior of the house is original and includes the bedroom of their daughter, Anna Ruby Nichols, for whom Anna Ruby Falls was named.

VISITING HELEN DURING OKTOBERFEST IS FUN. DRIVING THROUGH THE TOWN . . . NOT SO MUCH

ANNA RUBY FALLS IS ACTUALLY WATER FROM TWO DIFFERENT CREEKS

Dr. Lamartine G. Hardman purchased the property in 1903 and in 1999 the Hardman family donated the farm to the state of Georgia. The house and grounds are open for tours March 1 to December 18, Thursday through Saturday, 10 a.m.–4 p.m. Admission is $12 for adults, $10 for seniors, $7.50 for ages 6 to 17, and $3 for children under six.

Go 0.1 mile to the intersection with GA 75 and turn right for 0.4 mile to **Nora Mill**, on the right.

Constructed in 1876 by John Martin, who built a dam with a 100-foot sluiceway that conducts water to the turbine and installed 1500-pound French Burr millstones, the mill is very much a going concern, especially on a Saturday during Oktoberfest in nearby Helen, which was when I happened to stop by.

The name "Nora" was given by Hardman, who bought the mill in 1902 and named it after his sister. Hardman was later governor of Georgia from 1927 to 1931.

From the mill, continue on Main Street/GA 17/75 for 1.7 miles through downtown **Helen**.

In early 1969, some Helen businessmen were searching for a way to bolster the village's sagging lumber economy, possibly by finding a way to entice tourists to drop a few bucks in the town as they passed through on their way to the mountains. They consulted with an artist named John Kollock, who had some ideas. By fall of that same year, Helen had reinvented itself as an Alpine village, straight out of Bavaria. And the rest, as they say, is history. I do not recommend driving through Helen on an October weekend unless you have a lot of time to kill.

The **Helen Windmill** is on the right at the **Heidi Motel**, near the north end of town. Looking for information online, I found a surprising number of businesses that use windmills to distinguish themselves, but no information on this one. However, according to the hotel's website, you can actually rent a room in the windmill.

Stay on GA 17/75/Main Street for 0.8 mile and turn right on GA 356 for 1.8 miles. At that point, you can either bear left on Anna Ruby Falls Road for 3.4 miles to **Anna Ruby Falls Visitor Center** at 3455 Anna Ruby Falls Road, Helen, or you can continue straight to **Unicoi State Park**.

At Anna Ruby Falls, water from Curtis Creek drops 153 feet, while York Creek falls 50 feet. Both creeks begin on Tray Mountain and come together below the falls to form Smith Creek, which flows into Smith Lake in Unicoi State Park and then onward to the Chattahoochee River. Although it is necessary to go through the park to get to the falls, they are located in the Chattahoochee National Forest and are not part of the state park. A paved, 0.4-mile walk leads to the base of the falls, with benches along the way. Anna Ruby Falls is open 9 a.m.–5 p.m. daily. Admission is $5.

Unicoi State Park features a 100-room lodge and conference center, 30 cottages, 49 camp sites, picnic shelters, and a group shelter on its 1050 acres. There is also 53-acre Smith Lake, with a swimming beach, fishing docks, kayak and canoe rentals, 12 miles of hiking trails, 8 miles of mountain bike trails, a zipline, and a restaurant. Definitely something for everyone.

The park is open 7 a.m.–10 p.m. daily. There is no admission charge, but a $5 parking pass is required.

THE CHATTAHOOCHEE METHODIST CHURCH WAS THE SETTING FOR THE 1951 MOVIE *"I'D CLIMB THE HIGHEST MOUNTAIN"*

From Unicoi State Park, go back on GA 356 for 1.8 miles to GA 17/75 and turn right for 0.3 mile, then turn left on GA 75 ALT. Go 0.2 mile to the **Chattahoochee United Methodist Church**. Founded in 1860, the present building was built 1888–90 and looks the same as it did when it was the setting for the 1951 film *I'd Climb the Highest Mountain,* starring Susan Hayward, William Lundigan, and Rory Calhoun.

One of the first films to be photographed mostly on location, the movie was based on the autobiographical novel *A Circuit Rider's Wife,* by Cora Harris. It told the story of the trials and joys of the new, city-born wife of a circuit-riding Methodist preacher in the late-1800s North Georgia mountains. Many local people appeared as extras in the film.

From the church, continue on GA 75 ALT for about 3.7 miles and turn left on Asbestos Road. Go 3.6 miles, turn right on GA 75 for 0.9 mile, then turn right on Hulsey Road. Go a half-mile and turn right on N.O.K Drive for 0.3 mile to **Babyland General Hospital**, birthplace of Cabbage Patch dolls. Invented in the mid-1970s by a 21-year-old art student named Xavier Roberts, the soft-sculpture dolls became one of the most popular toy fads of the

1980s, and their creative advertising made them one of the most enduring doll franchises.

Babyland is the only place in the world where you can witness the "birth" of a hand-sculpted Cabbage Patch Kid. You can't "buy" one, but they're available for "adoption." You can take the Oath of Adoption and get a Certificate for an appropriate fee.

Visiting hours at Babyland are 9 a.m.–5 p.m. Monday through Thursday, 9 a.m.–6 p.m on Saturday and 10 a.m.–6 p.m. on Sundays. Admission is always free.

Leaving the hospital with your new baby (how could you resist?), go back to Hulsey Road and turn right. In 0.9 mile, turn left on US 129 and go 1.2 miles to downtown Cleveland and the historic **White County Courthouse**, built in 1859. A distinguished example of vernacular architecture, it stands proudly in the town square, although it has not been used for government business since 1962. It is now the home of the White County Historical Society.

From the courthouse, take Kytle Street/GA 115 east for 2 miles. Turn right on Black Road, go 0.8 mile and turn right on Cooley Woods Road for 0.1 mile to **Johnson Mill**, on the right at 424 Cooley Woods Road. It's just over the hill, and you will come upon it very suddenly.

Dating from the early 1800s, the mill is well-preserved and fully operational. The owners have taken a great deal of care with the landscaping,

THE OLD WHITE COUNTY COURTHOUSE IN CLEVELAND NOW HOUSES THE COUNTY HISTORICAL SOCIETY

THE EARLY 1800S JOHNSON MILL IS IN A BEAUTIFUL PARK-LIKE SETTING NEAR CLEVELAND

making this one of the loveliest settings I have seen for a mill. Walk across the footbridge, take a seat on a bench, and enjoy the peaceful ambience!

The mill property also includes a very nicely restored log cabin with rocking chairs on the porch, and across the street is a log double-pen barn and a covered bridge spanning the mill creek. This is altogether an idyllic place and a great way to end our tour.

From Johnson Mill, go back to the courthouse square in Cleveland. From there, if you're going south, you can take US 129 south to I-985 and points beyond.

IN THE AREA

Accommodations

GLEN-ELLA SPRINGS BED AND BREAKFAST INN, 1789 Bear Gap Road, Clarksville. 706-754-7295. glenella.com.

HEIDI MOTEL, 8820 North Main Street, Helen. 706-418-4169. www .heidimotel.com.

THE STOVALL HOUSE INN, 1529 GA 225 North, Sautee Nacoochee. 706-229-4434. www.stovallhouse.com.

Dining

BODENSEE, 64 Munich Strasse, Helen. 706-878-1026. www.bodensee restaurant.com.

FENDERS DINER, 631 Irvin Street, Cornelia. 706-776-2181. m.mainstreet hub.com/fendersrestaurant.

GLEN-ELLA SPRINGS RESTAURANT, 1789 Bear Gap Road, Clarksville. 706-754-7295. glenella.com.

HARVEST HABERSHAM, 1362 Washington Street, Clarkesville. 706-754-0058. www.harvesthabersham.com.

RIB COUNTRY, 2652 US 129 South, Cleveland. 706-865-1119. www.rib countrybbq.com/locations.

Attractions and Recreation

ANNA RUBY FALLS, 3455 Anna Ruby Falls Road, Helen. 706-878-1448.

BABYLAND GENERAL HOSPITAL, 300 NOK Drive, Cleveland. 706-865-2171. cabbagepatchkids.com/pages/babyland-general-hospital.

HARDMAN FARM HISTORIC SITE, 143 GA 17, Sautee Nacoochee. 706-878-1077.

SMITHGALL WOODS STATE PARK, 61 Tsalaki Trail, Helen. 706-878-3087.

UNICOI STATE PARK AND LODGE, 1788 GA 356, Helen. 706-878-2201. www.unicoilodge.com/ga-state-park.

For more information on any Georgia State Park or Historic Site, visit the state parks website: www.georgiastateparks.org.

Events

Banks County

Old Fashioned Day, Mt. Olivet Methodist Church, last Sunday in May.
Day at the Fort, Fort Hollingsworth-White House, May.

Habersham County

Mountain Laurel Festival, Clarkesville, May.
Chattahoochee Mountain Fair, Clarkesville, September.
Big Red Apple Festival, Cornelia, October.

White County

Oktoberfest, Helen, September–October.
Fall Country Fair at Hardman Farm, Nacoochee, October.
Agrifest Country Market, Cleveland, September.
Harvest Moon Dinner, Hardman Farm, Nacoochee, September.

15

OVER THE ROOF OF GEORGIA
The Northeast Georgia Mountains

This tour is about 145 miles in length and includes Stephens, Habersham, Rabun, Union, and Lumpkin Counties.

Begin at the Neoclassical Revival **Stephens County Courthouse** in Toccoa, built in 1907–08. If you're coming from Interstate 85, use exit 173 at Lavonia and follow GA 17 north for about 17 miles.

From downtown Toccoa, go east on Tugalo, the street that runs behind the courthouse. Shortly after passing the Presbyterian (a classically beautiful building), United Methodist, and Baptist churches on the left, bear right at the fork and continue onto Big A Road to the intersection with US 123/East Currahee Street. Go left for 5.3 miles and turn left again on Riverdale Road. In 0.3 mile, **Traveler's Rest Historic Site** will be on the right at Number 4339.

Traveler's Rest was built by James R. Wyly around 1815–16 as a stagecoach inn to serve travelers on the new Unicoi Turnpike. He operated the inn until 1833 then sold it to his neighbor, Devereaux Jarrett, who doubled the size of the house and made it the headquarters of his 14,400-acre plantation along the valley of the Tugaloo River.

Three generations of Jarretts lived at Traveler's Rest, gradually selling off pieces of the plantation over the years until the State of Georgia bought the house and the few remaining acres in 1955. The house contains many original artifacts and pieces of furniture, some of which were made by Caleb Shaw, a famous cabinetmaker from New England.

Traveler's Rest is open for tours on Saturdays and Sundays, 9 a.m.–5 p.m. Admission is $5 for adults, $4 for seniors, and $3 for ages 6–17. The charge is $1 for children under six.

LEFT: BRASSTOWN BALD MOUNTAIN, GEORGIA'S HIGHEST PEAK, AS VIEWED FROM GA 180 IN TOWNS COUNTY

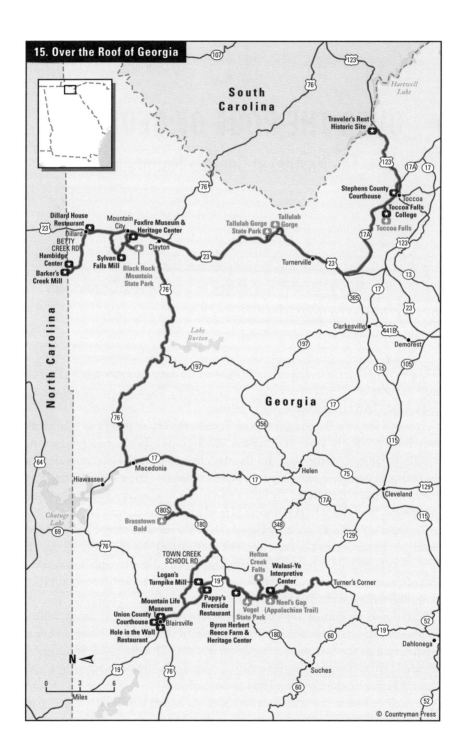

15. Over the Roof of Georgia

THE NEOCLASSICAL REVIVAL STEPHENS COUNTY COURTHOUSE IN TOCCOA WAS BUILT IN 1907–08

Leaving Traveler's Rest, take Riverdale Road and US 123 back to Toccoa. Turn right on Big A Road/GA 17 ALT and continue onto East Tugalo Street to downtown Toccoa. As you pass the courthouse on your left, the **Simmons-Bond Bed & Breakfast Inn** will be on the right at 74 West Tugalo Street. Built in 1903, the inn is furnished with period antiques and is known for its gourmet breakfasts.

One block past the Simmons-Bond Inn, turn right on Broad Street/GA 17 ALT and continue onto GA 17 ALT/Falls Road. About a mile from downtown, turn left on Kincaid Drive and enter the campus of **Toccoa Falls College**, a fully-accredited, four-year Christian liberal arts institution founded in 1907.

Keep left to continue on Forrest Drive for about a half-mile to the Gate Cottage and the easy, 100-yard trail to the 186-feet-high **Toccoa Falls**, the second-highest vertical-drop waterfall in Georgia and 19 feet higher than Niagara. Great boulders are piled around its base, where a clear pool receives the thundering water.

Taking in the serene beauty of the setting, it's difficult to grasp that this was once a scene of terror. In the early morning hours of November 6, 1976, five days of constant rain caused a rupture of the earthen dam that held a 40-acre lake above the falls, sending a wall of water surging through the campus, destroying much of the married students' on-campus housing, killing 39 people, and injuring 60 more. Prayers, expressions of sympathy, and

TOCCOA FALLS IS 19 FEET HIGHER THAN NIAGARA

THE GRISTMILL WAS BUILT NEAR COWETA, NC, AND MOVED TO FOXFIRE IN 1972

contributions to rebuild the campus poured in from all around the globe. Today, few signs of the physical damage remain. Admission to the falls is free. Call 706-886-7299 for hours.

From the campus, go back to GA 17 Alt and turn left for 10 miles to the intersection with US 23/441. Turn right and go 6.4 miles, then turn right on Old US 441 to drive along the rim of **Tallulah Gorge**, with several good overlook points. You will merge back into US 23/441 about a mile south of the entrance to **Tallulah Gorge State Park**.

One of the Seven Natural Wonders of Georgia, Tallulah Gorge is the 1,000-foot-deep canyon of the Tallulah River, which drops 490 feet in 1 mile in a series of six waterfalls as it flows through the gorge. Visitors to Tallulah Gorge State Park can hike easy trails along the rim to several overlooks and can also obtain a permit to hike the 1,099 steps to the bottom of the gorge (only easy going down), where a suspension bridge crosses 80 feet above the canyon floor.

In addition to the gorge, which of course is the main attraction, the 2,739-acre Tallulah Gorge Park has 50 campsites, a Pioneer Campground, a 63-acre lake with fishing and a swimming beach, picnic facilities, and rock climbing. There are also 20 miles of hiking trails and challenging trails for mountain biking. The park is open from 8 a.m. until dark every day. There is no charge for admission, but a $5 parking pass is required.

From Tallulah Gorge, continue on US 23/441 for 13.7 miles through Clayton to Black Rock Mountain Parkway in Mountain City. Watch carefully—the

UP TO 1,000 FEET DEEP, TALLULAH GORGE HAS BEEN A TOURIST ATTRACTION SINCE THE EARLY 1800S

turnoff is easy to miss. Turn left onto the Parkway, go 1 mile, and turn left again at the Foxfire sign. Go 0.5 mile (the road will become gravel—stay left at intersecting streets) to the **Foxfire Museum** on the right at 98 Foxfire Lane, Mountain City.

The Foxfire program was founded in 1966 by Eliot Wigginton, an English teacher at Rabun Gap-Nacoochee School, who, as a project with his students, began interviewing older residents of the area, learning about the pioneer culture of the Southern Appalachians and collecting old tools and artifacts. They began publishing a magazine that they named *Foxfire*, which led eventually to the best-selling series of *Foxfire* books.

With income from the books, the students began to expand their program, establishing a site and collecting old log cabins and outbuildings and moving them to the site. The oldest is a one-room log cabin built in the 1820s in which four generations of one family grew up. The museum now includes more than 20 cabins, a chapel, barn, blacksmith shop, and working gristmill, and a wagon built in the 1790s that was used on the Trail of Tears—the only one known to be still in existence.

Visitors to the Museum and Heritage Center take a self-guided tour along a walking trail that winds through the grounds. Foxfire is open Monday through Saturday 9 a.m.–4 p.m., and noon–4 p.m. on Sunday. Admission is $3 for ages 7–10, $6 for ages 11–18, $10 for ages 19–61, and $8 for those 62 and older. There is no charge for children 6 and under. All prices are plus 8% sales tax. Call 706-746-5828 for more information.

From the Foxfire Museum, go back to Black Rock Mountain Parkway, turn left, and go to the top of the mountain to 1,743-acre **Black Rock Mountain State Park**, at 3,640 feet the highest of Georgia's state parks. With spectacular views of the Blue Ridge Mountains, the park has 10 cottages, 44 campsites, 16 walk-in and backcountry campsites, picnic facilities, and a 17-acre

SYLVAN FALLS MILL HAS A 27-FOOT OVERSHOT WHEEL POWERED BY WATER FROM THE FALLS

lake with excellent fishing. It also has 11 miles of trails for hiking and back-packing. The park is open every day from 7 a.m.–10 p.m. but because of its altitude may close in icy weather. Admission is free, but a $5 parking pass is required.

Leaving the park, go back down the mountain to the Foxfire turnoff and go left on Taylor's Chapel Road. The road is well-maintained gravel until you get to Black Rock Lake, after which it's paved. **Sylvan Falls Mill** is on the left in 1.5 miles.

Built in 1840 of locally milled "wormy chestnut," the mill is intact and functioning. The original wheel was replaced in 1952 with a 27-foot overshot wheel that is one of the larger ones in the country, although not as large as the 42-foot wheel at the Berry College Mill near Rome.

Fed from springs atop Black Rock Mountain, water is channeled from the waterfall to power the wheel. The mill has been converted into a bed and breakfast inn, the **Sylvan Falls Mill Bed and Breakfast**, but the owners still grind a variety of grains for meal, grits, and flour.

From Sylvan Falls, continue on Taylor's Chapel Road for 0.2 mile. Turn right on Wolffork, go 2.2 miles, and turn left on US 23/441. Go 2.2 miles to the **Dillard House Restaurant** on the right.

Serving Southern cooking, family-style, all-you-can-eat meals, the

RABUN COUNTY'S CHATTOOGA RIVER IS ONE OF AMERICA'S PREMIER KAYAKING AND RAFTING STREAMS

BARKER'S CREEK MILL NEAR DILLARD STILL GRINDS MEAL ON THE FIRST SATURDAY OF EACH MONTH

Dillard House has been in business for nearly a hundred years and has become famous throughout the Southeast and beyond, feeding up to 3,000 people a day in peak season and listing many famous people among its clientele.

Leaving the Dillard House, turn right on US 23/441 for 0.2 mile, then turn left on Betty's Creek Road and follow it for 3.6 miles to the **Hambidge Center for the Creative Arts**, on the right. Continue on Betty's Creek Road

THE OLD UNION COUNTY COURTHOUSE IN BLAIRSVILLE IS NOW A MUSEUM

past the Center for 0.7 mile and, at the sign, turn left down a gravel lane to the beautiful **Barker's Creek Mill**, which is owned by the Hambidge Center. Built in 1940, the mill is powered by a 12-foot overshot wheel and is in excellent condition and still operating. In fact, meal is ground the first Saturday of each month, 10 a.m.–4 p.m.

Leaving Barker's Creek Mill, go back to Dillard and turn right (south) on US 23/441 for 6.7 miles to Clayton. Turn right on US 76 and go 23.7 miles through spectacular mountain scenery, beautiful any time of the year but especially in the fall.

Turn left on GA 17/75 for 3.6 miles, then turn right on Owl Creek Road. Go 4.2 miles and turn right on GA 180 for 1.3 miles. At that point, GA 180 Spur turns sharp right and goes 3 miles to the top of **Brasstown Bald Mountain**. The visitor center is located at the top, operated by the Cradle of Forestry in America Interpretive Association.

At 4,784 feet, Brasstown Bald is the highest point in Georgia. It's called a "bald" because, like many of the higher mountains in the Southern Applachians, it has no trees on its summit. With great views in every direction, you can even see the skyscrapers of Atlanta on a clear day.

The visitor center at Brasstown Bald is open every day, April through December, from 10 a.m. to 5 p.m., except in inclement weather. Admission is $5 for ages 16 and up and includes a shuttle ride to the summit if you prefer not to hike the half-mile paved trail.

Coming back down the mountain, go right on GA 180 for about 5 miles and turn right on Town Creek School Road. In 6.2 miles, turn right on US 19/129 for about 2.5 miles to downtown Blairsville.

The Romanesque Revival **Union County Courthouse** in the town square was built in 1899 and has recently been renovated with a new clock tower. Like many of Georgia's older courthouses, it has become a museum and is now the headquarters of the Union County Historical Society.

While you're on the square, you might like to check the **Hole-In-The-Wall Restaurant**. I haven't eaten there, but it comes highly recommended by someone whose judgment I trust.

From the square, go back south on Cleveland Street/US 19/129 for a block and go left on School Street. On your left will be the **Mountain Life Museum**, with the **Butt-Mock House**, built in 1906, and the **John Payne Cabin**.

Just before the Civil War, John Payne married Louisa Frady. In 1860, John and his brothers built a cabin for his new family. After that he went off to war, but fortunately came home to Louisa and their cabin, where they raised seven children. The cabin was moved to this site and reassembled by descendants of the Payne family.

The museum is open Thursday, Friday, and Saturday, 11 a.m.–4 p.m. There is no admission charge. The museum grounds are also the setting for the annual Mountain Heritage Festival on Labor Day Weekend.

THE 1860 JOHN PAYNE CABIN AND FARMSTEAD ARE PART OF THE MUSEUM OF MOUNTAIN LIFE IN BLAIRSVILLE

Continue on School Street to the four-way stop at School Circle. Just beyond is a small park on the left with the Union County Memorial to its generations of war dead. The Memorial is unusual in that it may be the only one in the South that honors Union soldiers as well as Confederate, and even to American Indians who fought against the white settlers.

From Blairsville, go back south on US 19/129 for about 9 miles to the **Byron Herbert Reece Farm and Heritage Center** on the right.

Born on a farm in Union County in 1917, Byron Herbert Reece was a writer and farmer who published four volumes of poetry and two novels in a life that ended when he was only forty. He was nominated for a Pulitzer Prize for his poetry, received two Guggenheim Fellowships, and was for a time writer-in-residence at The University of California at Los Angeles, but he never received wide recognition in his lifetime and never forsook his connection to the North Georgia land of his birth.

The Heritage Center at the remaining nine acres of Reece's family farm is a place to learn about the man, his work, and life in the Southern Appalachians in the mid-20th century. The site is open April–November, Wednesday through Saturday, 10 a.m. to 4 p.m. Admission is free.

From the Reece Center it's just over a mile to the entrance to **Vogel State Park**.

Built by the Civilian Conservation Corps in the 1930s, Vogel is one of Georgia's oldest and best-loved parks. Although only 233 acres, which is smaller than most, Vogel has 35 cottages, more than a hundred campsites, 17 miles of hiking trails, and gem-like, 17-acre Lake Trahlyta. An easy 1.2-mile loop trail around the lake leads to Trahlyta Falls, a 110-foot-high cascade.

The park is open every day, 7 a.m.–10 p.m. Admission is free, but a $5 parking pass is required.

Leaving Vogel State Park, turn right on US 19/129, go 1.2 miles, and turn left on Helton Creek Road, a gravel Forest Service road. Go 2.1 miles, park in the small parking lot at the trailhead, and take the fairly easy 300-yard hike to Helton Creek Falls, a beautiful double falls more than a hundred feet high, set in a deep hardwood forest.

From the falls, go back to US 19/129 and turn left up the mountain for 1.6 miles to Neel's Gap, 3,109 feet above sea level. The **Appalachian Trail** crosses the highway at this point, 30.7 miles from its beginning on Springer Mountain in Fannin County.

BYRON HERBERT REECE BUILT A ONE-ROOM HUT ON HIS FAMILY FARM AS A PLACE TO WRITE

TURNER'S CORNER, WHERE THE ROAD FORKS

The stone building at Neel's Gap is called the **Walasi-Ye Interpretive Center**, after a Cherokee village that once stood in the area. (The name means "Home of the Great Frog.") The land where the center sits was given to the State of Georgia by the Vogel family in the 1920s, and the building was erected by the Civilian Conservation Corps in the 1930s. Through the years it has been a restaurant, inn, and an artist's studio. Currently, it's a store selling supplies for tourists and hikers. The center also offers hostel and cabin rentals. A roofed passageway between the store and an adjoining building is directly on the route of the Appalachian Trail and is the only place on the entire 2,180-mile length of the trail from Georgia to Maine where it passes through a man-made structure.

THE APPALACHIAN TRAIL PASSES THROUGH A MAN-MADE STRUCTURE FOR THE FIRST AND ONLY TIME AT THE WALASI-YE CENTER AT NEEL'S GAP ON BLOOD MOUNTAIN

Continue on down Blood Mountain for 7.7 miles to **Turner's Corner**, where US 19 and US 129 divide. The Turner's Corner Cafe is closed now, but I remember when it was a gas station and the owner kept a pet bear in a cage in back of the store. More recently, after it became a restaurant, the deck overhanging the Chestatee River was a lovely place to eat.

But my most poignant memory is of the last day of my honeymoon. My wife and I had spent a week in the North Georgia mountains, the last several days in a small resort called Enotah Cottages across from Vogel State Park.

On this last day, we packed our Volkswagen and drove over the mountain to Turner's Corner. To the right, down US 19, lay home, responsibility . . . life. I can still feel, even now, the powerful urging of my heart to choose the left fork and stay in the mountains forever.

As Yogi Berra said, "When you come to a fork in the road, take it."

So I did. And life has been good.

This is the end of the tour. Take the right fork and follow US 19 south. If you have already taken Tour 13, which includes Dahlonega, you can bypass it and go on to connect with four-lane US 19/GA 400 to points south.

IN THE AREA

Accommodations

THE SIMMONS-BOND INN BED AND BREAKFAST, 74 West Tugaloo Street, Toccoa. 706-510-3573. www.simmons-bond.com.

SYLVAN FALLS MILL BED & BREAKFAST, 156 Taylors Chapel Road, Rabun Gap. 706-550-9638. www.sylvanfallsmill.com.

THE WHITE BIRCH INN BED AND BREAKFAST, 28 East Savannah Street, Clayton. 706-229-7254. www.thewhitebirchinn.net.

YOUR HOME IN THE WOODS BED AND BREAKFAST, 143 Timber Lane, Blairsville. 706-748-7496. www.yourhomeinthewoods.com.

Dining

THE CUPBOARD CAFE, 7388 US 441, Dillard. 706-746-5700. www.dillardgeorgia.com/cupboard-cafe.

DILLARD HOUSE RESTAURANT, 158 Franklin Street, Dillard. 706-746-5348. www.dillardhouse.com/restaurant.

HOLE-IN-THE-WALL RESTAURANT, 90 Town Square, Blairsville. 706-745-5888. www.holeinthewallga.com.

M&J HOME COOKING, 587 Mize Road, Toccoa. 706-282-0022.

RIB COUNTRY, Blairsville. 706-781-3530. www.ribcountrybbq.com/locations. Multiple locations in the area.

Attractions and Recreation

BLACK ROCK MOUNTAIN STATE PARK, 3085 Black Rock Mountain Parkway, Mountain City. 706-746-2141.

BRASSTOWN BALD MOUNTAIN VISITOR CENTER, GA 180 Spur, Blairsville. 706-896-2556. cfaia.org/brasstown-bald-recreation-area-visitor-centers -in-georgia.

BYRON HERBERT REECE FARM AND HERITAGE CENTER, 8552 US 19/129, Blairsville. 706-745-2034. reecefarm.org.

FOXFIRE MUSEUM AND HERITAGE CENTER, 98 Foxfire Lane, Mountain City. 706-746-5828. www.foxfire.org.

TALULLAH GORGE STATE PARK, 338 Jane Hurt Yarn Drive, Tallulah Falls. 706-754-7981.

TOCCOA FALLS, Toccoa Falls College Campus, Toccoa.

TRAVELER'S REST STATE HISTORIC SITE, 4339 Riverdale Road, Toccoa. 706-886-2256.

VOGEL STATE PARK, 405 Vogel State Park Road, Blairsville. 706-745-2628.

For more information on any Georgia State Park or Historic Site, visit the state parks website: www.georgiastateparks.org.

Events

Rabun County

Sassafras Artisan Market, Clayton, April. www.sassafrasartisanmarket.com.

Stephens County

Toccoa Harvest Festival, downtown Toccoa, last weekend in October.

Towns County

Georgia Mountain Fair, Georgia Mountain Fairgrounds, Hiawassee, July.

Georgia Mountain Fall Festival, Georgia Mountain Fairgrounds, Hiawassee, October.

Union County

Arts and Crafts Festival, Blairsville, Memorial Day Weekend.

Mountain Heritage Festival, Blairsville, Labor Day Weekend.

Index

Page numbers in *italics* refer to illustrations.